REAL CHARACTERS IN THE MAKING

Lorraine Peterson

BETHANY HOUSE PUBLISHERS

MINNEAPOLIS, MINNESOTA 55438
A Division of Bethany Fellowship, Inc.

Published by Bethany House Publishers
A Division of Bethany Fellowship, Inc.
6820 Auto Club Road, Minneapolis, Minnesota 55438

Printed in the United States of America

Library of Congress Cataloging in Publication Data

Peterson, Lorraine.
    Real characters in the making.

    (Devotionals for teens; #4)
    Summary: Stories of thirteen prominent Old Testament characters form the basis of thirteen weeks of daily lessons presenting issues common to today's teens and the Biblical heroes.
    1. Youth—Prayer-books and devotions—English.
2. Bible. O.T.—Biography—Meditations. [1. Prayer books and devotions.
2. Bible stories—O.T.] I. VanderWaal, Kent, ill. II. Title. III. Series.
BV4850.P463   1985   242'.63   85-7373
ISBN 0-87123-824-1 (pbk.)

About the Author

LORRAINE PETERSON was born in Red Wing, Minnesota, grew up on a farm near Ellsworth, Wisconsin, and now is a teacher at the American School in Guadalajara, Mexico. She received her B.A. (in history) from North Park College in Chicago, and has taken summer courses from the University of Minnesota and the University of Mexico in Mexico City.

Lorraine has taught high school and junior high. She has been an advisor to nondenominational Christian clubs in Minneapolis public schools and has taught teen-age Bible studies. She has written three best-selling devotional books for teens: *If God Loves Me, Why Can't I Get My Locker Open?*, *Falling Off Cloud Nine and Other High Places*, and *Why Isn't God Giving Cash Prizes?*

Preface

A recent magazine article said that in this age of disillusionment—and full press coverage of every mistake made by each famous person—young people have no heroes, because no one can be admired as an ideal or role model. Having no one to follow, the article continued, these teen-agers have trouble setting goals for their lives. As I read on, I realized the reason I had not faced that problem as a teen-ager was that I had been brought up on the Bible. The courage of Esther pleading with the Persian king to spare her people, the faith of Abraham starting out to an unknown land, and the effective prayers of Elijah, "a man just like us" (James 5:17), had thrilled and inspired me.

Jesus, of course, is the only perfect hero, the only One whom we can safely follow at all times. The Apostle Paul instructs us to "fix our eyes on Jesus, the author and perfecter of our faith" (Heb. 12:2). Yet, something in each of us wants to identify with "regular" people, just like ourselves, and to have examples of how God works in the lives of those who possess faults and weaknesses like ours. Knowing we needed human role models, God filled the Bible with them. "For everything that was written in the past was written to teach us, so that through endurance and the encouragement of the Scriptures we might have hope" (Rom. 15:4).

That is the first reason I wrote *Real Characters in the Making*. I trust this book will help its reader walk closer to Jesus by finding in the lives of real people examples to follow and actions to avoid. Joseph's faith and obedience in prison, Isaac's attitude toward marriage, or Jeremiah's courage in crisis demonstrate beautifully that with God all things are possible.

My second reason for writing this book is to interest young people in reading the Old Testament, allowing the Holy Spirit to reveal the great truths found within its pages. Many parts of it are very exciting, though the rest requires some digging to uncover its treasures. What a wonderful challenge for a young person! Since people haven't changed, and God hasn't changed either, the lives of the characters of the Old Testament offer great lessons.

I wish to express my appreciation to those who made the writing of this book possible. I owe much to Theodore Epp, J. Vernon McGee, Alan Redpath, and A. W. Pink, whose lifelong studies have become part of this book. I would especially like to thank Michael O'Connor for faithfully proofreading my manuscript and offering so many usable suggestions. Thank you to Sam Ovando, a student at the school where I teach, who helped with the map in this book. I want to tell my father I appreciate the way he helped me with so many details. I'd also like to express my gratitude to all the teen-agers who have been part of my life and in turn part of this book—my students at Edison High School, Northeast Junior High, and the American School of Guadalajara, Mexico; the members of my Student Life Clubs; girls who attended my Bible studies; teens who have written letters to me; and my favorite teen-agers, my nieces and nephews, Beth, Brett, Kaari, and Kirk.

Contents

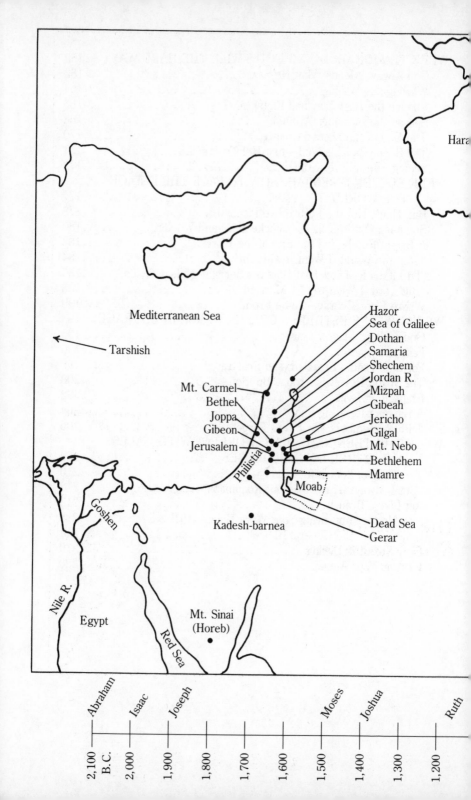

Mediterranean Sea

Tarshish

Hara

Hazor
Sea of Galilee
Dothan
Samaria
Shechem
Jordan R.
Mt. Carmel
Mizpah
Bethel
Gibeah
Joppa
Jericho
Gibeon
Gilgal
Jerusalem
Mt. Nebo
Bethlehem
Philistia
Mamre
Moab
Goshen
Dead Sea
Gerar
Kadesh-barnea

Nile R.
Egypt
Mt. Sinai
(Horeb)
Red Sea

Abraham   Isaac   Joseph   Moses   Joshua   Ruth

2,100
B.C.   2,000   1,900   1,800   1,700   1,600   1,500   1,400   1,300   1,200

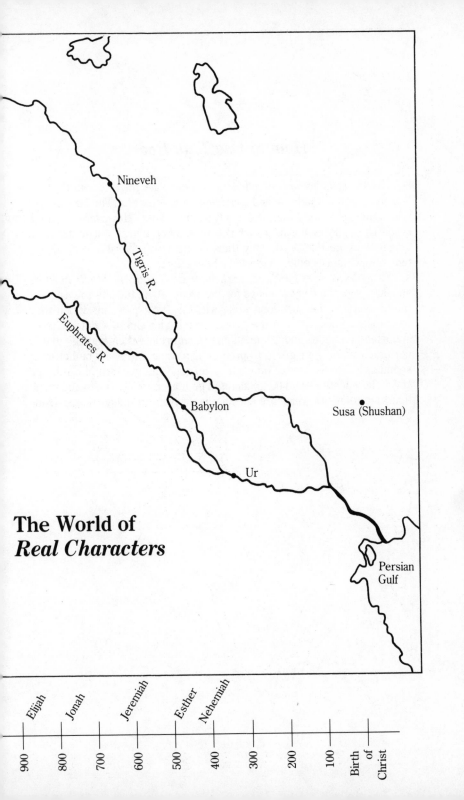

Nineveh

Tigris R.

Euphrates R.

Babylon

Susa (Shushan)

Ur

The World of
Real Characters

Persian
Gulf

Elijah	Jonah	Jeremiah	Esther	Nehemiah				Birth of Christ
900	800	700	600	500	400	300	200	100

How to Use This Book

To teen-agers for daily devotions: In order to get the most out of these lessons, keep a notebook and *write down* the answers. The lazy part of you is saying, "I don't want to—it's too much work." However, education research supports the idea that you remember things you write down longer than the things you only think about. God's Word is very important—important enough to get your best effort.

To youth workers for Sunday school or Bible study material: Leaders should assign the daily readings for the week. Ask students to write out the answers to the questions along with any new questions which they would like to discuss with the group. The leader can pick out the most important questions and ask members to contribute their findings. If it is not practical for your group to prepare in advance, it would be better to spend at least two weeks on each topic, read the material in class, and cover the questions as you go along. The teacher will want to add questions and thoughts which are specifically relevant to the particular group being taught.

ABRAHAM: THE UPS AND DOWNS OF A FRIEND OF GOD

Introduction

If you like to keep all the bases covered and minimize your risks, the life of Abraham will challenge you to break free and live by faith. If you thrive on stories of adventure and danger, reading about Abraham—and other heroes of faith—will teach you the difference between faith and foolishness. Either way you'll learn about faith. And since "without faith it is impossible to please God" (Heb. 11:6), these next chapters could change your life!

Obeying God When He Demands Sacrifice

God told Abraham to leave Ur, an important and prosperous city of ancient times, and go "to the land I will show you" (Gen. 12:1). Going meant saying good-bye to everything familiar, to family and friends. It meant leaving a nice house in a thriving city and camping in a tent for the rest of his life! And when Abraham's friends asked him where he was going, he didn't know, because God hadn't told him. How embarrassing. Abraham was obeying purely by faith.

Making a Stupid Decision

After leaving Ur, Abraham spent several years in Haran. Finally he reached Canaan, and there, at Shechem, he built an altar to God. Later he moved to Bethel.

Then famine struck Canaan. Egypt, however, had plenty of food because its water came not from local rainfall, but from the flooding of the Nile which gets its water supply from East Central Africa. Egypt often had crops when the rest of the area had none. Abraham therefore did what *he* thought was the logical thing: He moved to Egypt—and got into a lot of trouble with the king.

An ancient king was not above murdering the husband of a beautiful woman in order to add her to his harem. Well, Sarah, Abraham's wife, was beautiful. So in order to save his own skin, Abraham asked her to call herself his sister. Predictably, the king noticed her and brought her to the Egyptian palace, but he soon learned she was married. He swiftly exiled the couple from Egypt. What a dumb thing for Abraham to do. But God forgave him, and Abraham learned from his dreadful mistake.

Good and Bad Solutions to Problems

Abraham's nephew, Lot, was still living with Abraham, and both had large herds and many servants. This led to conflict. Because adequate pasture for so many animals was scarce, their servants began quarreling. Abraham decided to solve the problem by giving Lot first pick and then taking whatever land was left for himself. Their families would then separate. Ungrateful Lot chose the best land for himself, and left the scrubby desert for his uncle.

Childless at 86, Abraham received a promise from God: Abraham would have a son whose descendants would inherit the land of Canaan. Only faith could believe such a promise! Sarah was 76 at this time and found the promise hard to believe.

As years passed and no child appeared, Sarah gave up on a miracle. She resorted to the scheme used by childless wives of that day to insure that her husband had a son to carry on his name and to inherit his land. So she suggested her maid Hagar bear a son for Abraham. (Hammurabi, a Babylonian king who lived about two hundred years after the time of Abraham, included this kind of arrangement in his law code. One of his laws stated that the childless wife was responsible to find a woman to produce an heir for her husband. If the wife failed to do this, her husband could legally take a second wife. It is very possible that Sarah and Abraham lived under such a system. Even if they didn't, it was an attempt to settle Sarah's insecurity, using a human method to fulfill a heavenly promise.) Abraham also showed his lack of faith by consenting to Sarah's plan. And so he and Hagar produced a boy named Ishmael.

Ishmael caused nothing but trouble—and the problems continue to this day! Listen to the news and you'll hear about the descendants of Ishmael—the Arabs—fighting with the Jews. All this because Abraham and Sarah weren't willing to wait for God to provide them a son!

Yet God did not give up on Abraham and Sarah. When Abraham was 99 and Sarah was 89, Jesus made one of His Old Testament appearances. (The Bible says, "The Lord appeared to Abraham." Such an appearance of God to man is called a theophany. Most Old Testament scholars conclude that this was Jesus.) He announced that within a year Abraham and Sarah would have a son! When Sarah heard it she laughed, but she was reminded that nothing is too hard for God. And within a year she gave birth to Isaac, the miracle baby. He grew up to be an obedient boy who was a joy to his parents.

Then came another test of faith: God told Abraham to sacrifice Isaac, the miracle boy, as a burnt offering on Mount Moriah. Yes, God had promised Abraham a son. And He had kept that promise by giving Isaac. So why should He now want Abraham to destroy the fulfillment of the promise as a test of his faith? God didn't want Isaac dead. He just wanted Abraham to trust Him without question. By the time Abraham faced this greatest test of his faith, he had grown beyond the mistakes he'd made in earlier years. He no longer doubted God. This time he obeyed without question, reasoning that God could even raise Isaac from the dead. Even if he couldn't see his way clear, he could obey his way clear.

By giving a dramatic picture for your imagination (Isaac tied to a stone altar and Abraham, knife in his hand, ready to kill him), God demonstrated one of the premier principles of the Christian life: Spiritual life rises out of giving up to God everything you are and have. In other words, you must die to self. Yes, a substitute (for Isaac, a ram/for you, Jesus) did the physical dying. But in order to live a full, new life, you must act on the truth that the self-centered part of you died with Jesus on the cross. Only the things you sacrifice to God come back usable for His glory.

As a follower of God you must offer each "Isaac" (your most precious possession) on the altar of your heart. This sacrifice will move your life into a new dimension, for you will no longer view lightly the blessings God has given you. Just as Isaac became dearer to Abraham after selfish love for his son had been destroyed, so God's blessings will become dearer to you.

In addition to giving a major spiritual lesson, the sacrifice of Isaac also points to the coming of Christ. Man needed a sacrifice for sin, but no Isaac or ram was good enough to be that sacrifice. We don't know how much Abraham understood about Jesus the perfect sacrifice, but he must have had some knowledge, because Jesus said to doubting listeners, "Your father Abraham rejoiced at the thought of seeing my day; he saw it and was glad" (John 8:56).

To your modern mind, God's directing Abraham to sacrifice his son appears strange. You might be tempted to think God was commanding murder. It is doubtful, however, that Abraham ever thought, "How could God command me to do such a thing?" He lived in a society which commonly made child sacrifices to its gods. Since the law of Moses had not yet been given, and since such an offering carried such strong religious significance, Abraham probably didn't even associate child sacrifice with murder. Certainly the motives of hatred and revenge which lead to conviction of murder in today's courts were absent from these killings. Abraham's fellow countrymen, in their ignorance and desperation, gave their gods the best they had (in a crudely literal sense)—their sons and daughters. Certainly, worshipers of the true God could have sometimes thought, *If pagans are willing to offer up their children to gods of wood and stone, the living God surely deserves such a sacrifice.* Through Abraham's example, however, God showed the world, and especially the Israelites, that He detested human sacrifice. His warning to Abraham as the knife was poised above Isaac's throat, "Do not lay your hand on the lad," erases any doubt about the matter.

But God didn't put Abraham through this ordeal only for the sake of others, to show them His attitude toward human sacrifice. He did it as a supreme test of Abraham's faith. Would Abraham give the person he loved the most to God? Would he obey God even though he didn't understand the purpose of God's command? Abraham passed.

Abraham's life is marked by faith. By faith he made significant journeys: from Ur to Canaan, from his tent to the altar on Mount Moriah, from paganism to belief in the one true God, Jehovah. By faith he became "God's friend" (James 2:23). By faith he became righteous (Rom. 4:22). And by faith you can be a child of Abraham, the father of God's chosen people, "the father of all who believe" (Rom. 4:11).

Free to Receive

"The Lord had said to Abram, 'Leave your country, your people and your father's household and go to the land I will show you. I will make you into a great nation and I will bless you; I will make your name great, and you will be a blessing. I will bless those who bless you, and whoever curses you I will curse; and all peoples on earth will be blessed through you.' So Abram left, as the Lord had told him; and Lot went with him. Abram was seventy-five years old when he set out from Haran" (Gen. 12:1–4).

What if God asks you to break up with your boyfriend? What if you have to choose between going out for baseball and attending a series of great Bible studies and discipleship classes, which won't be offered again? What if you know you should stay home and attend the local junior college to ease your parents' financial load, even though you've been aching to get out on your own and attend the university? What if your mother needs help on Saturdays but you'd like to spend that time with your friends?

These decisions wouldn't be difficult if you had Abraham's faith. As Abraham, you must trust God enough to believe that if He takes something away from you, that it is for your good, that He has something better to give. This is part of the definition of faith in the great "faith chapter," Hebrews 11. It says those who come to God must believe He "rewards those who earnestly seek him" (v. 6). Do you believe that? Until you do, your Christian life will be full of constant struggles. You will be a Linus with all kinds of security blankets you're unwilling to give up.

If you're still wavering on this issue, the faith of Abraham can encourage you. God asked Abraham to leave everything—his house, his family, his friends, and his country. But He promised that the whole world would benefit if Abraham obeyed. It certainly didn't seem logical, but as Epp writes, God "seldom accompanies His commands with reasons or explanations, but He always accompanies them with wonderful promises."[1]

---

[1]Theodore Epp, *The God of Abraham, Isaac and Jacob.* Lincoln, Nebr.: Back to the Bible, p. 41.

God makes a similar promise to you: "For whoever wants to save his life will lose it; and whoever loses his life for me will save it" (Luke 9:24). Do you believe it? Read the verse again, substituting your name for "whoever."

No one would ever deny there is heartache in giving up something you value, but the Bible never says obeying God is painless. Even though it must have been very difficult for Abraham to leave everything as he headed for an unknown destination, he believed God's promise. His obedience made possible the formation of the Jewish people, through whom Jesus came into the world. Abraham, however, is not the only person who has given up everything to obey God and thus bless others. For instance, "By faith Moses, when he had grown up, refused to be known as the son of Pharaoh's daughter. He chose to be mistreated along with the people of God rather than to enjoy the pleasures of sin for a short time. He regarded disgrace for the sake of Christ as of greater value than the treasures of Egypt, *because he was looking ahead to his reward*" (Heb. 11:24–26). Moses' decision to sacrifice made possible the Israelites' escape from Egypt.

Are you willing to suffer, believing that God will reward you for your obedience? That obeying God in faith can lead to great and wonderful things? That God has a better life for you without your boyfriend? That getting to know Jesus better is more exciting than hitting home runs? That making sacrifices for other people will prove "it is more blessed to give than to receive" (Acts 20:35)? Only when you give up what you have in your hands can you be free to receive the greater gift God has for you.

The Apostle Paul, like Abraham, gave up what he had so he could receive better things from God:

"If anyone else thinks he has reasons to put confidence in the flesh, I have more: circumcised on the eighth day, of the people of Israel, of the tribe of Benjamin, a Hebrew of Hebrews; in regard to the law, a Pharisee; as for zeal, persecuting the church; as for legalistic righteousness, faultless. But whatever was to my profit I now consider loss for the sake of Christ. What is more, I consider everything a loss compared to the surpassing greatness of knowing Christ Jesus my Lord, for whose sake I have lost all things. I consider them rubbish, that I may gain Christ" (Phil. 3:4–8).

1. Make a list of each thing you might have to give up to follow Jesus. Can you give them up, believing God has something better to give you?
2. What did Paul think about all the things he gave up for Jesus?
3. Do you think giving up his great reputation may, at first, have been hard for Paul?
4. What lesson do the lives of Abraham, Moses, and Paul teach you?

About That F on the Faith Exam . . .

"Now there was a famine in the land, and Abram went down to Egypt to live there for a while because the famine was severe. As he was about to

enter Egypt, he said to his wife Sarai, 'I know what a beautiful woman you are. When the Egyptians see you, they will say, "This is his wife." Then they will kill me but will let you live. Say you are my sister, so that I will be treated well for your sake and my life will be spared because of you' " (Gen. 12:10–13).

Have you ever wished the teacher would give you one big exam, and after you'd passed that one, you'd never have to take another test? Well, there are some problems with that dream. First, good learning requires constant review to prevent forgetting, and tests motivate you to review. (For example, every math exam tests concepts you have learned in lower grades, as well as the new concepts you've just learned.) Second, you never know if you've mastered the new material unless you've been tested. (There may have been a time when you thought you knew a great deal—until a test proved you wrong.) Third, you learn a great deal by taking an exam. Sometimes the question you get wrong on the test is the very thing you'll remember longest. Fourth, constant tests keep you studying and learning new things. If you want to follow God, you might as well get

"If you learn from your mistakes, you won't have to flunk the next faith exam."

used to the idea of tests, because God uses them frequently. He tests faith for the same reasons that your teacher keeps giving exams.

The life of Abraham shows how—and how not—to take God's tests. Abraham's test, in this case, was a famine. A food shortage is a pretty serious problem, but Abraham's experience should have kept him from panic. God had provided for Abraham all the way from Ur to Canaan, a distance of several hundred miles; God had also protected and guided him. Therefore, the famine was only a review test for Abraham. But he failed.

A faith test is like a math test. If you use the wrong formula, you get all the problems wrong. The formula for solving faith problems is asking God what to do, then obeying Him out of faith rather than fear. In other words, attitude is all-important. The Apostle Paul told the Roman Christians what that attitude should be: "May the God of hope fill you with all joy and peace as you trust in him, so that you may overflow with hope by the power of the Holy Spirit" (Rom. 15:13).

Abraham failed because he used the wrong formula. He decided to solve the problem with his own plan—he moved to Egypt, which had plenty of food. What a bad trip! First he gave up the opportunity to learn to trust God more. Then he sinned to protect himself by indicating that Sarah was his sister and not his wife. (Sarah was very beautiful and in those days marriage was so highly respected that even a king couldn't take another man's wife. He could, however, murder anybody he wished. Thus, by making a beautiful woman a widow, he could take her into his harem.) Abraham fell, not only into fear and insecurity, but into selfishness that cared more about his own safety than his wife's welfare. This test showed Abraham that his faith was still weak, that he didn't know God as well as he thought he did.

Failing a test, however, is not nearly as important as your attitude about failing. Abraham failed but he learned from his mistakes. He admitted he was wrong, faced humiliation, and returned to face the famine and trust God. Are you willing to be humble, to admit you are wrong, and to go back and find out how to do the math problems (or the faith problems) correctly? Will you let God teach you from your failures?

The test also showed Abraham he needed to stay close to God so he could learn whatever was necessary to pass the next test. You, too, will have faith tests all your life. Learn all you can from God's Word. Let the Holy Spirit be your guide. If you learn from your mistakes, you won't have to flunk the next faith exam.

"Whoever loves discipline loves knowledge, but he who hates correction is stupid" (Prov. 12:1).

"He who ignores discipline comes to poverty and shame, but whoever heeds correction is honored" (Prov. 13:18).

"He who heeds discipline shows the way to life, but whoever ignores correction leads others astray" (Prov. 10:17).

"He who ignores discipline despises himself, but whoever heeds correction gains understanding. The fear of the Lord teaches a man wisdom, and humility comes before honor" (Prov. 15:32, 33).

"Our fathers disciplined us for a little while as they thought best; but God disciplines us for our good, that we may share in his holiness. No discipline seems pleasant at the time, but painful. Later on, however, it produces a harvest of righteousness and peace for those who have been trained by it" (Heb. 12:10, 11).

1. Are you stupid by God's definition? Do you have some changing to do?
2. What are the rewards for accepting discipline and correction?
3. Why is it hard to admit that you are wrong and receive correction?
4. What's the best way to avoid an *F* on the next faith exam?

Go-For-It Faith

"When Abram came to Egypt, the Egyptians saw that she was a very beautiful woman. And when Pharaoh's officials saw her, they praised her to Pharaoh, and she was taken into his palace. But the Lord inflicted serious diseases on Pharaoh and his household because of Abram's wife Sarai" (Gen. 12:14, 15, 17).

You've just passed your driver's test, and are ecstatically waiting for a chance to prove your skill as a licensed driver. Your grandmother congratulates you.

"I'm very proud of you. I know you'll be a safe and careful driver—not like the other teen-agers.

"Well, I do have an appointment with the doctor this afternoon, but—uh—I couldn't ask you to do that. It'll be during the worst rush-hour traffic of the day. I'll call a cab."

Crushed, you realize your grandmother has no faith in your driving ability—in spite of her encouraging comments. The words of faith must be acted on, or they mean nothing.

A simple man of great faith, named (don't laugh) Smith Wigglesworth, compared inactive faith to a robber who steals the good things God wants to give us. Faith doesn't drift along with the current, hoping things will turn out okay. Instead, it gets the map from God and follows the course with enthusiasm. It takes command of the situation, rides the rapids with God as co-pilot, and enjoys it—all the while letting God take you to the destination.

Faith requires initiative, but doesn't independently venture out. That is presumption. Because of this danger, the "go-for-it" element of faith is often overlooked. Abraham had to "go for it." God gave him the promise of the land, but God asked him to walk through the land, to claim it by a specific act of obedience. Theodore Epp lists the requirements of "go-for-it" faith:[2]

1. Helplessness—the realization that you can't please God by doing things in your own way or by your own strength.
2. Assurance—confidence that you are doing God's will and not your own.
3. Commitment—surrender of your desires, plans, and ideas to God.
4. Scripture—a passage of Scripture, a promise of God you can claim for the situation, and keep in your mind regardless of feelings or circumstances.
5. Boldness—daring to act, depending only on God's promises.

If you haven't taken the first four steps, your actions won't be based on faith. Usually, however, the problem is you never get to step five and thus miss the blessing. You do everything except thanking God and acting. God wants to give you "go-for-it" faith.

Now put it into practice. You and your mother have fought a hundred times about how often you are to stay home and take care of your younger brother and sister. The matter, still unsettled, sits like a bomb ready to explode. You must resolve the problem. First, admit to God that you're helpless, and in faith ask Him for the solution. Second, face God's word—"Children, obey your parents" (Eph. 6:1)—and realize disobeying your mother is never God's will. Third, give up your own desires and be willing to babysit every night—if that's God's plan. Fourth, find a Bible verse, a promise to claim (for example, "Blessed are the peacemakers, for they will be called sons of God."). Fifth, thank God that He wants to make you a peacemaker and that He has already done that. Then go with faith to your mother and discuss the babysitting situation. That's "go-for-it" faith. You have no need to fear; God rewards those who obey Him.

"Then Joshua told the people, 'Consecrate yourselves, for tomorrow the Lord will do amazing things among you.' And the Lord said to Joshua, 'Today I will begin to exalt you in the eyes of all Israel, so they may know that I am with you as I was with Moses. Tell the priests who carry the ark of the covenant: "When you reach the edge of the Jordan's waters, go and stand in the river." ' So when the people broke camp to cross the Jordan, the priests carrying the ark of the covenant[3] went ahead of them. Now the Jordan is at flood stage all during harvest. Yet as soon as the priests who carried the ark reached the Jordan and their feet touched the water's edge, the water from upstream stopped flowing. It piled up in a heap a great distance away, at a town called Adam in the vicinity of Zarethan, while the water flowing down to the Sea of the Arabah (the Salt Sea) was completely cut off. So the

---

[2]Theodore H. Epp, *Moses, Vol. 1, God Prepares His Man.* Lincoln, Nebr.: Back to the Bible, pp. 10, 11.
[3]The special gold-covered box containing tablets of stone with the Ten Commandments showing the covenant or agreement God had made with His people.

people crossed over opposite Jericho" (Josh. 3:5, 7, 8, 14–16).

1. How would you feel if you had to lead a million people across a flooding river and you had no boats?
2. Why did the people "sanctify" themselves (set themselves apart for God's special purpose)?
3. How did Joshua know this crossing was God's will? (If you read all of Joshua 3, you'll also find God had promised Joshua a dry crossing.)
4. What was the importance of breaking camp and having the priests step into the flooding river before seeing any results? Ask God to show you which situation in your life will require believing God's promise and acting in faith before you'll see signs of God working.

The Faith-Obedience Plan

"So Abram said to Lot, 'Let's not have any quarreling between you and me, or between your herdsmen and mine, for we are brothers. Is not the whole land before you? Let's part company. If you go to the left, I'll go to the right; if you go to the right, I'll go to the left.' The king of Sodom said to Abram, 'Give me the people and keep the goods for yourself.' But Abram said to the king of Sodom, 'I have raised my hand to the Lord, God Most High, Creator of heaven and earth, and have taken an oath that I will accept nothing belonging to you, not even a thread or the thong of a sandal, so that you will never be able to say, "I made Abram rich" ' " (Gen. 13:8, 9; 14:21–23).

Why do you obey? You might answer that no one gets through life without obeying somebody sometime. And you're right. But such an attitude won't do much for your life, because the quality of life you'll have depends on the *reasons* you have for obeying.

Consider the variation in your attitudes toward certain tasks. You follow your English teacher's instructions for writing a term paper to the letter to avoid getting an *F*—and hate her all the time you are doing it. You obey crabby Aunt Bessie's instructions for mowing the lawn because your mother said it's your duty—but you can't stand Aunt Bessie. But when your girlfriend gives you strict instructions on impressing her grandparents, you obey because you love her and trust her—and you enjoy doing it! You know she won't lead you astray, and you have a good reason for gaining the confidence of her grandparents. As you can see, obedience can be out of fear, out of duty, or out of love and faith.

People obey God for different reasons. Some forget that their relationship with God and their motives for obeying Him are as important as the obedience itself. They obey God only because they are afraid of what He will do to them if they don't obey. Or they just do their duty. Obviously, these people don't consider God their intimate friend. This is as absurd as a wife obeying her husband only out of fear or duty. Obedience which comes from love and faith is the only kind that satisfies. If you obey God because you know He loves you completely and has your best interests at heart, obeying is easy. Obedience doesn't have to be a drag. It wasn't for Abraham.

Just casually reading about Abraham's generosity to Lot might convince you he was a very poor businessman, or that he was a good guy with a white hat who went around doing unselfish things because that's what good guys are supposed to do. Actually, Abraham's generosity came neither from ignorance nor from duty. Instead, he obeyed in faith. He knew that the God who loved him owned everything, so God would take good care of him, even if Lot received first choice of the land. And he knew better than to place his confidence in the generosity of people, such as the king of Sodom who wanted to give him gifts. "Lest you should say, 'I made Abram rich,' " reveals Abraham's attitude. He loved God and had full confidence in Him, not in people. He chose to obey God because God would give him the very best. Abraham knew that accepting presents from the powerful king of Sodom could obligate him to that king. Abraham wanted to be obligated only to God.

Abraham's view of material possessions clearly shows an obedience based on faith. First, Abraham left a big, beautiful house in Ur. (We can safely assume this because archaeologists have uncovered foundations of spacious homes in ruins of the ancient city.) Second, he lived in a tent. A tent won't hold much, so a person can't store up anything for the future. He must trust God for his needs each day. Abraham believed that the God who owned the whole world had plenty of riches to supply his needs. So in faith he obeyed God's instructions.

Abraham found that the faith-obedience plan worked very well. You must try it. Put God first and trust Him for your worn-out wardrobe, your empty billfold, or your school tuition. He will take care of you.

"And why do you worry about clothes? See how the lilies of the field grow. They do not labor or spin. Yet I tell you that not even Solomon in all his splendor was dressed like one of these. If that is how God clothes the grass of the field, which is here today and tomorrow is thrown into the fire, will he not much more clothe you, O you of little faith? So do not worry, 'What shall we eat?' or 'What shall we drink?' or 'What shall we wear?' For the pagans run after all these things, and your heavenly Father knows that you need them. But seek first his kingdom and his righteousness, and all these things will be given to you as well" (Matt. 6:28–33).

1. What kind of relationship with God can take worry out of your life?
2. What is the difference between putting God and His kingdom first because of obligation, and doing it because of love and faith?
3. What is God really like? Do you think of Him like that?

22

Is Your God As Good As His Word?

"Now Sarai, Abram's wife, had borne him no children. But she had an Egyptian maidservant named Hagar; so she said to Abram, 'The Lord has kept me from having children. Go, sleep with my maidservant; perhaps I can build a family through her.' Abram agreed to what Sarai said. So Hagar bore Abram a son, and Abram gave the name Ishmael to the son she had borne. Abram was eighty-six years old when Hagar bore him Ishmael" (Gen. 16:1, 2, 15).

Someone has said, "Hope says, 'God will do it,' but faith says, 'God has already done it.' " That is a statement of confidence. If you really trust someone when he says, "I'll do it," you can declare, "It's as good as done."

You probably have friends you trust implicitly, but do you include God in that category? Imagine God's great disappointment when He sees the puny faith you put in Him. How preposterous to think God needs your help to fulfill His promises. How silly to grow discouraged if you don't see God's answer right away. This implies that God has forgotten all about His promises! What God has said is as good as done. Although you realize the logic of trusting an all-powerful, all-wise, all-loving God to carry out His promises, you probably succumb to the human tendency to figure things out for God and give Him some help. Even Abraham, a great man of faith, was guilty of this.

When God promised Abraham a son, he was 86 years old—and his wife was 76. Only a miracle could make this happen. As years passed, however, and the promise remained unfulfilled, Abraham and Sarah began to wonder. They didn't have enough faith to believe that a promise from God was as good as done. Therefore, they slipped into the world's way of thinking—"God helps those who help themselves."

According to the law code of Hammurabi (a king who lived 200 years after Abraham), if a wife was childless, she was expected to find a woman who could produce a son for her husband. If the wife didn't find such a woman, the husband could legally bring home a second wife. This official law, written 200 years after Sarah's time, was probably a social custom in her day. Such a custom probably made her insecure about her status as a wife, and she allowed this fear to get the best of her—after all, Abraham could bring home some beautiful young woman any day. So Sarah advised Abraham to have a son by her maid, Hagar. This was the logical, culturally acceptable way to solve the problem.

Unfortunately, Abraham never asked God what was right. It never dawned on him that God was true to His word and had already decided how to fulfill His promise of a son for Abraham. Probably, Abraham and Sarah both thought they were helping God fulfill the promise.

What a disaster! Not only did Sarah and Hagar become enemies, but their sons, Isaac and Ishmael, became enemies. To this day, the sons of Ishmael (the Arabs) are still fighting the sons of Isaac (the Jews). Abraham and Sarah's sin of unbelief had terrible consequences. But God didn't give up on them. He forgave them, built up their faith, and sent them a son when Abraham was 100 and Sarah was 90—an even greater miracle than it would have been before.

Now compare yourself with Abraham and Sarah. When God says, "So do not fear, for I am with you" (Isa. 41:10), do you believe He can help you pass final exams without one second of worrying on your part? When God says, "By His [referring to Jesus] wounds you *have been* healed" (1 Pet. 2:24), do you trust Him to make you healthy without your deciding exactly when and how He will do it? When God says, "He who began a good work in you will carry it on to completion" (Phil. 1:6), do you still insist you must have a good-looking husband, a BMW, and a big bank account? To "help" God is to distrust Him. Because He is the most trustworthy person in the universe, He doesn't need any help. Whatever He has promised isn't "as good as done"; it's *already done*. Your God is as good as His word.

"The centurion replied, 'Lord, I do not deserve to have you come under my roof. But just say the word, and my servant will be healed. For I myself am a man under authority, with soldiers under me. I tell this one, "Go," and he goes; and that one, "Come," and he comes. I say to my servant, "Do this," and he does it.' When Jesus heard this, he was astonished and said to those following him, 'I tell you the truth, I have not found anyone in Israel with such great faith' " (Matt. 8:8–10).

1. This Roman soldier realized that once Jesus gave His word, the thing was as good as done. Do you believe that?
2. Why was the Roman soldier satisfied, though he hadn't seen his servant healed?
3. Why was Jesus so impressed with this man's faith?
4. Find a promise in the Bible that applies to a problem you are facing. By faith believe that Jesus has already done what He said He would.

Stop Laughing and Start Listening

"The Lord appeared to Abraham near the great trees of Mamre while he was sitting at the entrance to his tent in the heat of the day. Then the Lord said, 'I will surely return to you about this time next year, and Sarah your wife will have a son.' Now Sarah was listening at the entrance to the tent, which was behind him. Abraham and Sarah were already old and well advanced in years, and Sarah was past the age of childbearing. So Sarah laughed to herself as she thought, 'After I am worn out and my master is old, will I now have this pleasure?' Then the Lord said to Abraham, 'Why

did Sarah laugh and say, "Will I really have a child, now that I am old?"
Is anything too hard for the Lord? I will return to you at the appointed time
next year and Sarah will have a son' " (Gen. 18:1, 10–14).

How would you react if someone suggested something impossible?
With laughter? If someone said you could get rid of your explosive temper,
would you laugh and exclaim, "Me? Never!"? If someone suggested you
could be organized, calm, and efficient, would you treat it as a big joke
and excuse yourself with, "Once a scatterbrain, always a scatterbrain"?
Would you chuckle if your English teacher said you could overcome your
shyness and become a great speaker? Do you picture yourself still biting
your fingernails in some rest home someplace down the road? "Impossible" is sometimes spelled L-A-U-G-H-T-E-R.

You're not the only one who uses laughter to cover up lack of faith.
Sarah did, too. When Jesus made one of His Old Testament appearances
and told Abraham (who was then 99) that within a year he and Sarah (then
89) would have a son, Sarah laughed. (Of course, the idea of a woman
having a child at 90 *is* rather funny.) The Lord reminded Sarah that she
was forgetting that God was all-powerful—"Is anything too hard for the
Lord?" This made Sarah think about an omnipotent God and helped build
up her faith. The Bible says, "Consequently, faith comes from hearing
the message, and the message is heard through the word of Christ" (Rom.
10:17). That is what happened to Sarah. She listened to the message the
Lord gave and believed it. Her laughter turned to listening, and through
listening she learned faith.

God could have formed Isaac in heaven and sent him down in a blanket,
but that's not His way. He performs His impossible miracles through
ordinary people—such as you—who believe Him. So Sarah, at age 90,
gave birth to a beautiful, healthy boy. And she named him Laughter—
that is what Isaac means. Maybe she chose the name to remind herself
that this living miracle was once a laugh of unbelief.

You, too, must leave behind your laugh of unbelief and begin listening
to the words of a God who can do anything. You must learn to trust Him
completely. Nothing is too hard for God—not even your temper, your
disorganization, your shyness, or your gnawed fingernails! Stop laughing
right now and start listening.

"God also said to Abraham, 'As for Sarai your wife, you are no longer
to call her Sarai; her name will be Sarah. I will bless her and will surely
give you a son by her. I will bless her so that she will be the mother of nations;
kings of peoples will come from her.' Abraham fell facedown; he laughed
and said to himself, 'Will a son be born to a man a hundred years old? Will
Sarah bear a child at the age of ninety?' " (Gen. 17:15–17).

"Against all hope, Abraham in hope believed and so became the father
of many nations, just as it had been said to him, 'So shall your offspring
be.' Without weakening in his faith, he faced the fact that his body was as

good as dead—since he was about a hundred years old—and that Sarah's womb was also dead. Yet he did not waver through unbelief regarding the promise of God, but was strengthened in his faith and gave glory to God, being fully persuaded that God had power to do what he had promised. This is why 'it was credited to him as righteousness' " (Rom. 4:18–22).

1. How did Abraham get from laughter to believing?
2. Why is it good to come to the place where there is NOTHING you can do about the situation?
3. Why did Abraham praise God BEFORE the miracle took place?
4. Work on your own faith project. What seems so impossible now that the very idea makes you laugh? Is there anything too hard for God? Keep listening to God and His words and learning to trust Him for the impossible.

Mighty Miracles and Mickey Mouse

"Some time later God tested Abraham. He said to him, 'Abraham!' 'Here I am,' he replied. Then God said, 'Take your son, your only son Isaac, whom you love, and go to the region of Moriah. Sacrifice him there as a burnt offering on one of the mountains I will tell you about.' Early the next morning Abraham got up and saddled his donkey. . . . When they reached the place God had told him about, Abraham built an altar there and arranged the wood on it. He bound his son Isaac and laid him on the altar, on top of the wood. Then he reached out his hand and took the knife to slay his son. But the angel of the Lord called out to him from heaven, 'Abraham! Abraham!' 'Here I am,' he replied. 'Do not lay a hand on the boy,' he said. 'Do not do anything to him. Now I know that you fear God, because you have not withheld from me your son, your only son' " (Gen. 22:1–3, 9–12).

It's hard to read the account of Abraham starting out early in the morning to offer up his son Isaac as a sacrifice, in obedience to God's command, without something pulling at your heartstrings. (For a fuller discussion of this strange command of God, read the introduction to these chapters on Abraham.) Abraham's faith should fill you with awe; his faith was so mature, so serene, that he did not question God, or even procrastinate. Abraham knew God so well he couldn't help but trust God. The Bible doesn't indicate Abraham had any fear. Instead, he looked at the situation in the light of his close acquaintance with God; and he reasoned that God could raise Isaac from the dead (Heb. 11:19).

The greatest evidence of Abraham's solid faith was the confidence of Isaac, by this time a teen-ager and stronger than his father. (Note that Isaac, not Abraham, carried the wood up the mountain.) Isaac must have caught his father's miracle-believing faith, because he allowed himself to be bound to the altar when he easily could have escaped. If Abraham had been obeying God out of obligation or tradition, Isaac would have pointed out that this was a good time to break with tradition and do some independent thinking! But tradition wasn't Abraham's motive. He believed that God could do anything and he trusted God's judgment. So he and Isaac counted on a miracle, and that's what they got.

You need the mature faith that Abraham displayed, faith which counts on miracles in impossible situations. You need mature faith especially when your emotions are deeply involved—such as having to sacrifice the son you love. Abraham could easily have let his love for Isaac keep him from obeying God. Instead, his belief in God's power enabled him to obey in spite of his emotions.

You may be facing several "mouse in a maze" situations in which you cannot obey God unless you are expecting miracles. For instance, how can you follow God's command "Children, obey your parents" (Eph. 6:1) if your alcoholic father becomes utterly unreasonable? Only by expecting a miracle. How can you practice "Be still, and know that I am God" (Ps. 46:10) when there is constant tension and arguing in your home? Only by expecting a miracle. How can you "love your enemies" (Matt. 5:43) when your non-Christian family and classmates constantly ridicule and tease you? Only by expecting a miracle. (Remember that God is free to work whatever miracle He wishes. He may choose to make you strong and courageous, rather than dealing with the people who are causing your problems.)

No matter how difficult your predicament, it is not too difficult for God. You may feel as if you were Mickey Mouse caught in the world's biggest mouse trap, but whoever said that mighty miracles and Mickey Mouse don't go together?

"How great is your goodness, which you have stored up for those who fear you, which you bestow in the sight of men on those who take refuge in you. In the shelter of your presence you hide them from the intrigues of men; in your dwelling you keep them safe from the strife of tongues" (Ps. 31:19, 20).

"Therefore let everyone who is godly pray to you while you may be found; surely when the mighty waters rise, they will not reach him. You are my hiding place; you will protect me from trouble and surround me with songs of deliverance" (Ps. 32:6, 7).

1. Write down the promises in the above verses which assure you of mighty miracles for tough situations.
2. In what situations do you need to allow God to keep you safe "from the strife of tongues"?
3. In what situation do you need to be "encompassed [surrounded] with deliverance"?
4. What miracle can you expect from God this week?

Week Two

ISAAC: GOD'S BLESSINGS ON AN ORDINARY LIFE

Introduction

As you read this book, you may notice many great heroes of faith were strong-willed, natural leaders. Therefore, if you're easy-going, happy-go-lucky, and not overly ambitious, you may have trouble identifying with some of them. Don't despair. Not all people of great faith were leaders.

Isaac was not a leader. Gentle and passive, he didn't like to make decisions or tell other people what to do. He lived an ordinary, uneventful life. But to God, Isaac was as important as his remarkable father. When God introduced himself to Moses, He said, "I am the God of your father, the God of Abraham, the God of Isaac, and the God of Jacob" (Exod. 3:5). Isaac's life shows that God is just as interested in the average student, the second string football player, and the unpopular kid as He is in the senior voted most likely to succeed. So, whatever your personality, you can learn from Isaac.

Because Sarah, Isaac's mother, was ninety when he was born, Isaac was a miracle baby, a child who would grow up with a sense of destiny. He was the fulfillment of God's promise. Through him, Abraham would become the father of many nations and the ancestor of the Messiah, Jesus.

When God's Command Seems Illogical

As a young man, Isaac's faith in God received a severe test when God commanded Abraham to sacrifice his son on an altar.[1] Isaac "aced" the test. Although he was physically strong enough to resist his father, and although this command seemed to contradict everything God had promised to his father, Isaac obeyed. But when Abraham was about to stab Isaac, a voice from heaven directed that his life be spared. Isaac learned that God always keeps His promises.

Forty and still unmarried, he again passed a great faith test. Abraham did not want him to marry a woman who worshiped idols—thus narrowing the selection drastically. In fact, the only eligible women would be among Abraham's relatives, far away in Haran. So, Abraham sent his trusted servant to find the right girl, certain that God had already chosen a bride

---

[1]See pages 12-14 for a discussion of this command.

for his son. Isaac, however, was not allowed to go along. In obedience and faith he stayed home, believing God would overrule any chance of error in this seemingly risky procedure. God rewarded his faith and obedience. For Isaac found that he truly loved Rebekah, the wife chosen for him by God.

After twenty years of marriage, Isaac and Rebekah had no children, though God had promised to make Abraham the father of many nations. So Isaac reminded God. Soon, Rebekah conceived, and then gave birth to twins, Esau and Jacob. Even before their birth, God told her ". . . the older will serve the younger" (Gen. 25:23). Jacob, the younger, would therefore receive the inheritance and the special blessing usually reserved for the firstborn son.

When a famine ravaged the land, Isaac moved (sound familiar?) elsewhere in Canaan to Gerar, governed by Abimelech, king of the Philistines. But Isaac wasn't satisfied. Because the annual flooding of the Nile meant good crops and plenty of food in Egypt, Isaac began thinking of going there. Such a move, however, would mean leaving the land God had promised Abraham. As Isaac was pondering his idea, God appeared and told him not to go to Egypt. Moving from a land of famine to a land of plenty seemed sensible, but God had other plans. Isaac obeyed God.

Temptation to Take the Easy Way Out

Isaac did not trust God for every problem he encountered in Gerar. Scared that some man might kill him in order to marry beautiful Rebekah, Isaac employed a scheme his father had used—he lied, telling everyone Rebekah was his sister. This plan backfired for Isaac just as it had for Abraham. One day, King Abimelech looked down from his window and saw Isaac necking with Rebekah—definitely not brother-sister stuff. Realizing that Rebekah was Isaac's wife, the king called Isaac in and chewed him out for lying. How humiliating for Isaac, a man who knew God, to be admonished by a pagan!

Faith grows only when a person actively seeks God and puts faith into practice. In his later years, Isaac grew careless, neglecting to put his faith into action. Those years were characterized by blunders. First, Isaac showed favoritism by doting on his older son Esau, the strong outdoorsman. He failed to recognize favoritism as a sin. Second, Isaac didn't attempt to prevent Esau from marrying a pagan woman. Because of Isaac's carelessness and weakness, Esau married two Hittite women. Third, Isaac embittered his wife, Rebekah, against himself—he favored Esau the outdoorsman, and she favored Jacob the homebody. A divided family always leads to trouble.

Fourth, Isaac, because of his favoritism, did not take seriously God's word which said the older son would serve the younger. Tradition required that the older son receive the inheritance and a special oral blessing, so Isaac did not have faith or courage to defy tradition and disappoint his favorite son. When the time came for the blessing, Isaac told Esau to kill wild game and prepare him a special meal. To correct Isaac's disobedience, Rebekah resorted to deceit: She cooked goat meat as Esau would cook his game, disguised Jacob in Esau's clothes, and sent Jacob in to dishonestly receive the blessing from his blind father. The scheme worked perfectly. When Isaac realized he had been tricked, it was too late. The enraged Esau vowed to kill his brother, so Jacob fled for his life.

Isaac's life shows the value of great faith and the need to exercise faith always, even in everyday matters. Heed the warning of Isaac's life: Put faith into practice or suffer the consequences.

The Vision and the Visible

"Abraham took the wood for the burnt offering and placed it on his son Isaac, and he himself carried the fire and the knife. As the two of them went on together, Isaac spoke up and said to his father Abraham, 'Father?' 'Yes, my son?' Abraham replied. 'The fire and wood are here,' Isaac said, 'but where is the lamb for the burnt offering?' Abraham answered, 'God himself will provide the lamb for the burnt offering, my son.' And the two of them went on together. When they reached the place God had told him about, Abraham built an altar there and arranged the wood on it. He bound his son Isaac and laid him on the altar, on top of the wood. Then he reached out his hand and took the knife to slay his son. But the angel of the Lord called out to him from heaven, 'Abraham! Abraham!' 'Here I am,' he replied. 'Do not lay a hand on the boy,' he said. 'Do not do anything to him. Now I know that you fear God, because you have not withheld from me your son, your only son.' Abraham looked up and there in a thicket he saw a ram caught by its horns. He went over and took the ram and sacrificed it as a burnt offering instead of his son" (Gen. 22:6–13).

Sometimes God calls you, as He called Isaac, to obey without explaining to you the outcome. When this happens, you must not start trying to give God "help." You'll get into big trouble if you try to work out the details and plan the steps that will lead to God's ultimate goal for your life. You may not see, for instance, how mopping the floor at Taco Bell every night will make you an effective Christian leader, but God does. You may not see how studying chemical formulas or practicing on your tuba can affect your future, but God does. As you live out the plot for the story of your life, you won't know how things are going to turn out, but God sees far ahead.

God's ways can seem very puzzling. Joseph found that the path to the palace led through prison. Moses discovered that leading God's people meant leading sheep first. David learned that becoming king required him first to spend years in the wilderness hiding like a common criminal. Young

Isaac found that living a deeper life with God meant facing death.

As he walked up the mountain with his father, Isaac finally realized *he* was the sacrifice. The father who had always shown him great love and tenderness now explained that God had commanded him to sacrifice his only son—but Abraham believed there would be a miracle. (For a discussion of this sacrifice, see the introduction to "Abraham: The Ups and Downs of a Friend of God.") Isaac could have justified running away at that point. He could have thought, *If God went to all the trouble to work a miracle for me to be born, why would He want me sacrificed? After all, God needs me to carry on the family line which He promised my father. Maybe my father is imagining he heard God—Dad is getting old. Besides, it hurts to get stabbed. I don't think I want to be part of this faith experiment.*

But Isaac didn't succumb to such thoughts. He knew he'd been a miracle baby, and that he owed his entire life to God. He had complete faith. Theodore Epp writes about such faith: "[It] can subdue every passion of the human heart and every imagination of the carnal mind by bringing everything into an obedient subjection to God."[2] As the child of promise, the heir through whom God would bless the world, Isaac could see no reason why he should become a burnt offering. In fact, it seemed to contradict the plan God had revealed. But he complied. As he felt the ropes tightening around his wrists, the firewood poking his back, and his muscles tensing in anticipation of his father's knife, Isaac gave up the right to think things through for himself, and instead trusted God.

God had planned the plot with a wonderful surprise ending. He knew exactly what He was doing—just as He always does. What a wonderful walk down the mountain Abraham and Isaac must have had! Imagine how close to God they felt, how glorious the plan of God seemed. Yet it never would have happened without faith which reached beyond human understanding. All this joy could have been spoiled by a little logical scheming and manipulating.

Keep the vision God gives you, but don't forget to obey Him right now, even when that obedience seems to be leading in another direction. When God expects you to obey without your seeing how He'll work things out, your job is not to connect the visible with the vision. God will do that. Your job is to make certain you hear God's voice and obey without question.

"He said to me: 'It is done. I am the Alpha and the Omega, the Beginning and the End' " (Rev. 21:6).

" 'For I know the plans I have for you,' declares the Lord, 'plans to prosper you and not to harm you, plans to give you hope and a future' " (Jer. 29:11).

"In him we were also chosen, having been predestined according to the

---

[2]Theodore Epp, *The God of Abraham, Isaac and Jacob.* Lincoln, Nebr.: Back to the Bible, 1981, pp. 167, 168.

plan of him who works out everything in conformity with the purpose of his will, in order that we, who were the first to hope in Christ, might be for the praise of his glory" (Eph. 1:11, 12).

1. Why don't you have to work out your own future, and each step from the present reality to the goal God has for you?
2. Write down the promises contained in the above verses.
3. How can the promises in your list help you when something happens that apparently spoils all your dreams and plans?
4. Talk to God, telling Him you want to trust Him with your future.

An Arranged Marriage—God's Way

"He said to the chief servant in his household, the one in charge of all that he had. '. . . I want you to swear by the Lord, the God of heaven and the God of earth, that you will not get a wife for my son from the daughters of the Canaanites, among whom I am living, but will go to my country and my own relatives and get a wife for my son Isaac.' 'The Lord . . . will send his angel before you so that you can get a wife for my son from there.' He set out for Aram Naharaim and made his way to the town of Nahor. Then he prayed, 'O Lord. . . . May it be that when I say to a girl, "Please let down your jar that I may have a drink," and she says, "Drink, and I'll water your camels too"—let her be the one you have chosen for your servant Isaac.' Before he had finished praying, Rebekah came out with her jar on her shoulder. The servant hurried to meet her and said, 'Please give me a little water from your jar.' 'Drink, my lord,' she said, and quickly lowered the jar to her hands and gave him a drink. After she had given him a drink, she said, 'I'll draw water for your camels too, until they have finished drinking.' Then the man bowed down and worshiped the Lord, saying, 'Praise be to the Lord, the God of my master Abraham, who has not abandoned his kindness and faithfulness to my master' " (Gen. 24:2–4, 7, 10, 12, 14, 15, 17–19, 27).

You probably have imagined it all: Someday you'll meet him, or her—attractive, polite, charming, intelligent, with interests like yours. You'll look into this person's eyes and feel special. As you get to know each other you'll fall in love, and you'll know *this* is the one for you! But maybe you've forgotten the most important ingredient in your idea of a "marriage made in heaven"—God's will and plan for your life.

Isaac trusted God to choose a wife for him. According to the custom of that time, parents arranged a marriage, usually with the consent of the children they'd matched up. Abraham wanted to make sure his son didn't marry a local idol-worshiper, so he sent his servant to Abraham's relatives to find the woman God had chosen for Isaac. God arranged it beautifully, and everyone recognized God's guidance. When the servant asked that

Rebekah come with him to marry Isaac, her brother answered, "This is from the Lord; we can say nothing to you one way or the other. Here is Rebekah; take her and go, and let her become the wife of your master's son, as the Lord has directed" (Gen. 24:50, 51).

God's choice was the best. The Bible says they were married ". . . and he loved her" (Gen. 24:67). Their love didn't fizzle out after the honeymoon, either, as King Abimelech of the Philistines could testify. He looked out his window one evening "and saw Isaac caressing his wife Rebekah" (Gen. 26:8). After forty years of marriage Isaac still couldn't keep his hands off her!

God chose the right woman for Isaac. Isaac was quiet and easy-going, but Rebekah had spunk—any girl who offered to water ten camels must have been hard-working and decisive! Isaac and Rebekah therefore complemented each other. No one can arrange a marriage better than God can.

Read Genesis 24—then reread it. Ask the Holy Spirit to show you how the principles in that chapter apply to the issues of dating and marriage in your life. Then change your attitudes. Decide not to date the girl you're first attracted to; instead, ask God whom to date. Determine not to trap the guy you have a crush on, but instead ask God to sort out your emotions and to give you the dates that would be best for you.

Make up your mind now that you will not date or marry anyone— unless God tells you to. Don't make a list of qualifications and start hunting. Seek God's will, remembering He is all-powerful. Isaac was forty years old and living in a country without one suitable marriage partner! But that posed no problem for God. Even if you, like Isaac, live in a Christianless wilderness, God can find for you the right friends and the right person to date—if you're willing to wait in faith and cooperate with Him.

"So they called Rebekah and asked her, 'Will you go with this man?' Then Rebekah and her maids got ready and mounted their camels and went back with the man. So the servant took Rebekah and left. Now Isaac had come from Beer Lahai Roi, for he was living in the Negev. He went out to the field one evening to meditate, and as he looked up, he saw camels approaching. Rebekah also looked up and saw Isaac. She got down from her camel and asked the servant, 'Who is that man in the field coming to meet us?' 'He is my master,' the servant answered. So she took her veil and covered herself. Then the servant told Isaac all he had done" (Gen. 24:58, 61–66).

1. List all the prerequisites you've decided are necessary for perfect marriage. Read Genesis 24:50. Cross out your list and write "Genesis 24:50" in its place.
2. In what ways did Isaac and Rebekah demonstrate great faith?
3. In what ways do you need to exercise faith about your desires for dating or marriage?

Conquering Confusion

"Isaac prayed to the Lord on behalf of his wife, because she was barren. The Lord answered his prayer, and his wife Rebekah became pregnant. The babies jostled each other within her, and she said, 'Why is this happening to me?' So she went to inquire of the Lord. The Lord said to her, 'Two nations are in your womb, and two peoples from within you will be separated; one people will be stronger than the other, and the older will serve the younger' " (Gen. 25:21–23).

Isaac and Rebekah had no children, and in their culture, childlessness was a tragedy. This bothered Isaac. But he also was bothered because God had promised to bless the whole world through his descendants. Yet, after twenty years of marriage, Isaac and Rebekah had no children. The situation confused him.

When she became pregnant, Rebekah had a problem that was very personal, something women who had birthed many children might have laughed about—there seemed to be a fight going on in her womb. This confused her.

Isaac and Rebekah knew what to do about the things that bothered them. They prayed. Instead of stewing and worrying, instead of seeking advice and sympathy from neighbors, they asked God. Their prayers weren't "Dear Abby" sessions, spent trying to help God clarify the problem, but were requests to an Almighty God who had the right answers. They prayed expecting God to intervene. And, as He always does, God answered such prayers.

Isaac preferred meditating in the field to planning decisive action. He was prone to accept whatever came along instead of taking positive steps to change things. Praying, for him, meant bucking the routine he preferred—endlessly mulling over the problem. Praying meant leaving his thoughts behind and, in faith, asking God to clarify the situation. And God did just that.

This episode in the lives of Isaac and Rebekah teaches that you can pray about anything and expect God to clear up your confusion. If you're wondering how to get along better with your parents, how to view capital punishment, how to handle feelings of inferiority, or how to be more outgoing, God is ready to help you. But, so often, you do everything but study what the Bible says about the issue and pray. You worry, read books on the problem, get everyone's advice, spend hours trying to think things through—everything, except pray. And if you do pray, you don't expect an answer. You only think of God as one more friend who will listen to your explanation of the problem.

With God, you are not helpless, for that situation is controlled by Jesus, not the devil. When Jesus died on the cross and rose again, He defeated the devil and his demons (Col. 2:13–15). Now Jesus is the head of the church, which is the body of people who truly believe in Him (Eph. 1:22, 23), and has put within each believer the same power that raised Jesus from the dead (Eph. 1:8–10). That power is available to you! As a Christian, you have been transferred from Satan's realm to the kingdom of light ruled by Jesus (Col. 1:13). The devil, therefore, has no legal power over you, so you can resist him and he will run from you (James 4:7). You have the authority.

When you face confusion, here's what to do: say out loud, "Devil, in the name of Jesus and by the power of His blood, I command you to leave." Then thank God that He will rule completely in this matter. Next, ask God if there is sin you must confess, or wrong attitudes and habits you must change. And let Him change you. Next, ask Him if you've been blinded by ingrained responses to problems. Ask for new ways to handle problems—God has promised for the Christian that "the old has gone, the new has come" (2 Cor. 5:17). Finally, pray for other people who may be involved in your problem. Pray they would see God's will and follow it—so God will be glorified, not so your life will be easier!

You don't have to continue to accept confusion, because God has provided all the power you need to deal with it. Confusion can be conquered in Jesus' name!

"Whatever you have learned or received or heard from me, or seen in me—put it into practice. And the God of peace will be with you" (Phil. 4:9).

"May God himself, the God of peace, sanctify you through and through. May your whole spirit, soul and body be kept blameless at the coming of our Lord Jesus Christ" (1 Thess. 5:23).

"You will keep in perfect peace him whose mind is steadfast, because he trusts in you" (Isa. 26:3).

1. Since God is a God of peace, is it His will that you stay confused?
2. What proof do you have that God cares about every part of you—body, soul, and spirit?
3. What formula does Isaiah 26:3 give for coming out of confusion and into peace?
4. Are you confused about something? Take a stand in faith now that God will clear away that confusion.

Angelic Visitors, Neon Lights, and Thunder from Heaven

"Now there was a famine in the land—besides the earlier famine of Abraham's time—and Isaac went to Abimelech king of the Philistines in Gerar. The Lord appeared to Isaac and said, 'Do not go down to Egypt; live in the land where I tell you to live. Stay in this land for a while, and I

will be with you and will bless you. For to you and your descendants I will give all these lands and will confirm the oath I swore to your father Abraham' " (Gen. 26:1–3).

A famine is no fun. People will do almost anything to avoid being hungry. Isaac learned about the hardship of famine by experience. When lack of rainfall caused a crop failure and a shortage of grass for his animals, he had to make a decision. Egypt had plenty of grain, so he considered going there. God, however, had promised Isaac's father Abraham that Canaan was the land for him and his descendants. If Isaac moved to Egypt he would leave this Promised Land. He would also leave God's special blessing, for God wanted Isaac to trust Him, and life in Egypt wasn't conducive to trust—Egypt symbolized luxury, ease, worldly pleasure, and spiritual compromise. While Isaac was trying to decide what to do, God appeared and told him to avoid Egypt, even though it meant giving up the security of knowing where his food would come from.

You may wish life could be that simple for you—if only you could hear a voice from heaven thundering out God's commands, or see an angel, or read flashing neon signs in the sky, you'd obey God perfectly. Everything would be clear if God would communicate His desires to you. Wrong. You're forgetting a couple of things.

First, you're forgetting communication involves receiving a message as well as sending it. Unless you are in tune with the Holy Spirit, who interprets God's Word for you, neon sky-signs won't impress you a bit.

Second, you're forgetting that you already have God's message—His Word. If your father wants you not to use the car for a month, it doesn't matter how he tells you. Whether he walks into your room, or calls you on the phone, or writes you a letter, the command is the same: You can't use the car. People would consider you weird if you said, "If only Dad would walk into my room and tell me not to use the car, then I would know what he wants. But all I have is a letter." Your father's word is enough. It's the same with God. When you have His Word—and the Holy Spirit to make it real to you—that's all you need.

One command God has made clear is not to "go to Egypt"—in other words, not to pursue the first idea that pops into your head. He has said, "Do not conform any longer to the pattern of this world, but be transformed by the renewing of your mind. Then you will be able to test and approve what God's will is—his good, pleasing and perfect will" (Rom. 12:2).

Don't let the world squeeze you into its mold. Instead, let God's Word guide you. Here's how it works: "His divine power has given us everything we need for life and godliness through our knowledge of him who called us by his own glory and goodness. Through these he has given us his very great and precious promises, so that through them you may participate in the divine nature and escape the corruption in the world caused by evil desires" (2 Pet. 1:3, 4).

To escape evil you must stick close to God's Word. Some people get out of balance by creating "One-Hundred-and-Fifty-Rigid-Rules-for-Righteousness" lists, instead of asking the Holy Spirit to guide them as they study and obey God's Word. Others try to control their environment by having contact only with Christians, instead of letting God's Word make them strong against temptation. The Bible doesn't say you will escape the corruption of this world through legalism, or tradition, or isolation. It says He has given wonderful promises so you can "escape the corruption in the world" (2 Pet. 1:4).

If you apply God's Word to your life, He will keep you from filth and corruption. If you rejoice in the Lord always (Phil. 4:4), make the joy of the Lord your strength (Neh. 8:10), and pray in Jesus' name so your joy will be complete (John 16:24), you won't be tempted to attend the party where everybody gets high, because the emptiness you once felt will be gone.

If you give thanks in all things (Eph. 5:20), show contentment with what you have (1 Tim. 6:6–8), and trust God to provide your needs (Phil. 4:19), you won't be tempted to shoplift.

If you practice "love your enemies" love (Matt. 5:44), you won't be tempted to spread the gossip you heard or to say something nasty to get even with your classmate.

If you keep your mind on whatever is true, honorable, just, pure, lovely, gracious, excellent, and praiseworthy (Phil. 4:8), you won't be tempted to see the movie loaded with sex and violence, or to visit the pornographic bookstore.

You don't need an angel, or a thundering voice, or neon lights to tell you not to go to Egypt. You already have God's clear command. You can know what to do and how to live because you have the Holy Spirit to lead you into the truth of God's Word. And that is enough.

"You are already made clean because of the word I have spoken to you. Remain in me, and I will remain in you" (John 15:3, 4).

"How can a young man keep his way pure? By living according to your word. I seek you with all my heart; do not let me stray from your commands. I have hidden your word in my heart that I might not sin against you" (Ps. 119:9–11).

1. Why are God's commands the same whether they are spoken audibly from Mount Sinai or read from the Bible?
2. Why will hearing, absorbing, declaring, and obeying God's commandments enable you to live a pure life?
3. Are you straying from one of God's commandments and heading toward "Egypt"? Get this matter straightened out with God right away.

New Software for Old Habits

"So Isaac stayed in Gerar. When the men of that place asked him about his wife, he said, 'She is my sister,' because he was afraid to say, 'She is my wife.' He thought, 'The men of this place might kill me on account of Rebekah, because she is beautiful.' When Isaac had been there a long time, Abimelech king of the Philistines looked down from a window and saw Isaac caressing his wife Rebekah. So Abimelech summoned Isaac and said, 'She is really your wife! Why did you say, "She is my sister"?' Isaac answered him, 'Because I thought I might lose my life on account of her.' Then Abimelech said, 'What is this you have done to us? One of the men might well have slept with your wife, and you would have brought guilt upon us' " (Gen. 26:6–10).

A friend of mine says, "Your greatest strength is your greatest weakness." This is often true. It was true of Isaac.

Isaac's easy-going nature made it easy for him not to rebel against his parents or his God. He showed great obedience and faith as he allowed his father to bind him to an altar as a sacrifice, and as he trusted his father's servant to carry out the all-important task of choosing his wife. Trust and obedience came naturally to him.

But such a temperament was also a pitfall. When obeying God required pioneering a new path and standing against pressure, Isaac didn't have the "right stuff"; in the land of the Philistines, he followed his father's example, right into trouble. Just like Abraham had told people his wife was his sister in order to keep himself safe, Isaac told people Rebekah was his sister—for the same reason. He knew it was wrong. But instead of praying about the danger he was facing, and finding God's solution, Isaac jumped at the only solution he knew. When the king saw Isaac embracing Rebekah, he knew Isaac had lied. So Isaac, the man of God, had to face the humiliation of being corrected by a pagan.

Isaac did what many children do. He repeated the mistakes of his parents whom he respected, and found out it's sometimes better not to be "a chip off the old block."

Statistics show that children who were abused by their parents often become child abusers, that children from divorced parents often end their own marriages in divorce. This is puzzling, for young people usually have lofty dreams of doing things very differently from what their parents did. Why, then, does this scenario occur? Because the first idea that comes to a person's mind when a problem strikes is to work it out the way he has seen someone else handle a similar crisis. Very often that someone else is a parent.

Isaac did exactly that. He and his beautiful wife were in a foreign land, and he felt himself in danger. He no doubt had heard how his father told everyone Sarah was his sister. Without thinking, Isaac did the same.

You, however, don't have to repeat your parents' mistakes. The Bible says, "For you know that it was not with perishable things such as silver or gold that you were redeemed from the empty way of life handed down to you from your forefathers, but with the precious blood of Christ, a lamb without blemish or defect" (1 Pet. 1:18, 19). Your parents' bad habits were not passed to you from their genes. You acquired those habits. But Jesus has set you free from the natural inclination to follow the easiest and familiar answers to problems.

To start walking in this freedom, to begin solving problems Jesus-style, you must retrain yourself to think as the new creation in Christ which the Bible says you are (2 Cor. 5:17). You're no longer bound by tradition, or by the examples of others, such as the method your mom uses to handle her emotions. You are free in Jesus. But you must learn to use this freedom. You must reprogram your mind as you would a computer. Instead of reacting according to the computer disks stored from previous experiences, learn to pray, "Jesus, how would you solve this problem?"

God's Word is the secret of the reprogramming process. It renews your mind and gives general guidelines for problem-solving: "Overcome evil with good," "serve one another in love," "share with God's people who are in need," and so on. As you meditate on God's Word it will fill your "software" with God's guidelines for action, and God's methods will become your natural reactions. After that, when you meet a problem you'll know the general guidelines, so you'll simply ask God to fill in the specifics.

All this is not to say you should start cutting down your parents. You are to respect, love, and obey them, not point out their shortcomings. You can, however, channel that special ability (which all teen-agers seem to possess) to see the inconsistencies of authority figures by looking for similar tendencies in yourself. Ask God to show you which undesirable traits you observe in others are present in you. (For example, if you think your mother yells at you for every little mistake, forgive her, then see if you may be treating your little sister the same way.) And let Him show you how to avoid falling into a similar pattern.

Isaac's bad habit, using the first reaction which popped into his mind, led to lying. Dishonesty, as always, is hard to hide. The hug he gave Rebekah gave him away. As a result, his pagan neighbors weren't impressed by Isaac's God who apparently couldn't protect one of His followers. But you can learn from Isaac. Decide not to repeat his mistake. The Lord has freed you from the tendency to automatically react according to familiar patterns. Give God a chance to reprogram your mind.

"You were taught, with regard to your former way of life, to put off your old self, which is being corrupted by its deceitful desires; to be made new in the attitude of your minds; and to put on the new self, created to be like God in true righteousness and holiness" (Eph. 4:22–24).

1. What are you commanded to do with old reactions and methods of handling problems?

2. Would God command you to do something He hasn't given you the power to do?
3. What is the next command?
4. Since you can get new attitudes only by letting God's Word become part of you, you must spend much time meditating on passages from the Bible. Are you willing to do that?

Personality Plus, Personality Minus, and Too Weird to Categorize

"The boys grew up, and Esau became a skillful hunter, a man of the open country, while Jacob was a quiet man, staying among the tents. Isaac, who had a taste for wild game, loved Esau, but Rebekah loved Jacob" (Gen. 25:27, 28).

How do you feel about teachers who have "pets"? If you have ever taken a class where *A's* were reserved for apple polishers, you know the anger favoritism causes.

The same problem occurs elsewhere, such as in families. Maybe your parents give your little brother all the attention and allow him to do things you never were permitted to try. As a result, you feel neglected and

"God doesn't put people into categories, and you mustn't either."

forgotten. Favoritism also occurs at work, and even at church, when those in charge make special allowances for the people they like best. Sometimes, however, you may be the favorite, and the jealous person becomes your enemy even though you have tried hard to prevent it.

Before you judge others for the sin of preferring someone over another, examine yourself. Playing favorites is one of the easiest traps to fall into. Do you go through the yearbook classifying the seniors—personality plus, personality minus, and too weird to categorize? Do you resent the history teacher's assigning you to work with George on the Civil War project—because George just isn't your type? Do you refuse to do your geometry homework because you have a "personality clash" with the teacher? Do you avoid the new girl at church because she makes nerdy remarks and doesn't dress in style? Do you plan to witness to Jill because she's the kind of person you'd like to have for a friend, but ignore Ellen because you don't especially care for her? You, as everyone, are tempted to cater to the people you enjoy, and to ignore the people you don't like.

Isaac was guilty of the sin of favoritism; he loved Esau more than Jacob. He was proud of this brave, athletic hunter, and he enjoyed the wild game which Esau prepared for him to eat. Isaac made his choice only on personal preference. Jacob, however, was quiet, and he enjoyed staying around the tents—nothing wrong with that. But Isaac admired an expert hunter, so he loved the son who fulfilled *his* expectations.

Isaac failed to deal with his sin, and thus caused great trouble in his family. Because Isaac found it hard to say no to Esau, his favorite, the rejected Jacob followed the example of his father. (In Gothard's seminar, he has said a child tends to acquire the parental traits which he most resents.) Out of his twelve sons, Jacob favored Joseph. The next chapter shows how much trouble that caused.

If you don't deal with your tendency to choose one person over another, and thus withhold your friendship from people whom you don't appreciate, you, like Isaac, will cause friction and heartache. Remember, you are a child of the God who sends rain on the just and the unjust, the God who shows no partiality. You, therefore, are to act like your heavenly Father. Scripture is very clear on this issue—"do nothing out of favoritism" (1 Tim. 5:21).

Examine yourself before God. Have you been trying hard to impress someone, while ignoring other people? Is there somebody you just can't stand? God doesn't put people into categories, and you mustn't either. God is in the business of changing people and He wants to use your love and acceptance to help someone become likable and friendly. Think about it. Can you serve a God who "does not show favoritism" (Acts 10:34) if you befriend only those who favorably impress you?

"Live in harmony with one another. Do not be proud, but be willing to associate with people of low position. Do not be conceited" (Rom. 12:16).

"My brothers, as believers in our glorious Lord Jesus Christ, don't show favoritism" (James 2:1).

"If you really keep the royal law found in Scripture, 'Love your neighbor as yourself,' you are doing right. But if you show favoritism, you sin and are convicted by the law as lawbreakers" (James 2:8, 9).

"These also are sayings of the wise: To show partiality in judging is not good" (Prov. 24:23).

1. Why is favoritism sin?
2. What are some ways in which you excuse your favoritism? What's wrong with these excuses?
3. Ask God to convict you of any preference you have shown for one person over another. Thank God for the good friends He has given you and determine that you and your friends will not make anybody else feel left out.

Whom Are You Leading into Temptation?

"When Isaac was old and his eyes were so weak that he could no longer see, he called for Esau his older son and said to him, 'My son.' 'Here I am,' he answered. Isaac said, 'I am now an old man and don't know the day of my death. Now then, get your weapons—your quiver and bow—and go out to the open country to hunt some wild game for me. Prepare me the kind of tasty food I like and bring it to me to eat, so that I may give you my blessing before I die.' Rebekah said to her son Jacob, 'Look, I overheard your father say to your brother Esau. . . . Go out to the flock and bring me two choice young goats, so I can prepare some tasty food for your father, just the way he likes it. Then take it to your father to eat, so that he may give you his blessing before he dies.' After Isaac finished blessing him and Jacob had scarcely left his father's presence, his brother Esau came in from hunting. He too prepared some tasty food and brought it to his father. Then he said to him, 'My father, sit up and eat some of my game, so that you may give me your blessing.' His father Isaac asked him, 'Who are you?' 'I am your son,' he answered, 'your firstborn, Esau.' Isaac trembled violently and said, 'Who was it, then, that hunted game and brought it to me? I ate it just before you came and I blessed him—and indeed he will be blessed!' " (Gen. 27:1-4, 6, 9, 10, 30-33).

Although Isaac showed great faith when God required passivity, he had a hard time exercising faith when God required action. God had told Rebekah before the twins were born, "The elder shall serve the younger" (Gen. 25:23). This was God's plan. The inheritance and the blessing would be Jacob's. In carelessness and weakness, however, Isaac ignored

God's word and prepared to give the blessing to Esau. Obeying God in this matter would mean bucking tradition and trying to explain the reasons to Esau, the strong-willed son whom he loved more than Jacob. Instead of acting in faith, Isaac took the easy way out.

Rebekah was dead wrong in devising a scheme which involved deceit in order to ensure God's will was fulfilled. She wanted Jacob to receive his blessing. "She was not going to leave anything to chance. However, neither did she leave anything to faith."[3] Her lack of faith was sin, but since we're talking about Isaac, it's only fair to note that wishy-washy, indecisive people who just let things slide, valuing convenience above all else, make life very difficult for others. A person, such as Isaac, who is out of the will of God puts great temptation in the way of others. The people close to Isaac found obeying God very hard because he was disobeying.

How about checking your life for omissions that make other people want to step in and do "God's will" for you, even if their method is wrong? Your mother may be trying to run your life for you, but maybe your laziness and irresponsibility tempt her beyond endurance. Your father may not trust you as much as your older brother, but maybe your carelessness and indecision keep him from giving you important responsibilities. Your parents and teachers may be constantly nagging you, but maybe your endless procrastinating leaves them no choice. That pushy girl may always be trying to run the youth group which elected you president, but maybe your poor performance constrains her to act before things fall apart.

Don't be an Isaac who sets things up so some Rebekah finds it easy to sin. Examine your life. Whom are you leading into temptation? Determine by God's grace to root out the things in your life that invite others to sin. Then live to encourage those around you to do God's will. Your example should be leading people into victory, not into temptation!

"When Peter came to Antioch, I opposed him to his face, because he was in the wrong. Before certain men came from James, he used to eat with the Gentiles. But when they arrived, he began to draw back and separate himself from the Gentiles because he was afraid of those who belonged to the circumcision group. The other Jews joined him in his hypocrisy, so that by their hypocrisy even Barnabas was led astray" (Gal. 2:11–13).

1. In the above case, how did Peter make it easy for others to sin?
2. Can you recall an instance in which you sinned because someone you respected made it easy for you to disobey God?
3. Prejudices, customs, and traditions can be very blinding. Ask God to show you if your lack of courage in standing up for something that is right, rather than following your group of friends, is helping someone else to follow the wrong path.
4. Which is more important to you, what's right or what people think?

---

[3]*Ibid.*, p. 202.

JOSEPH: THE LEMONADE PRINCIPLE MAKES DREAMS COME TRUE

Introduction

Question: What should you do if life throws you a lemon?
Answer: Make lemonade.

Not a bad principle. You need to learn to make the best of even a bad situation, and the life of Joseph provides Lesson One. But first, a bit of background.

A Difficult Homelife

Joseph was born in the sixteenth century B.C., the eleventh son of Jacob who had two wives—the rivalry was fierce, and, Joseph's mother, Rachel, was the favorite. She died after the birth of Benjamin, the youngest child in the family. Because Joseph was the oldest son of Jacob's favorite wife, Jacob gave him special attention and thus infuriated the boy's ten half brothers. He even gave this son a beautiful long-sleeved coat which was worn only by the noblemen of that time.

Joseph dreamed the sun, moon and eleven stars (symbolizing his parents and brothers) bowed down to him; then, rather than silently wait for God to fulfill this prophecy, he blabbed about the dream, only adding to his brothers' jealousy. One day Joseph's father sent him to check on the ten brothers who were tending Jacob's flocks several miles away in Dothan. When Joseph found them, some of the brothers wanted to kill him. They finally compromised by throwing him in an empty cistern, used to collect rain water, and leaving him there to die. When a caravan of traders passed by, Judah got the bright idea of selling his brother as a slave! After the caravan left with their kid brother, the rascals killed a goat, dipped Joseph's gorgeous coat in the blood, and brought it to Jacob. The brothers convinced him they had found it beside the road and Joseph had been killed by a wild animal.

Unfair Treatment

The traders hauled Joseph to Egypt and there sold him to Potiphar, commander of the king's Not-So-Secret Service. Joseph remained obedient to God, working faithfully at his duties. As the months passed,

Potiphar noticed Joseph was a trustworthy and gifted administrator, so he placed him in charge of his entire household.

Potiphar's wife noticed something different—Joseph's good looks, and set out to seduce him. Unwilling to sin against God or her husband, Joseph refused her advances. But he could not escape her, for he was a slave in that house. One day, in desperation, the woman grabbed him by his jacket and pleaded with him to come to bed. He ran, leaving the jacket—and his fate—in her hands.

Angered by Joseph's rejection, she told her husband his slave had tried to rape her. She showed the jacket as evidence and Potiphar threw Joseph in the dungeon.

Even in prison Joseph kept trusting God and performed his duties faithfully. Like Potiphar, the warden soon recognized Joseph's character and ability and placed him in charge of all the prisoners. One day the Pharaoh's baker and cupbearer (he checked all the king's beverages for poison) became inmates. Before long they each had a dream which Joseph interpreted. And exactly as Joseph had predicted, the baker was soon executed and the cupbearer returned to his position in the palace. But he forgot to mention Joseph to the Pharaoh.

Making It Big

Two years after his cupbearer's return, the Pharaoh dreamed that seven fat cows were devoured by seven scrawny ones. Puzzled, he mentioned the dream to various people. Then the cupbearer remembered Joseph.

At the king's request Joseph came from the prison to stand before him and interpret the dream. The seven fat cows would be seven years of good crops, he said, but the skinny cows were seven years of famine. Then Joseph suggested a plan to store food for the dry years. The Pharaoh recognized a born leader in Joseph and named him prime minister. Quite a leap from prison. And Joseph set about constructing warehouses and filling them with surplus grain.

When the famine finally came, it affected neighboring countries as well. Jacob's family also suffered from the draught, and he sent his sons to buy grain in Egypt. They had to deal directly with Joseph. But they didn't recognize him, and he didn't reveal his identity until he had tested them and arranged circumstances that brought them to repentance for their deeds against him.

Finally Joseph exposed his identity. He harbored no bitterness. Instead, he had seen God's hand working in all his hard times. He then invited the brothers to move their entire family to Egypt.

Egyptians despised shepherds so the family of Jacob was not accepted by these idol worshipers. This was God's way of keeping His people set apart for himself.

Three Strikes Against You—So You Hit a Home Run!

"So Rachel died, and she was buried on the way to Ephrath (that is, Bethlehem). . . . Now Israel loved Joseph more than any of his other sons, because he had been born to him in his old age; and he made a richly ornamented robe for him. When his brothers saw that their father loved him more than any of them, they hated him and could not speak a kind word to him. Then he had another dream, and he told it to his brothers. 'Listen,' he said, 'I had another dream, and this time the sun and moon and eleven stars were bowing down to me.' His brothers were jealous of him, but his father kept the thing in mind. So Joseph went after his brothers, and found them near Dothan. They saw him in the distance, and before he reached them, they plotted to kill him. . . . Judah said to his brothers, 'What will we gain if we kill our brother and cover up his blood? Come, let's sell him to the Ishmaelites.' . . . Now Joseph had been taken down to Egypt. Potiphar, an Egyptian who was one of Pharaoh's officials, the captain of the guard, bought him from the Ishmaelites who had taken him there" (Gen. 35:19; 37:3, 4, 9, 11, 17, 18, 26, 27; 39:1).

Have you ever thought your tough home situation, bad grades, and lack of talent make your life almost hopeless? Well, you need to meet Joseph. Theodore Epp, a respected Bible teacher, wrote of him: "In Joseph, God wanted to show us how a person can live honorably before God regardless of his heredity and environment."[1]

Perhaps your parents are divorced and you don't get along with your stepfather. On the other hand, you may be a spoiled brat who has developed selfish habits and attitudes which are now ruining your social life. Perhaps alcoholism, mental illness, or drug abuse has ruined your home life. Whatever the problem, here's good news: God is in the business of remaking people, healing broken hearts, and putting together the shattered pieces of mixed-up families.

The life of Joseph proves God can work out His great purpose despite difficult circumstances. And his were difficult. His father's wives, who were sisters, hated each other. Joseph had to live with the consequences of the disobedience to God which had caused this horrible home situation. To make matters worse, his father favored him. This not only inspired his brothers to hate him, but probably left him spoiled and untrained to face tough breaks of adult life. Because Joseph lost his mother during Benjamin's birth, Jacob no doubt gave him an extra dose of coddling. The fancy coat and the dream which Joseph couldn't keep secret finally caused the half brothers' jealousy to explode—they sold their own brother to

---

[1]Theodore H. Epp, *Joseph: God Planned It for Good.* Lincoln, Nebr.: Back to the Bible, 1982, p. 9.

some traders, and Joseph found himself on the auction block in Egypt.

If someone who didn't know the end of Joseph's story heard only this much, he would assume Joseph became a drug addict, had a nervous breakdown, or became very bitter. This probably would have been the case without God. But God surprised everyone and made Joseph a forgiving, prosperous, highly-respected man.

What will be the end of your story? God can transform your life, no matter how messed-up it is. You may feel you have three strikes against you, but with God you still can hit a home run!

"The Lord will fulfill his purpose for me; your love, O Lord, endures forever—do not abandon the works of your hands" (Ps. 138:8).

"I cry out to God Most High, to God, who fulfills his purpose for me. He sends from heaven and saves me, rebuking those who hotly pursue me; God sends his love and his faithfulness" (Ps. 57:2, 3).

"His divine power has given us everything we need for life and godliness through our knowledge of him who called us by his own glory and goodness. Through these he has given us his very great and precious promises, so that through them you may participate in the divine nature and escape the corruption in the world caused by evil desires" (2 Pet. 1:3, 4).

1. What do the above verses say to a person who feels unable to overcome a bad background?
2. Notice these verses say God promises to fulfill *His* purpose for you, not the goals you've set for yourself. Are you willing to let God determine your future?
3. In order to live above your background, how must you receive what you need for "life and godliness"?
4. Which of the above Bible promises will you hang onto this week? How will you apply it to the problems you'll face?

The Way Out of Temptation City

"So he left in Joseph's care everything he had; with Joseph in charge, he did not concern himself with anything except the food he ate. Now Joseph was well-built and handsome, and after a while his master's wife took notice of Joseph and said, 'Come to bed with me!' But he refused. 'With me in charge,' he told her, 'my master does not concern himself with anything in the house; everything he owns he has entrusted to my care. No one is greater in this house than I am. My master has withheld nothing from me except you, because you are his wife. How then could I do such a wicked thing and sin against God?' And though she spoke to Joseph day after day, he refused to go to bed with her or even be with her. One day he went into the house to attend to his duties, and none of the household servants was inside. She caught him by his cloak and said, 'Come to bed with me!' But he left his

cloak in her hand and ran out of the house" (Gen. 39:6–12).

How do you respond to temptations too hard to resist? With excuses? Maybe you can relate to some of the following statements:

"Whenever I see my old friend, I start smoking again."

"If I really acted as a Christian at school, I wouldn't have one friend."

"My girlfriend and I can't hold out much longer. We love each other too much."

If anyone could have used these kinds of excuses for yielding to temptation, it was Joseph. He was far away from home, with no one around who knew him. In fact, he lived in a society that approved of premarital and extramarital sex—he wouldn't have to explain to anyone. He might have reasoned, "Can I help having sex appeal?" Besides, he was a slave, bound to do whatever Mrs. Potiphar ordered. He could try to avoid her, but he was her property and thus had to work in her house every day. He knew the possible consequences of refusing her commands. Nonetheless, Joseph resisted. Why?

First, he based his actions on God's Word, rather than on the opinions and views of other people. He refused the woman's invitation to adultery, not on the basis of logic which could be refuted, or customs which vary from country to country and decade to decade, but on the basis of God's command: adultery is sin. The biblical argument against illicit sex is not the possibility of pregnancy or V.D. It is: "The body is not meant for sexual immorality, but for the Lord. . . " (1 Cor. 6:13). New antibiotics or birth control methods will not change this kind of reasoning.

Don't ever judge God's commandments through the eyes of logic, tradition or majority opinion. Use those commandments, as Joseph did, to guide your life.

Second, Joseph could resist temptation because he took a strong stand against it from the beginning. Epp notes: "By a definite act of Joseph's will he refused to yield to what he knew was sin. Once we have said no to sin, it is easier to reject it the next time."[2] Because Joseph had the Spirit of God living in him, he knew "to set the mind on the flesh is death, but to set the mind on the Spirit is life and peace" (Rom. 8:6). Had he allowed his mind to be preoccupied with sex, he would easily have fallen prey to sin. Instead, he filled his mind with God's commandments.

Third, Joseph could resist temptation because he chose to be popular only with God—no matter what the price. He knew the fury of a rejected woman could throw him into serious trouble. But he didn't care. Temptation isn't so hard to resist if you really want to obey God.

Fourth, he could resist because he was willing to run from temptation, to avoid it at all cost. You must do the same. Don't read a few pages in that novel with a sexy cover to see if it actually is dirty. Walk away. Stay miles away from the party that will tempt you back into drugs. Carefully

---

[2]*Ibid.*, p. 39.

plan your dates to avoid any possibility of sexual temptation. Vow that popularity with the kids at school will not control your life.

The way out of Temptation City is the steepest and least-traveled road, but the end leads to heaven, and there are some beautiful rest stops along the way.

"Test everything. Hold on to the good. Avoid every kind of evil" (1 Thess. 5:21, 22).

"No temptation has seized you except what is common to man. And God is faithful; he will not let you be tempted beyond what you can bear. But when you are tempted, he will also provide a way out so that you can stand up under it" (1 Cor. 10:13).

"If you love me, you will obey what I command. And I will ask the Father, and he will give you another Counselor to be with you forever" (John 14:15, 16).

"This is love for God: to obey his commands. And his commands are not burdensome" (1 John 5:3).

1. Is it hard to obey someone you really love?
2. If you don't enjoy obeying God's commandments, check out your relationship with Jesus. Ask Him to show you where you need to improve that relationship.
3. The key to avoiding temptation is setting your mind on a clear goal: being like Jesus. Using the above verses as a guide, write down the principles by which you intend to live a "Jesus life."
4. What attitudes and actions must you change in order to resist temptation?

The Minus that Makes a Real Plus

"When his master heard the story his wife told him, saying, 'This is how your slave treated me,' he burned with anger. Joseph's master took him and put him in prison, the place where the king's prisoners were confined. But while Joseph was there in the prison, the Lord was with him; he showed him kindness and granted him favor in the eyes of the prison warden. So the warden put Joseph in charge of all those held in the prison, and he was made responsible for all that was done there. The warden paid no attention to anything under Joseph's care, because the Lord was with Joseph and gave him success in whatever he did" (Gen. 39:19–23).

How do you handle the teacher who picks on you, the boss who gives you all the dirty work, and the little brother who gets away with murder while you're expected to do things right? Have you learned the secret of handling these predicaments successfully? Joseph's stay in prison reveals it.

After surviving his father's favoritism, his brothers' hatred, and finally slavery, Joseph was unjustly imprisoned—just when it seemed God should have given him a gold medal for resisting temptation. Joseph's secret was a life minus bitterness. He certainly had reason to be bitter. But he wasn't.

Hidden bitterness always leaks out—as disrespect for authority; or as an everybody-picks-on-me or I-never-get-a-fair-shake attitude. Or it shows on one's face. But Joseph's jailer didn't detect any of these in Joseph. Instead, he noticed "the Lord was with Joseph and gave him success in whatever he did" (Gen. 39:23).

Later, when Joseph—as prime minister—had authority even to kill his brothers, he never tried to repay their evil deeds. Although he tested them to see if their characters had changed, he was never bitter. Instead, he told them, "You intended to harm me, but God intended it for good to accomplish what is now being done, the saving of many lives" (Gen. 50:20).

This was part of Joseph's secret. He believed everything fit into God's purpose, that God can use even evil attitudes and sinful deeds to bring people closer to Him, to fit them for His purpose, and to mold them into His image.

With such an outlook you also can overcome bitterness. Someone in your geometry class needs to see you react with love when the teacher unfairly accuses you. Humility and a helpfulness will touch the heart of your boss who gives you the hard jobs because you don't complain. And maybe your little brother needs a role model for his life.

Joseph not only trusted God's long-range plans, he knew how to receive power from God for each day. He didn't say, "I'm supposed to be a good boy so I'll act nice, keeping in all my pent-up anger." Instead, he trusted God to give him an attitude of forgiveness. He decided not to brood over the wrongs done to him and attacked the job at hand with the Holy Spirit's enthusiasm and energy. He had no time left to be bitter.

Someone has said hardships either make you bitter or better. Let Joseph be your example for the "better." Don't let injustice, tragedy, or indifference sour you. A life minus bitterness is a real plus.

"See to it that no one misses the grace of God and that no bitter root grows up to cause trouble and defile many" (Heb. 12:15).

"Get rid of all bitterness, rage and anger, brawling and slander, along with every form of malice. Be kind and compassionate to one another, forgiving each other, just as in Christ God forgave you. Be imitators of God, therefore, as dearly loved children and live a life of love, just as Christ loved us and gave himself up for us as a fragrant offering and sacrifice to God" (Eph. 4:31—5:2).

1. How can bitterness keep you from receiving all of God's kindness and love?

2. With what are you to replace bitterness?
3. From where does the love that erases bitterness come?
4. Ask God to show you what things you are bitter about. Decide to receive His power and love so healthy attitudes can replace your bitterness.

Is God Your Partner?

" 'I cannot do it,' Joseph replied to Pharaoh, 'but God will give Pharaoh the answer he desires' " (Gen. 41:16).

Joseph had just walked out of prison and was standing before the Pharaoh, the most powerful king in the world. And now he was expected to interpret the king's dream. Kicking a field goal from the 50-yard line in the final thirty seconds of a tied Super Bowl game would have been easier. The words Joseph spoke in that tight spot revealed another secret of his life, a secret that enabled him to trust God to bring him through tough circumstances victoriously. He told the king, "I can't do it. But God will." Joseph was in partnership with God.

You face "pharaohs": the driver's license exam; an oral report in chemistry class; batting with the bases loaded and two out in the bottom of the ninth inning; witnessing to friends at school; family squabbles. And God will perform miracles when you face those trials—if you cooperate.

Making way for a miracle is a bit like walking to the bus station while lugging two heavy suitcases, a guitar, and a tennis racket. You're certain your body can't endure the remaining eight blocks—you need a miracle. Just then a world-class weightlifter appears.

He says, "I'd be glad to carry everything for you. Just tell me where you're headed."

The offer troubles you. You'd love the help, but you're unsure the man can be trusted. Will he steal your possessions? Will he carefully handle your new guitar? You must choose between freedom from the load and control over your possessions. But miracles don't come when you're in control.

If Joseph had thought, *I'd better say everything right—my whole future depends on it*, he would have been under great strain. His mind would have been on himself and possible failure, and he wouldn't have received God's revelation. But he trusted God, and the insight Joseph received catapulted him to the position of prime minister.

You can do the same. Relax and let God help you through the driver's test. It won't be such a terrible ordeal. Give that chemistry report to glorify God—not to impress your classmates. If you flub a few times, He'll understand, and you won't feel so much tension. If you're in partnership with God, you can calmly enjoy the ball game, even if you strike out in the bottom of the ninth with the bases loaded. If you're witnessing to friends or trying to keep your cool at home, the Holy Spirit will make it happen—if you give Him your reputation and allow Him to work through you in His own way.

Partnership with God develops through a learning process. By spending time with Him you learn to know what He wants. Through hard times you learn to be broken of attitudes that hinder the relationship: selfishness; wanting to be right; unwillingness to change; ignorance; impulsiveness; passivity; and pride. This learning process isn't easy, but it's worth the effort. Joseph couldn't enter the palace until he'd been a slave and prisoner, and you can't expect God to deliver you during that exam if you've been skipping His classes and ignoring His homework.

Partnership with God is a binding commitment, not something you can jump in and out of like a swimming pool. It is more like being a canvas and letting the Master Artist paint anything He wishes on your life. It is a partnership in which your only duty is to cooperate. If you are that kind of partner you can stand before any "pharaoh" and expect your divine Partner to come through.

"When you are brought before synagogues, rulers and authorities, do not worry about how you will defend yourselves or what you will say, for the Holy Spirit will teach you at that time what you should say" (Luke 12:11, 12).

"Now to him who is able to do immeasurably more than all we ask or imagine, according to his power that is at work within us, to him be glory in the church and in Christ Jesus throughout all generations, for ever and ever! Amen" (Eph. 3:20, 21).

"But thanks be to God, who always leads us in triumphal procession in Christ and through us spreads everywhere the fragrance of the knowledge of him" (2 Cor. 2:14).

"The Lord is my light and my salvation—whom shall I fear? The Lord is the stronghold of my life—of whom shall I be afraid?" (Ps. 27:1).

1. What can God do through you if you let Him?
2. What attitudes and actions can prevent God from doing His work through you?
3. What "pharaoh" must you face this week? Pick a truth from one of the above verses and use it to guide you as you face your tough challenge.

Are You a Product of God's Remodeling Factory?

"So Pharaoh asked them, 'Can we find anyone like this man, one in whom is the spirit of God?' Then Pharaoh said to Joseph, 'Since God has made all this known to you, there is no one so discerning and wise as you' " (Gen. 41:38, 39).

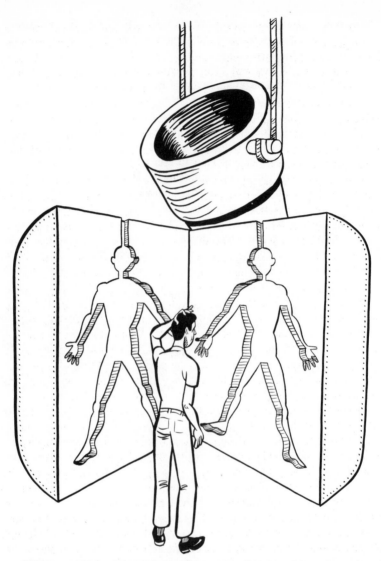

"Do you often jump from the mold that would reshape your character and improve your personality?"

"I'm just a country clutz."

"What more can you expect of an inner-city idiot?"

"It's my suburban stupidity."

"I'm nervous, just like my mother."

"I inherited my bluntness from my father."

"Oh, well, everybody in my family hated to study and thus earned bad grades in school."

Do these statements sound familiar? Do you feel as if you can't do anything right when under pressure? Do displaying poise in social situations, giving appropriate replies, and handling emergencies calmly seem to be skills only other people possess? And it probably never occurred to you God might be able to do something about your lack.

If you are thinking this way, you are limiting God who has the ability to change you. You expect Him to help you stop sinning—even tough sins such as drug abuse and dishonesty. And He will. But you've probably thought He can do nothing to change your personality defects. Not true. Here again, you can learn from the life of Joseph.

Joseph grew up among shepherds, then endured slavery and imprisonment. Imagine yourself coming from such a background—then being instantly promoted to the palace! That would be a pressure situation. But Joseph didn't cave in under the pressure. Instead, the pagan king was amazed, and he recognized Joseph's poise and inner strength had come from God. He even was impressed by the discreetness of Joseph—who had once blurted out all his dreams to anyone within earshot. Joseph certainly had experienced a miracle, but how?

First, the miracle occurred because Joseph had willingly gone through God's remodeling factory. He believed God could remake him completely. That is why he could later tell his brothers, "You intended to harm me, but God intended it for good. . . ." Joseph had seen that from any heartache, scar, or nasty circumstance, God could forge the jewels of character: compassion, patience, and understanding of others. So Joseph had sustained pain and suffering, always trusting God to do His work.

Second, the miracle occurred because Joseph learned the lesson of patient waiting. Slaves and prisoners, of course, have no choice but to wait, so Joseph was in an ideal situation for remodeling—personality remakes take time. And he learned to wait for God's perfect moment, even though Joseph, as prime minister, had complete authority over people. When his brothers appeared to buy grain, he could have pulled rank on them. He could have confronted them with their sin of selling him, extracted a confession, and vented all his emotions within an hour. And don't think the temptation to do so never entered his mind. Instead, Joseph obeyed God and step by step placed his brothers in circumstances that brought them to repentance. This probably took at least two years. That's patience!

Do you often jump from the mold that would reshape your character and improve your personality? Do you insist on clearing up a misunderstanding today? Demand a hearing immediately? Try forcing your parents to conform to your viewpoint? Do you forget people's emotions are delicate and must be handled with God's wisdom, and impatiently fumble each chance God gives for learning tact and poise? Would you prefer to improve your study habits by rubbing Aladdin's lamp, rather than by consistent hard work? Would you prefer to receive an injection that will instantly heal your broken heart, rather than slowly learn God's lessons?

Would you like to acquire gracious speech habits without having to listen to others and be sensitive to their feelings?

If you find yourself guilty of any of these attitudes, it's time for you to start acting like a product, rather than a boss, in God's remodeling factory. If you want to be a Joseph, you must obey like Joseph.

"And we, who with unveiled faces all reflect the Lord's glory, are being transformed into his likeness with ever-increasing glory, which comes from the Lord, who is the Spirit" (2 Cor. 3:18).

"And we know that in all things God works for the good of those who love him, who have been called according to his purpose" (Rom. 8:28).

"A student is not above his teacher, but everyone who is fully trained will be like his teacher" (Luke 6:40).

"The Sovereign Lord has given me an instructed tongue, to know the word that sustains the weary. He wakens me morning by morning, wakens my ear to listen like one being taught" (Isa. 50:4).

1. Where does the power for a changed personality come from?
2. Jesus has a perfect personality. Since He has the power to be perfect, why don't you pray and ask Him for power to do things like lose weight, be understanding toward others, and the ability to make new friends?
3. Once in God's remodeling factory, can you expect to specify the method He uses to change you? If not, are you willing to place yourself in His hands to do as He pleases?
4. Find a statement in one of the above verses which you can claim as a promise. On the basis of that promise, trust God for a specific change in your personality.

How Far Is It from Under the Pile to on Top of the World?

"So the chief cupbearer told Joseph his dream. 'This is what it means,' Joseph said to him. ' . . . Within three days Pharaoh will lift up your head and restore you to your position . . . But when all goes well with you, remember me and show me kindness; mention me to Pharaoh and get me out of this prison. For I was forcibly carried off from the land of the Hebrews, and even here I have done nothing to deserve being put in a dungeon.' Now the third day was Pharaoh's birthday, and he . . . restored the chief cupbearer to his position. . . . The chief cupbearer, however, did not remember Joseph; he forgot him" (Gen. 40:9, 12–15, 20–23).

"Sir, can you tell me how to get from under the pile to on top of the world?" Sounds like an introduction to a kid's cartoon feature. But if you're honest, you may admit having thought those very words about your own life. In fact, you feel like a permanent resident of "under the pile."

You know what that means. Just when you wish you could take things a bit at a time, everything comes at once. Sixth-hour Biology gets more boring by the day. The depressing ramifications of nuclear war have been discussed in Social Problems class for six weeks. Your ex-boyfriend's new chick just moved into the locker on your left. Your family has serious money problems and your father fears he'll be losing his job. When life overwhelms you, you're under the pile.

How can you handle overwhelming problems that seem as if they'll never go away? Again, take a good look at Joseph.

For Joseph, both slavery and imprisonment appeared hopelessly permanent. First came the loss of freedom and never-ending work with no paycheck at the end of the week. Then chains and dungeon gloom darkened the picture. And just when a ray of hope entered—the king's butler returned to his palace job, where he could have put in a good word—Joseph had to endure two more years of darkness, dirt and depression. How could he be victorious in all this? He had a formula: Victory = Faith + Faithfulness.

Faith made Joseph successful, even in prison, enabling him to bring cheer to others. You need such faith which believes God will never allow you to experience trials greater than He will give strength to handle. (This guarantee won't hold if you attempt to face problems in your own strength.) Claim God's promise: "Therefore let every one who is godly offer prayer to thee; at a time of distress, in the rush of great waters, they shall not reach him. Thou art a hiding place for me, thou preservest me from trouble; thou dost encompass me with deliverance" (Ps. 32:6, 7). Never let the devil convince you God doesn't care, or can't give you strength for the problem you're facing.

Faithfulness, according to Epp, is "the duty of life."[3] Displaying faithfulness in all you do is not only your responsibility to God and others, it's good for you. Because Joseph faithfully performed his tasks in prison, he lived victoriously, and unknowingly prepared for a glorious future.

Faithfulness will bless you. If you carefully complete your Biology assignment, keeping your mind on Jesus, you can rejoice as you observe how God planned each organism perfectly. And your boredom will disappear. If you pray about how to approach your project on the dangers of nuclear war, God can not only help you turn out good work, He can make you a member of the "We-will-not-fear-though-the-earth-give-way-and-the-mountains-fall-into-the-heart-of-the-sea" Club (Ps. 46:2).

Concentrating on doing your best for God in each class and task will give you little time to nurse your broken heart. And it will give God a chance to reveal your future "on top of the world." You can get there, regardless of your circumstances, if you follow the formula of faith plus faithfulness.

"If this is so, then the Lord knows how to rescue godly men from trials

---

[3]*Ibid.*, p. 83.

and to hold the unrighteous for the day of judgment, while continuing their punishment" (2 Pet. 2:9).

"Dear friends, do not be surprised at the painful trial you are suffering, as though something strange were happening to you. But rejoice that you participate in the sufferings of Christ, so that you may be overjoyed when his glory is revealed. If you are insulted because of the name of Christ, you are blessed, for the Spirit of glory and of God rests on you. If you suffer, it should not be as a murderer or thief or any other kind of criminal, or even as a meddler. However, if you suffer as a Christian, do not be ashamed, but praise God that you bear that name" (1 Pet. 4:12–16).

1. What kind of suffering do you unnecessarily bring on yourself? Ask God to show you which of your sufferings are due to lack of faithfulness. Now confess your sin and decide to change your ways.
2. From the above verses, what promise can you claim for times you must suffer?
3. How can trials and suffering be a blessing?

Watch Out for Falling Stars

"Then Joseph said to his brothers, 'Come close to me.' When they had done so, he said, 'I am your brother Joseph, the one you sold into Egypt! And now, do not be distressed and do not be angry with yourselves for selling me here, because it was to save lives that God sent me ahead of you. For two years now there has been famine in the land, and for the next five years there will not be plowing and reaping. But God sent me ahead of you to preserve for you a remnant on earth and to save your lives by a great deliverance. So then, it was not you who sent me here, but God' " (Gen. 45:4–8).

When your friend is voted captain of the football team, is crowned Apple Blossom Queen, or gains the lead part in the school play, you find out what he or she is made of—especially if you don't run around with the popular crowd. Does your friend still have time for you? Or are you lucky to get an appointment with the new star six months in advance? The temptations that accompany sudden power, prestige, or popularity can ruin a once-nice person. Authority and influence are easily misused.

Joseph was propelled instantly to the peak of authority and influence, the ultimate rags-to-riches story. Now he had the power to even the score with his brothers. But the same truth that sustained Joseph through slavery and imprisonment kept him from caving in under the temptation to misuse his authority. He knew God had promoted him in order to fulfill His purpose. For that reason Joseph was not impressed with his own importance or anxious to use his great power for selfish goals.

When his brothers feared he might try to get even after their father was dead, Joseph assured, "Don't be afraid. Am I in the place of God?" (Gen. 50:19). He meant to do God's will, not his own. He realized God had sent him to Egypt and granted his high position to save God's chosen people. So Joseph identified himself with his relatives and invited them to live in Egypt. By doing this he risked losing the Egyptian's respect, for they despised shepherds. The Bible says, ". . . all shepherds are detestable to the Egyptians" (Gen. 46:34). Now all Egypt would know Joseph grew up as a shepherd. God protected Joseph's reputation, however, and caused Pharaoh to support his prime minister.

God used the Egyptians' attitude to keep His chosen people separate from the idolatrous religions in the country. And He used Joseph's high position to keep them alive. Christ would come from these people, and His coming would be history's most important event. All of this hinged on Joseph's willingness to let God control and use his life.

You must leave the possibility of stardom in God's hands. If He gives you popularity and influence, remember a star's purpose is to *give light*. You can show God's light by obeying His orders, by associating with people other kids look down on, by risking your popularity. God makes you popular because He wants to use you for His Kingdom, not because you're more intelligent or more talented than others.

Humbly thank God for your being elected to the National Honor Society or being chosen as class president. Thank Him for your solo in the upcoming concert or your Most Valuable Athlete award. Then determine to use each honor, each position, each talent for God and His Kingdom. Don't become a falling star.

"No one from the east or the west or from the desert can exalt a man. But it is God who judges: He brings one down, he exalts another" (Ps. 75:6, 7).

"The Lord sends poverty and wealth; he humbles and he exalts" (1 Sam. 2:7).

"Suppose a man comes into your meeting wearing a gold ring and fine clothes, and a poor man in shabby clothes also comes in. If you show special attention to the man wearing fine clothes and say, 'Here's a good seat for you,' but say to the poor man, 'You stand there,' or, 'Sit on the floor by my feet,' have you not discriminated among yourselves and become judges with evil thoughts?" (James 2:2–4).

1. What do the verses above have to say about smugness or jealousy? Are you guilty of either attitude?
2. Do you constantly strive to be popular? Ask God what He thinks about your efforts.
3. What does Jesus think about your youth group clique which only admits new members if they "make the grade"?
4. Thank God for being exactly who and where you are. Determine to live for Him right where He has put you.

Week Four

MOSES: A GOOD LEADER IS A GOOD FOLLOWER

Introduction

Your mind may be cluttered with questions: What college should I attend? Should I go out for track? Should I quit my job? Should I sign up for physics? Everyone faces questions such as these. So did Moses. And the choices he made can teach you some very useful lessons. But first, take a short look at his life.

Making Big Decisions

Moses' parents were Israelite slaves in Egypt. At the time of his birth, Egyptian law required all male Israelite babies be killed, but Jochebed, his mother, hid him for three months, then in faith launched him in a waterproof basket on the Nile river. Downstream, the Pharaoh's daughter was taking a bath and spotted the strange little boat. After retrieving the basket and discovering the baby inside, she decided to keep him, even though he was from the Hebrew slave class. Moses' big sister, Miriam, had been watching from behind the marsh grass along the bank, and bravely approached the princess who had now claimed Miriam's brother. Would her highness like to hire a Hebrew nursemaid until the boy was old enough to be weaned? The princess thought this a great idea. So Jochebed was paid to nurse and raise her own son! Thus Moses was raised as an Israelite but became a member of the pagan Pharaoh's royal family.

The Pharaoh had a large harem, and thus had many children. The princess who adopted Moses was one of many royal children, and Moses may not have had any throne rights. In any case he would have been trained for an important position in the Egyptian government. But we do know the Egyptian throne was inherited through the queen, so in light of the passage in Hebrews 11, "By faith Moses, when he was grown up, refused to be known as the son of Pharaoh's daughter" (v. 24), many people believe Moses was scheduled to be the next Pharaoh. However, he gave up the throne to free his people, the Hebrews.

It seems Moses first planned to deliver his people by force, for he killed an Egyptian taskmaster who was beating a Hebrew slave. Maybe he thought this would spark a revolt. But as soon as word of Moses' foolish act reached the authorities, he had to flee to the desert. There, amidst sand and scrub brush, God spent forty years teaching Moses *His* plan for bringing His chosen people to the Promised Land.

Watching Plans Fail

In the desert Moses became a shepherd, the Egyptian equivalent of the scum of the earth. There he married a native woman and fathered two sons. For years he wandered up and down rocky hillsides with his sheep, until one day God finally got his attention with a flaming bush— that didn't burn. From the bush God told Moses to lead His people out of Egypt, and Moses immediately replied with a pile of excuses. But God countered each excuse. However, Moses wouldn't accept the fact that God would be with him and teach him how to speak. So God sent Aaron— who later proved to be a hindrance. But, finally, Moses agreed to go to Egypt.

When Moses first appeared before the Pharaoh and demanded the Israelites be freed, he laughed in Moses' face and ordered the slaves to work even harder—weary people don't revolt. Now Moses was unpopular not only with the Pharaoh, but also with his own people. He was in too deep to quit, however, so he decided to obey and trust God no matter what.

Expecting Miracles

Because Moses trusted God, he succeeded. Pharaoh stubbornly resisted Moses' demands, but after ten plagues, each one worse than the last, he conceded defeat and let the people go.

True to form, however, Pharaoh again changed his mind and decided to give chase. Without the Israelites he would have no work force. He cornered the Israelites at the Red Sea, but God intervened and opened up the sea so His people could walk through, then unleashed the waters as Pharaoh and his charioteers thundered along the sea bottom. Once the people were in the desert, God protected them and fed them daily with bread from heaven.

Moses had a thankless job as leader, for in spite of constant miracles the Israelites weren't impressed. Even when God spoke from heaven with the Ten Commandments, their attitude was, "Big deal." And when Moses returned from the mountaintop after spending forty days receiving God's law, he found his people worshiping a golden calf idol. God had endured enough. He told Moses He would destroy these rebels for smearing their God's name. Moses was probably as weary of their disobedience as God, but he refused to give up on them. He prayed. Desperately he told God he would rather lose his own soul than see God's people annihilated, giving the pagan world cause to bad-mouth God for abandoning His people. God listened and spared the Israelites.

Although a strong leader, Moses was humble. When criticized he never defended himself. He ignored even Aaron and Miriam's jealous accusations. But God didn't—He gave Miriam leprosy. The forgiving Moses came through again, though, and prayed successfully for her recovery.

Moses was extremely patient with his complaining people, tolerating their grumbling for forty years through the desert. One time, however, he lost his cool and plainly disobeyed God's orders. God had told him to call a torrent of water from a certain rock by speaking to it. Instead, in a blaze of temper against the murmuring multitude, Moses hit the rock twice with his walking stick. God graciously supplied the water anyway, but because of Moses' disobedience, God never allowed Moses to enter the Promised Land. He only let Moses see it from the top of Mt. Nebo, where Moses then died.

In spite of some moments of disobedience, Moses made many good decisions. And those decisions changed time and eternity.

Are You Listening to a "From-the-Pit" Recording?

"By faith Moses, when he had grown up, refused to be known as the son of Pharaoh's daughter. He chose to be mistreated along with the people of God rather than to enjoy the pleasures of sin for a short time. He regarded disgrace for the sake of Christ as of greater value than the treasures of Egypt, because he was looking ahead to his reward. By faith he left Egypt, not fearing the king's anger; he persevered because he saw him who is invisible" (Heb. 11:24–27).

There seems to be a tape recording inside each of us, repeating, "You're not very important and what you do doesn't really matter to anybody. So do whatever you feel like at the moment. You can't change your life no matter what you do." Unfortunately, most people don't realize this message was produced and distributed by the Human Demolition Department of the From-the-Pit Recording Company.

Contrary to the recorded message, you are constantly making choices of great consequence—eternal consequence. If you choose to be kind to your mother after she bawls you out for something you didn't do, you grow closer to God and pave the way for some member of your family to accept Jesus. If you choose to spend time with God every morning, you will find out what He wants you to do, and others will notice you've been with Jesus and will think about accepting Him as their Savior. On the other hand, if you choose to lash out when accused, or clam up when you have a chance to talk about your faith, or use your time and money selfishly, you may keep people from giving their lives to God.

Moses had to make a drastic choice. Becoming the Pharaoh would require identifying himself with the pagan Egyptian religion. Becoming the Pharaoh would mean abandoning his people in their slavery. He had to either give up his right to the Egyptian throne with its vast power and wealth (the treasures found in King Tut's tomb indicate the Pharaohs at the time of Moses were swimming in wealth) or compromise with God. He chose God's way. And history has been changed because of his choice.

You, like Moses, must make important decisions that affect your life, and even others' lives, so you need to establish a standard by which every

"... this message was produced by and distributed by the Human Demolition Department of the From-the-Pit Recording Company."

decision can be made. You must make every decision in the light of *eternity*. If you choose God's will and His kingdom above everything else, making each choice count for eternity, your life will be different. Letting Jesus direct your life is the one decision that will change everything.

As you apply eternity's values to your daily decisions, think of what will change! Will you study the Bible more or watch more TV? Will you cheerfully obey your parents or argue and complain? Will you pray for and witness to your non-Christian friends, or pretend you're no different from them and follow their ways? Will you spend your money carefully and give away more of it, or spend it carelessly on yourself?

In the light of eternity, as you think about college, are you considering how to better yourself for serving God, or how to get a plush job? As you consider a marriage partner, will you leave the decision to God, or will you look for the person who satisfies your 25–point checklist? Because no matter what that nasty recording keeps telling you, the choices you make do make a difference.

So don't listen to that "From-the-Pit" recording. You are extremely important to God. You're part of the greatest enterprise in the world: spreading God's good news to all people. The world can be different because of your choices. As Moses did, make decisions that will count for eternity.

"Choose for yourselves this day whom you will serve. . . . But as for me and my household, we will serve the Lord" (Josh. 24:15).
"But seek first his kingdom and his righteousness, and all these things will be given to you as well" (Matt. 6:33).
"For God so loved the world that he gave his one and only Son, that whoever believes in him shall not perish but have eternal life" (John 3:16).
"For the wages of sin is death, but the gift of God is eternal life in Christ Jesus our Lord" (Rom. 6:23).

1. What is the most important decision you will ever make?
2. What are the consequences of failing to choose Christ?
3. Have you decided to give your *whole* life to Jesus and make Him the Lord of your life?
4. What other decisions will you be making that will count for eternity?

It's What's Inside That Counts

"One day, after Moses had grown up, he went out to where his own people were and watched them at their hard labor. He saw an Egyptian beating a Hebrew, one of his own people. Glancing this way and that and seeing no one, he killed the Egyptian and hid him in the sand. The next day he went out and saw two Hebrews fighting. He asked the one in the wrong, 'Why are you hitting your fellow Hebrew?' The man said, 'Who

made you ruler and judge over us? Are you thinking of killing me as you killed the Egyptian?' Then Moses was afraid and thought, 'What I did must have become known.' When Pharaoh heard of this, he tried to kill Moses, but Moses fled from Pharaoh and went to live in Midian" (Ex. 2:11–15).

Sometimes you may think choices are merely an external matter—deciding which college to attend or considering whether or not to buy a car. In reality, the external, the outward is only the result. Heart attitude is much more important than outward action, for if the attitude is correct the decision is apt to be correct. But you can make "the right" decision and still be a failure in God's eyes if your attitude is wrong, because God looks deep inside for your motive. Only the right motive pleases Him.

Moses made "the right" decision—he renounced the Egyptian throne in order to identify with his people. He knew God had promised that Abraham's descendants would be freed after 400 years of slavery, so he meant to assist God in His plan for their deliverance. Yet, though his choice was admirable, his attitude was not.

Moses intended to deliver God's people in his way, and in his strength. As heir to the throne he had received much military training, so he decided to exploit that training with a show of force. This certainly would make the Israelites claim him as leader in a revolt. So when he spotted an Egyptian beating up an Israelite, he used Incredible Hulk tactics and simply killed the Egyptian. Moses did not bother to check with God first. Consequently, he messed up everything.

Moses hadn't learned to die to self and live for God. Fifteen hundred years later, Jesus explained that a seed has to be buried in the ground and die before it can produce new life (John 12:24). If you've given your life to Jesus, just as a seed you have new life within you. But a seed must die, allowing its outer shell to disintegrate, so its life can sprout and become a beautiful plant able to produce many more seeds. It can't argue, "No, I won't let my lovely brown shell crack and rot. I have an image to maintain." If a seed persisted in such an attitude, it would eventually dry up and be useless. Neither can you resist death to self and yet remain alive and useful.

The certain road to a dead end is the attitude which says, "I'll do great things for God. After all, I'm rather good-looking and popular; I get excellent grades; I'm good at sports; and many people tell me I'm a natural leader." If this is your attitude, get off your cloud, because Moses had more going for him than you do, and he had a zero success rate. He was the adopted grandson of the Pharaoh; he received the finest education available at the time; he was trained to be a king. But in spite of physical strength, leadership ability, and great intellect, he failed miserably by attempting to do God's work in his own way.

There are two steps in learning to work God's way. First, you must *die to self.* You must stop depending on any of your abilities or training. You must wait for God's time rather than rushing into things as Moses did. For instance, you may be able to bombard some poor atheist with superior, brainy arguments that defend Christianity. However, if Jesus isn't in control of your argument, if His love isn't shining through, the atheist will most likely run away from you rather than endure humiliation. And you'll have blown your chance to witness.

But dying to your old self and realizing you are nothing apart from God is not enough. You also must *receive the life, power, and guidance of the Holy Spirit.* You must continually say, "Holy Spirit, show me exactly how to witness to this person," instead of depending on some method you've learned. Your witnessing must include your inside, not just your outside.

If you think you've surrendered the outward parts of your life to Christ, you'd better check things out inside. Don't be like the rebellious little boy who, after being told to sit, declared to his mother, "I'm sitting down on the outside, but on the inside I'm still standing up." Learn to obey from the depths of your heart. As Moses, you'll find it's what's inside that counts.

"For we know that our old self was crucified with him so that the body of sin might be rendered powerless, that we should no longer be slaves to sin—because anyone who has died has been freed from sin. Now if we died with Christ, we believe that we will also live with him. For we know that since Christ was raised from the dead, he cannot die again; death no longer has mastery over him. The death he died, he died to sin once for all; but the life he lives, he lives to God. In the same way, count yourselves dead to sin but alive to God in Christ Jesus. Therefore do not let sin reign in your mortal body so that you obey its evil desires" (Rom. 6:6–12).

1. When was the old self (which lives to sin) crucified? (v. 6).
2. If your old self has been crucified with Christ, how can you make that fact a reality in your life? (v. 11).
3. The first step in learning God's ways is dying to your old self. What is the second step?
4. Why can't the life of Jesus in you break out if your old self is still in the way?

Rejecting the Miracle-Speech Therapist

"The Lord said to him, 'Who gave man his mouth? Who makes him deaf or dumb? Who gives him sight or makes him blind? Is it not I, the Lord? Now go; I will help you speak and will teach you what to say.' But Moses said, 'O Lord, please send someone else to do it.' Then the Lord's anger burned against Moses and he said, 'What about your brother, Aaron

the Levite? I know he can speak well' " (Ex. 4:11–14).

What do you dislike the most about yourself? Those forty excess pounds? Your stuttering? Your shyness? Your lack of organization?

Imagine someone saying, "Okay, you can conquer shyness—just trust me. I'll tell you exactly what to say, and here's your audience: a crowd of 10,000 people." Or, "I'll help you lose forty pounds. All you need to do is live at my house for two months and eat only cabbage and tuna. The diet's never failed yet!" Would you jump at the chance for help, even if these people were known worldwide for their successful cures? The problem is that change requires risk-taking and self-discipline.

You probably at times try to hide behind your weaknesses. For example, being overweight can be used as an excuse for a shabby wardrobe and lack of popularity. Stuttering or shyness are excuses to avoid giving an oral report and meeting new people. "Neatness makes me uncomfortable" seems to justify your messy room. Beneath these alibis, however, lies the real reason: You despise work, discipline and consistency. In fact, you sometimes enjoy your sense of inadequacy and want to keep your crutches.

Such thinking, which comes from a lack of faith, keeps God from doing some wonderful things for you. That's what Moses did. He turned down one of God's great miracle offers—and lived to regret his decision.

When God told Moses to confront Pharaoh and demand the freedom for God's people, Moses made excuses. One of them was, "I'm slow of speech." Maybe he had a speech defect or had difficulty putting ideas into words. Whatever Moses' problem, God had the power to remedy it. And He quickly reminded Moses He had made man's mouth, and Moses could trust Him for whatever words he should say. But Moses turned down God's offer of a miracle.

Moses wasn't intending to be rebellious, for he wanted to do God's will. Forty years in the wilderness had taught him that brash self-confidence has nothing to do with faith. Now Moses was a humble man who believed he in himself could do nothing. He had finished step one of the two-step process, but things would not go right until he had finished step two: to acknowledge, "I can do everything through him who gives me strength" (Phil. 4:13). Moses would not take this step of faith; and lack of faith which limits God's power is *sin*. No wonder God became angry when Moses refused to be His spokesman!

Because Moses refused, God appointed big brother Aaron to speak for Moses. And more than once, Aaron caused major problems for Moses. The worst thing Aaron did was supervise the making of a golden calf idol during Moses' forty days on the mountain with God. Moses would have saved himself much trouble if he had accepted God's task for him, and allowed his weakness to be overcome by God.

How about your weaknesses? God wants to help you conquer your problem of overweight, stuttering, shyness, disorganization, or whatever.

He'll do it if you'll trust and obey Him. You will have to face some of your excuses squarely, renounce wrong behavior patterns, and by faith step into a life of obedience. Change may come slowly, and God's ways of accomplishing change may surprise, even shock you, but be assured He knows what He is doing. Don't refuse the services of the miracle therapist. Be willing to dump your crutches—and your excuses.

"He gives strength to the weary and increases the power of the weak. Even youths grow tired and weary, and young men stumble and fall; but those who hope in the Lord will renew their strength. They will soar on wings like eagles; they will run and not grow weary, they will walk and not faint" (Isa. 40:29–31).

"Now a man crippled from birth was being carried to the temple gate called Beautiful, where he was put every day to beg from those going into the temple courts. Peter said, 'Silver or gold I do not have, but what I have I give you. In the name of Jesus Christ of Nazareth, walk.' Taking him by the right hand, he helped him up, and instantly the man's feet and ankles became strong. He jumped to his feet and began to walk. Then he went with them into the temple courts, walking and jumping, and praising God" (Acts 3:2, 6–8).

"Jesus looked at them and said, 'With man this is impossible, but with God all things are possible' " (Matt. 19:26).

1. What characteristics of God are shown in the above verses?
2. Do you have any weaknesses you need to overcome? What are they?
3. Can you believe a God with so much power can change you completely?
4. Claim one of these verses as yours. Then, in faith and willingness to obey, ask God to start changing your weaknesses.

All You Need Is a Blank Check

"But the king of Egypt said, 'Moses and Aaron, why are you taking the people away from their labor? Get back to your work! . . .' That same day Pharaoh gave this order to the slave drivers and foremen in charge of the people: 'You are no longer to supply the people with straw for making bricks; let them go and gather their own straw. But require them to make the same number of bricks as before; don't reduce the quota. They are lazy. . . .' Then the Israelite foremen went and appealed to Pharaoh: 'Why have you treated your servants this way? Your servants are given no straw, yet we are told, "Make bricks!" Your servants are being beaten, but the fault is with your own people.' Pharaoh said, 'Lazy, that's what you are—lazy!' . . . The Israelite foreman realized they were in trouble. . . . they found Moses and Aaron waiting to meet them, and they said, 'May the Lord look upon you and judge you! You have made us a stench to Pharaoh and his servants and have put a sword in their hand to kill us' " (Ex. 5:4, 6–8, 15–21).

You're puzzled. You broke up with your non-Christian boyfriend and you haven't had a date for a year. Or you studied hard for the World Literature test, resisted a perfect chance to cheat, and still received a D–. Or you resolved to always obey your parents, because you knew that was God's will, but now your mother is asking you to do all the housework in order to avoid all the excuses your brother gives her. You've made a big sacrifice for God and everything has gone wrong. Why?

Moses felt the same way. He had chosen to obey God, thus risking his life by facing Pharaoh, leader of the world's strongest army, and risking his sanity by leading an entire nation across a waterless, foodless desert. He had tremendous faith to willingly accept such danger and responsibility. But the whole project blew up in his face.

Pharaoh's stubbornness came as no surprise. God had warned Moses this would happen. But Moses did not expect the king would retaliate by forcing the Hebrews to work harder, to fill the same quota of bricks—but find their own straw. It was an impossible task. And the Egyptians beat the Israelite foremen whenever their crews failed to deliver the required number of bricks. So the Israelites blamed Moses. They sent a delegation to Pharaoh to beg for mercy, and as they left the fruitless discussion, they ran into Moses and Aaron. In their frustration they gave Moses a piece of their minds and told him they hoped God would punish him. Poor Moses! He was willing to give his life for his people, but now they wouldn't even give him the benefit of the doubt. In the midst of rejection he had to make his most important decision ever: Would he stick with God when everything was going against him? Or would he give up?

Unlike forty years earlier, Moses did not run from this crisis. Now he was certain that God had sent him. Moses was also certain he had no selfish motives, and that only God's will mattered anymore. And since he could depend on no person, even among his own people, he turned to God.

Moses discovered his God was almighty. When God had spoken to him in the desert, He called himself, "I AM." Epp comments: "In revealing Himself to Moses as I AM, God was telling him: 'I will be to you whatever you need,' " like a blank check which can be filled in by faith.[1] God was saying, I AM your strength. I AM your security. I AM your wisdom. I AM the one who loves you. So Moses staked his life on I AM.

And I AM proved to be all Moses needed. Moses could do nothing about his predicament; God had to do it all. And He did by sending a series of ten awesome, horrible miracles. The Egyptians were finally convinced, and the Israelites left Egypt in style. The Egyptians even gave the Israelites their gold—just to get rid of them!

You'll face situations just as discouraging as those Moses faced. You'll make a major decision to obey God, and everything seemingly will fall apart. Will you stick with God when times get tough? Or will you turn

[1]Theodore H. Epp, *Moses, Vol. 1, God Prepares His Man*. Lincoln, Nebr.: Back to the Bible, 1975, p. 105.

away? Your God is almighty, for He hasn't changed since He spoke to Moses. His name is still I AM. I AM _____(whatever you need). It's a blank check you can fill in by faith.

"Then Jesus declared, 'I am the bread of life. He who comes to me will never go hungry, and he who believes in me will never be thirsty' " (John 6:35).

"When Jesus spoke again to the people, he said, 'I am the light of the world. Whoever follows me will never walk in darkness, but will have the light of life' " (John 8:12).

"Jesus answered, 'I am the way and the truth and the life. No one comes to the Father except through me' " (John 14:6).

"It is because of him that you are in Christ Jesus, who has become for us wisdom from God—that is, our righteousness, holiness and redemption" (1 Cor. 1:30).

"And my God will meet all your needs according to his glorious riches in Christ Jesus" (Phil. 4:19).

1. Using the above verses, list all the things Jesus can be for you.
2. List the things in your life you have not asked Him or permitted Him to be because your heart has been set on something else.
3. How about asking Jesus to fill the needs in your life? How about using your blank check?

Why Not Choose the Best?

"The next day Moses said to the people, 'You have committed a great sin. But now I will go up to the Lord; perhaps I can make atonement for your sin.' So Moses went back to the Lord and said, 'Oh, what a great sin these people have committed! They have made themselves gods of gold. But now, please forgive their sin—but if not, then blot me out of the book you have written.' The Lord replied to Moses, 'Whoever has sinned against me I will blot out of my book' " (Ex. 32:30–33).

How important on your agenda is God? What sacrifices are you willing to make for Him, for His work and kingdom? The choices you make show where your priorities lie. For instance: Will you befriend the new kid at church, or stay with your clique? Will you fork over a few dollars for your church's missionary in Nigeria, or spend them on pizza? Will you spend your afternoon visiting a classmate in the hospital or playing tennis? Be honest now, where are your priorities? Are you doing God's work or pursuing your own interests? Moses has a chariot-load of lessons to teach about priorities.

After God gave the Israelites the Ten Commandments, one of which prohibits idol worship, Moses went to the top of Mt. Sinai to talk with

God. There he spent the most amazing forty days any man had ever experienced—only to return to the most horrifying sight he could imagine: his people dancing around and worshiping a gold calf, just like the calf idols in Egypt. They were rebelling against the God who had performed mind-blowing miracles to bring them out of Egypt! What do you think went through Moses' mind?

Moses first must have thought, *Get rid of the whole bunch. I won't put up with such a thankless lot.*

So God gave Moses a big test to discover if Moses was truly committed to leading God's people to the Promised Land. "Maybe," He told Moses, "it would be a good idea to destroy these people and raise up a new group from your descendants." Not only was God testing Moses' commitment, He was testing his ego. (Wouldn't you be tempted by the chance to father God's chosen people?) But even in his great distress, Moses didn't jump at such a chance.

Moses responded by praying for the people. He knew God had promised a great nation would come from Abraham, and from that nation would come the Messiah. He also realized God would not be glorified in the eyes of the surrounding nations if God's miracle people were simply destroyed. So he pleaded with God to let them live.

He knew from his own experience God was merciful, so he asked God to forgive His people. Moses was willing not only to put up with such rebellious people and give up the chance for his descendants to be God's chosen people, but he was willing to live in hell so these people could be saved. His is perhaps one of the greatest prayers in the Bible: "But now, please forgive their sin—but if not, then blot me out of the book you have written" (Ex. 32:32).

Nowhere can we find greater identification with God's cause. Moses was willing to make the ultimate sacrifice—which only Jesus, the sinless man, could make. Moses could pray like this because of his close relationship with God. God had become so important to him that nothing else mattered.

You, too, need to spend time with God. You must get to know Him and love Him so much that choosing His work, His honor, and His will above your own interests becomes automatic. If you know God like that, you, like Moses, will experience God's glory. Since you have a choice, why not choose the best?

"I am the good shepherd. The good shepherd lays down his life for the sheep. . . . No one takes it from me, but I lay it down of my own accord. I have authority to lay it down and authority to take it up again. This command I received from my Father" (John 10:11, 18).

"I speak the truth in Christ—I am not lying, my conscience confirms it in the Holy Spirit—I have great sorrow and unceasing anguish in my heart. For I could wish that I myself were cursed and cut off from Christ for the sake of my brothers, those of my own race" (Rom. 9:1–3).

"Brothers, my heart's desire and prayer to God for the Israelites is that they may be saved" (Rom. 10:1).

"For this reason, since the day we heard about you, we have not stopped praying for you and asking God to fill you with the knowledge of his will through all spiritual wisdom and understanding" (Col. 1:9).

1. How did Jesus illustrate to His followers His love and concern for them?
2. How did Paul feel toward the people he worked with?
3. From where did Paul get his great love and concern for people and God's work?
4. Tell Jesus you want His concern for God's work in the world. Tell Him His kingdom is more important than your affairs (if you mean it). Then ask Him for a specific way to show that concern.

Let God Be Your Defense Lawyer

"Miriam and Aaron began to talk against Moses because of his Cushite wife, for he had married a Cushite. 'Has the Lord spoken only through Moses?' they asked. 'Hasn't he also spoken through us?' And the Lord heard this. (Now Moses was a very humble man, more humble than anyone else on the face of the earth.) At once the Lord said to Moses, Aaron and Miriam, 'Come out to the Tent of Meeting, all three of you.' So the three of them came out. The anger of the Lord burned against them, and he left them. When the cloud lifted from above the Tent, there stood Miriam—leprous, like snow. Aaron turned toward her and saw that she had leprosy; and he said to Moses, 'Please, my lord, do not hold against us the sin we have so foolishly committed. Do not let her be like a stillborn infant coming from its mother's womb with its flesh half eaten away.' So Moses cried out to the Lord, 'O God, please heal her!' " (Num. 12:1–4, 9–11, 13).

You like to feel important. Everyone does. You want people to respect you and think well of you. You want them to need you. But God wants to fill these longings with Himself.

You have a very important position in God's strategy for changing the world. Possibly, one of the reasons God has chosen to work through you is to fulfill your desires for belonging and being needed. When God's power is working through you to touch other people, and you are fully occupied with bringing glory to God, you won't care whether people notice you or not. God will be noticing, and what else could matter?

Unfortunately, it is too easy to shift your focus from God to people. You can be too impressed by compliments, then fall apart at criticism. And if falsely accused, you probably lash out in anger. It's too easy to spend a great deal of time fretting over your popularity rating.

Moses decided never to gauge his life by the opinions of others. He chose to live for God, and nothing else. He was never jealous of others and he did not erect walls around himself, bristling with self-defense cannons to bombard anyone who hurled advice, criticism, or false accusations at him. He placed his reputation in God's hands and let God defend him. And God did a very good job.

Miriam and Aaron jealously resented their younger brother's leadership. And as you know, jealousy loves to find fault. First they gossiped about Moses' wife and then criticized him for marrying an Ethiopian woman. Then they questioned his exclusive authority, claiming God could speak through them just as well as through Moses.

Throughout this verbal abuse, Moses remained humble and meek. And God dealt with the accusers. He called the two brothers and their sister before Him and asked Miriam and Aaron why they had been unafraid to speak against God's chosen leader. Aaron admitted his sin, but Miriam apparently didn't, so she received an instant case of leprosy.

Even when Miriam got her just reward, Moses didn't say, "You deserved that for bad-mouthing me." Instead of rejoicing in God's revenge, Moses prayed for her and God healed her. Moses didn't allow his life to be ruined by hurt feelings, lack of respect for others, and self-pity. Only serving God was important to him.

Decide while you're young to receive your sense of importance and security from God alone, and you'll save yourself great heartache. Because people are fickle, they'll disappoint you. They'll misjudge you. But God is faithful and will always be just and honest with you. You'll save yourself much trouble if you'll always let God be your defense lawyer.

"Commit your way to the Lord; trust in him and he will do this: He will make your righteousness shine like the dawn, the justice of your cause like the noonday sun. Be still before the Lord and wait patiently for him; do not fret when men succeed in their ways, when they carry out their wicked schemes. Refrain from anger and turn from wrath; do not fret—it leads only to evil" (Ps. 37:5–8).

"Vindicate me, O God, and plead my cause against an ungodly nation; rescue me from deceitful and wicked men" (Ps. 43:1).

1. What should be your attitude when people let you down or criticize or falsely accuse you?
2. What promise does God make to you in Ps. 37:6?
3. When you are falsely accused, do you ask God to show people you are right? Or do you run about trying to be your own defense lawyer? (Even before you ask God to defend you, ask Him if some of the accusations are true. As part of the human race, you tend not to see your own faults.)
4. Are you resenting anyone for something he has said about you? Forgive him and start letting God handle your reputation.

"Quick, Give Me a Patience Pill!"

"Now there was no water for the community, and the people gathered in opposition to Moses and Aaron. The Lord said to Moses, 'Take the staff, and you and your brother Aaron gather the assembly together. Speak to that rock before their eyes and it will pour out its water. You will bring water out of the rock for the community so they and their livestock can drink.' So Moses took the staff from the Lord's presence, just as he commanded him. He and Aaron gathered the assembly together in front of the rock and Moses said to them, 'Listen, you rebels, must we bring you water out of this rock?' Then Moses raised his arm and struck the rock twice with his staff. Water gushed out, and the community and their livestock drank" (Num. 20:2, 7–11).

You've never needed lessons on how to make excuses. Children barely able to talk concoct imaginative reasons for why they do (or don't do) something. We all use the same excuses: "But I was exhausted"; "It's just that I had a bad day at school"; "I don't feel very good, so don't expect much of me today"; "Well, she just got on my nerves"; "I couldn't stand it anymore, and besides, I had shown her a lot of patience all day long"; and the list goes on.

Excuses are used to cover up an inability to handle pressure. However, with the Holy Spirit in you, you can obey God regardless of the pressure. You can choose no longer to make excuses, not to be ruled by fear, irritation, or laziness. God expected this kind of obedience from Moses, and he expects the same from you; and He never will ask you to do something for which He has not given you sufficient strength.

Moses met one of those pressure situations in the desert. The people had run out of water and began grumbling, which drove Moses and Aaron to prayer. At which point God gave them clear instructions to solve the problem: (1) Take out the rod. (2) Gather the people. (3) Talk to the rock and it will gush water. God wanted to impress the people with His power and holiness as they prepared to enter the Promised Land, and this was a perfect opportunity. They needed a fresh sense of God's greatness.

But the people were getting frantic, and Moses was getting upset, so he yielded to the pressure of the moment. Instead of calmly speaking to the rock, he yelled and whacked it twice with his rod.

Moses could have had a lot of excuses. After all, he had patiently put up with these rebellious people for nearly forty years, so he had a right to blow his cool. Besides, in a previous incident, he had hit a rock (as God instructed) and it had produced water. Maybe Moses just hadn't understood the instructions. We have no record of what Moses said when God came and told him what he had done wrong. But whether he instantly admitted his wrong or made excuses, he had disobeyed. He had chosen to give way to his natural reactions rather than let the Holy Spirit give peace. And once a person loses his cool, he loses his ability to think straight. The leader of God's chosen people had made a fool of himself. God severely punished Moses by not permitting him to enter the Promised Land.

One reason for this severe measure was to teach future generations that the God who has all power expects His children to depend on that power at all times. Lack of faith is always sin. And some of the best chances for practicing faith come in everyday incidents—such as when you lose your purse; or when everyone laughs at the inappropriate statement you made; or when you studied the wrong chapter for the test. These are the times when you can let the Holy Spirit take over so you can live above life's ordinary irritations.

In order to start living above these irritations, you must do two things: First, you must reject Satan's lie that God can't change your natural reactions which seem automatic. *Nothing* is too hard for God. Second, you must trust the Holy Spirit each time you hit a situation that has you crying, "Quick, I need a patience pill!" Tell the devil to takeoff, then give the Holy Spirit a chance to handle the whole thing—and you won't need any kind of pill.

"Put to death, therefore, whatever belongs to your earthly nature: sexual immorality, impurity, lust, evil desires and greed, which is idolatry. Because of these, the wrath of God is coming. You used to walk in these ways, in the life you once lived. But now you must rid yourselves of all such things as these: anger, rage, malice, slander, and filthy language from your lips. Do not lie to each other, since you have taken off your old self with its practices and have put on the new self, which is being renewed in knowledge in the image of its Creator. Therefore, as God's chosen people, holy and dearly loved, clothe yourselves with compassion, kindness, humility, gentleness and patience" (Col. 3:5–10, 12).

1. Jesus died to give you an all-new self. Are you choosing that new self by letting Jesus live through you?
2. On a paper make two columns, one titled "Actions of the Old Self," and the other, "Actions of the New Self." Then list, from the above scripture passage, what those actions are. Now ask yourself, is it ever worth rejecting God to give the old self a chance?
3. List the commands given in the scripture passage. To obey these, you must consciously choose to give each situation over to God's control.
4. What situation in your life needs to be turned over to God? Now do it. And each time the devil haunts you about it, tell him, and yourself, that it is now in God's hands.

Week Five

JOSHUA: YOU CAN'T BE AWESOME WITHOUT FAITH

Introduction

Having trouble living above your circumstances? Then get better acquainted with Joshua, because his life was full of obstacles. He began as a slave in Egypt. Then he became Moses' assistant, enduring the complaints and grumblings from unthankful, rebellious Hebrews as they wandered in the barren desert. When Moses died, Joshua led the people in battle against the strong armies and well-fortified cities of Canaan. But Joshua lived a life of victory and obedience. And once you've learned Joshua's secret of an overcoming life, you, too, can live in victory.

What If Life Is One Big Obstacle Course?

Moses was one of the greatest leaders in history. What a hard act for Joshua to follow! But he had great faith. When God told him, "As I was with Moses, so I will be with you" (Josh. 1:5), Joshua believed Him. When things got tough, he never complained about not being Moses, because Joshua was willing to let God work through him. And his job required incredible courage. He was to destroy an entire nation so the Israelites could take the land.

Many people have wondered why a loving God would order the Canaanites to be destroyed. Archaeology helps to explain this problem. Excavations have shown that these people were more immoral than any other nation of the ancient world. If they had been allowed to continue their sexual permissiveness their physical and spiritual disease would have infected the entire world. So, however disagreeable the task might be, Joshua was required to destroy the Canaanites in order to protect God's world and to give His people the land promised to Abraham.

Joshua's first obstacle was the Jordan River—at flood stage. (It's not a very deep river in the dry season.) How was he to get all those people across the rushing waters? After all, none had learned to swim while trekking through the desert. So Joshua got his instructions from God: The priests carrying the Ark of the Covenant, the symbol of God's presence, were to walk right into the water. Unusual instructions, yes, but when the priests' feet touched the water, the river's flow was cut off until everyone had crossed over. No one even got his feet wet.

To insure the people wouldn't forget this miracle, Joshua had twelve stones (one for each tribe) piled in the middle of the Jordan River. Then he had twelve stones taken from the middle of the Jordan and erected as a monument on the Canaan side. When future generations would ask about the stones, they would be told the story of the miracle. The story would live on.

But right on the heels of this miracle followed another huge obstacle: the mighty fortress of Jericho. If they did not conquer Jericho, the Israelites would never take Canaan. But when Joshua went down to look over the situation, Jesus[1] appeared to him—and gave him history's strangest battle instructions. So, in faithful obedience Joshua organized a silent military parade to march around Jericho. After seven days and thirteen laps around the city, the priests blew their horns, everyone shouted, and Jericho's walls fell down.

Now only a little town named Ai prevented Israel from taking the center of the country and cutting Canaan in half. Israelite spies reported only a few people at Ai—only two or three thousands soldiers could easily finish off the town. But soon after they attacked, these Israelites were running in terror. Thirty-six of their men were killed by the soldiers of tiny Ai. Why?

The humiliating defeat at Ai would always remind Israel of the cost of disobedience. God had commanded that all the wealth of Jericho be put in a special treasury to support the priests and the worship services. But a soldier named Achan stole some gold and silver and a stylish Babylonian garment and buried the loot under his tent. God had warned that a person stealing any of these things would die and bring disaster on all Israel. So Achan was stoned. Then with fresh instructions from God, the soldiers conquered Ai and destroyed it. The people of Israel then took time out for spiritual renewal and listened to Joshua read the law of Moses.

But What If You Get Tricked into Sin?

Soon representatives of the Gibeonites, next in line to be destroyed, paid a visit to the Israelite camp. Wearing old clothes and worn shoes, and carrying moldy bread and tattered wineskins, these men claimed to be from a far country and requested a peace treaty with the Israelites. Regrettably, Joshua and the leaders didn't bother to pray about the request and signed a treaty. When they realized they had been tricked, the Israelites were "stuck." They were obligated to keep their word. So, when five southern kings attacked Gibeon for siding with the enemy, Joshua went out with his army to rescue Gibeon. Joshua's men slaughtered the enemy—while God gave extra hours of sunshine, preventing the enemies of Israel from escaping in the darkness and returning to fight another day.

---

[1]He is referred to as the Captain of the Lord's army—most Bible scholars conclude that this was an OT appearance of Jesus.

After defeating the five main southern kings, Joshua routed a coalition of thirty-one northern kings. (One of the cities he burned, Hazor, has been excavated by modern archaeologists who have found ashes left from the time of Joshua.)

With the big enemies defeated, all that remained were a few pockets of resistance, so the Israelite leaders divided the land among the different tribes. The tribes were to trust God to help them drive out every last Canaanite. Some completed that assignment. Others did not. Because they failed to annihilate the Canaanites, the Israelites had to contend with guerrilla warfare and enemy occupations for years to come.

Joshua, however, kept his faith strong and kept encouraging the Israelites to obey God in everything, thus to receive God's blessing. In his famous farewell address, Joshua challenged the Israelites, "Choose for yourselves this day whom you will serve. . . . But as for me and my household, we will serve the Lord" (Josh. 24:15). These words were not just a dramatic speech; they were the testimony of Joshua's life.

Under the Circumstances, Over a Barrel, or in Jesus?

"After the death of Moses the servant of the Lord, the Lord said to Joshua son of Nun, Moses' aide: 'No one will be able to stand up against you all the days of your life. As I was with Moses, so I will be with you; I will never leave you or forsake you. Be strong and courageous, because you will lead these people to inherit the land I swore to their forefathers to give them. Be strong and very courageous. Be careful to obey all the law my servant Moses gave you; do not turn from it to the right or to the left, that you may be successful wherever you go. Do not let this Book of the Law depart from your mouth; meditate on it day and night, so that you may be careful to do everything written in it. Then you will be prosperous and successful' " (Josh. 1:1, 5–8).

Do you feel imprisoned by your circumstances—by tension at home, temperamental friends, hard subjects in school, and a cat who refuses to be housebroken? Joshua could have felt imprisoned, too. He had a high-pressure job trying to fill the shoes of Moses, one of the very greatest leaders in history. He had to lead a nation of stubborn complainers. He was caught between the scorching desert behind him and the fierce, fortified armies before him. There seemed to be no way out—without God. So the Lord gave Joshua a great promise (the above verses). Joshua believed that promise, acted on it, and God worked miracles.

God has promises for you, too, but Satan doesn't want you to know about them. Jesus said, "If you abide in me, and my words abide in you, ask whatever you will, and it shall be done for you" (John 15:7). The devil wants such promises for a victorious Christian life kept secret. He wants you running around feeling discouraged and helpless because of your circumstances, rather than having faith in God's promises and receiving deliverance.

How do you find God's "This Way Out" sign in each tough situation? Theodore Epp says it this way: "Faith lays hold of a promise and is therefore the basis for courage."[2] In other words, you first must find a Bible verse that applies to your situation. (If you don't know the Bible very well, ask someone to help you find an appropriate verse.) And remember, this is God's promise. God never fails. He always fulfills His promises.

Next, make that promise part of you. As God told Joshua, "Meditate on it day and night" (Josh. 1:8). As you continually think about that special promise you've found in Scripture, the Holy Spirit will make that promise real to you. You then can act on it, and in faith take the path labelled "This Way Out."

Here's an example of how this principle works. If someone has spoken harsh words to you in anger or thoughtlessness, there's now a "tape recorder" in your brain playing those words over and over. Now you need a remedy from the Bible: "Cast all your anxiety on him because he cares for you" (1 Pet. 5:7). This promise says you can get rid of that terrible feeling caused by the "tape recording" in your head. So meditate on the promise, asking the Holy Spirit to teach you exactly what it means. For example, in the verse we chose, "cast" really means throw. Therefore God is really saying, "Throw every worry on me and I'll take care of it." If we're playing catch and you throw the ball to me, you don't have it any longer. God wants you to deal with your problems and worries in the same way, by throwing them to Him. And you don't have to do it problem by problem; you can roll them all up in one ball for Jesus to worry about— and He never worries. Besides all this, the verse is a command. It doesn't say, "*Try* to give your problem to Jesus." It simply tells you to do it. So decide to throw the whole problem to God, and each time the devil reminds you of the harsh words, tell him, "That's God's problem, not mine."

Like Joshua, learn to believe and claim God's promises, to meditate on and make them part of you, and to act on them. If Joshua had not done this, the rest of the book of Joshua, with all its miracles, would never have been written. If you're really in Jesus and His word is in you, you won't be living under the circumstances and nothing will put you over a barrel.

"Praise be to the Lord, who has given rest to his people Israel just as he promised. Not one word has failed of all the good promises he gave through his servant Moses" (1 Kings 8:56).

---

[2]Theodore H. Epp, *Joshua: Victorious by Faith.* Lincoln, Nebr.: Back to the Bible, 1968, p. 43.

". . . he has given us his very great and precious promises, so that through them you may participate in the divine nature and escape the corruption in the world caused by evil desires" (2 Pet. 1:4).

" 'If you can?' said Jesus. 'Everything is possible for him who believes' " (Mark 9:23).

1. What are the characteristics of God's promises?
2. What can we receive through His promises? (See 2 Pet. 1:4.)
3. How do we cash in on God's promises?
4. Find one of God's promises, meditate on it, believe it, and act on it.

Crossing River Impossible

"Then Joshua told the people, 'Consecrate yourselves, for tomorrow the Lord will do amazing things among you.' Joshua said to the priests, 'Take up the ark of the covenant and cross over ahead of the people.' 'As soon as the priests who carry the ark of the Lord—the Lord of all the earth—set foot in the Jordan, the water flowing downstream will be cut off and stand up in a heap.' So when the people broke camp to cross the Jordan, the priests carrying the ark of the covenant went ahead of them. . . . Yet as soon as the priests who carried the ark reached the Jordan and their feet touched the water's edge, the water from upstream stopped flowing. . . . So the people crossed over opposite Jericho. The priests who carried the ark of the covenant of the Lord stood firm on dry ground in the middle of the Jordan" (Josh. 3:5, 13–17).

Ann Kiemel Anderson, a popular Christian author, loves impossibilities. (She even wrote a book called, *I Love the Word Impossible.*) But most of us don't. We feel overwhelmed: "I won't ever pass the algebra final"; "I can't possibly forget the way he hurt me"; "Trying to witness at my school is hopeless"; and the list goes on. There seems to be no way to conquer these circumstances. But there is *one* way: Jesus.

God told the Israelites to cross the Jordan River at flood stage without as much as a rowboat—a seemingly impossible order! In addition, they were told to do things that most people would consider crazy. First, the Israelites were to keep their eyes on the Ark of the Covenant and follow it. (The Ark of the Covenant was a gold-covered box containing the original copy of the Ten Commandments and other objects which symbolized God's power, presence, and promises.) Second, the priests carrying the Ark were to walk into the overflowing Jordan River—and the waters from upstream would stop flowing so the people could walk across on dry ground. Talk about conquering the impossible!

The God of Joshua can do the same today for you. This story teaches two principles, and if you obey them you also can win victories over the impossible. The first principle is to keep your eyes on Jesus. The Ark of the Covenant represents Jesus who is "God with us." If you look to Jesus, your "ark," rather than to your Jordan River of impossibility and to your daydreams about the Promised Land, you can walk boldly across the rushing waters of hopelessness. Even Peter, the disciple, walked on water as long as he kept his eyes solely on Jesus—and you can too!

The second principle, one people often fail to recognize, is to go ahead and act on God's promise before there is any evidence that God will come through. This is real faith that grabs God's promise to Jeremiah: "I am the Lord, the God of all mankind. Is *anything* too hard for me?" (Jer. 32:27). Do you believe God even can help you understand algebra? He can. So meditate on God's power, His ability to give knowledge. Then act on it. Instead of saying, "I'll flunk the final for sure," say in faith, "With God's help I'll pass it." Then you can study (faith is never a cop-out from work) in faith instead of frustration, and take that test in peace instead of panic. And you'll find out nothing is too hard for God.

But what about that person who hurt you? How can you possibly love him? By faith. In the same way you learned to understand algebra. God commands you to love: ". . . love each another as I have loved you" (John 15:12), not "Love unless the person has hurt you." So in faith obey this command. Defy your emotions and put your feet into the Jordan by deliberately doing something to show love for that person. Pray for him every day. Don't avoid him. Be friendly. Then ask God what you can do for that person that would help him. Take conscious steps of faith to forget that hurt.

You can witness by faith as well. Jesus said, "You will be my witnesses" (Acts 1:8). This is a promise. Therefore, go out on a limb and say in a faltering voice, "There's something that changed my life and I want to tell you about it." God won't let you fall. He'll come to your rescue, but first you'll have to get your feet wet. Then God will open the Jordan.

Next time something seems impossible, remember how the Israelites crossed the Jordan at flood stage. In good weather your River Impossible can seem bad enough, but when thunderstorms of problems soak you, and the river starts to overflow, panic comes easily. But don't give in. Instead, do as the Israelites and keep your eyes on the Ark—Jesus' presence. But always remember you must also act in faith on God's promise to you.

"During the fourth watch of the night Jesus went out to them, walking on the lake. When the disciples saw him walking on the lake, they were terrified. 'It's a ghost,' they said, and cried out in fear. But Jesus immediately said to them: 'Take courage! It is I. Don't be afraid.' 'Lord, if it's you,' Peter replied, 'tell me to come to you on the water.' 'Come,' he said. Then Peter got down out of the boat and walked on the water to Jesus. But when he saw the wind, he was afraid and, beginning to sink, cried out, 'Lord, save me!' Immediately Jesus reached out his hand and caught him. 'You of little

faith,' he said, 'why did you doubt?' " (Matt. 14:25–31).

1. What circumstances, as the waves on the Sea of Galilee, would scare you if you focused your attention on them?
2. Find a Bible promise for each one of those problems and claim those promises.
3. Now, in the best way you know how, give the problem to Jesus and take His hand just like Peter did.

Living by Dying

"So Joshua called together the twelve men he had appointed from the Israelites, one from each tribe, and said to them, 'Go over before the ark of the Lord your God into the middle of the Jordan. Each of you is to take up a stone on his shoulder, according to the number of the tribes of the Israelites, to serve as a sign among you. In the future, when your children ask you, "What do these stones mean?" tell them that the flow of the Jordan was cut off before the ark of the covenant of the Lord. When it crossed the Jordan, the waters of the Jordan were cut off. These stones are to be a memorial to the people of Israel forever.' So the Israelites did as Joshua commanded them. They took twelve stones from the middle of the Jordan, according to the number of the tribes of the Israelites, as the Lord had told Joshua; and they carried them over with them to their camp, where they put them down. Joshua set up the twelve stones that had been in the middle of the Jordan. . ." (Josh. 4:4–9).

The Israelites placed stones in the Jordan River so they and their descendants would never forget what God did for them the day they crossed on dry ground. They memorialized the event, not because God had performed a miracle, although that was wonderful, but because crossing the Jordan put them into an entirely new kind of life: victory. Wandering in the wilderness symbolized the life of a defeated, me-first Christian, a person who has accepted Jesus as Savior but hasn't died to self-centeredness. The Israelites, although they didn't return to Egypt, selfishly grumbled and complained their way through the desert. Their self-centered attitudes created most of their misery, and prevented them from knowing victory.

God asked the Israelites to cross the Jordan, to leave behind their life which had catered to selfish desires, and to enter a new life of obedience and victory. It meant dying to everything in the old life and beginning over again. This didn't mean God hadn't been with them. He had—the Ark of the Covenant they had been following symbolized His presence. In the same way, if you have received Jesus Christ, but continue to live selfishly, you can still have Jesus in your heart. But Jesus died not only to forgive sins, but to destroy sin. The selfish part of you which likes to sin, the source of sin in your life, was crucified with Jesus when He died. However, you can consider the selfish part of you dead only by faith, just as the Jordan had to be crossed by faith. But stubbornness and unbelief caused the Israelites to wait forty years, even though they could have entered the Promised Land immediately. So don't be stubborn. Your sinful self was crucified with Christ. Believe it and act on it, and you, too, will enter the land of victory.

This, however, is not a one-time experience that you never need to think about again. You must constantly keep in mind the death of your me-first life. Realizing this was true for his people, Joshua commissioned a visible reminder of the Israelites' death to the self-life of the wilderness and their entry into the faith-life of the Promised Land. So he ordered two piles of stones built as memorials—one in midstream as a memorial to the death of the old life, and one on the bank of the new land as a reminder of their new life.

Water-skiing helps illustrate the truth of death to the self-life. If you try using your snow skiis on the lake, you'll say skiing on water is impossible. To water-ski, you have to completely scrap the notion of using your snow skiis. Winter is gone. In the same way, the victorious Christian life is impossible if you continue to pamper your sinful desires. They'll drag you under, just as snow skiis on water. Instead, you must die to self, and then let the resurrection of victory take over in you.

You can't, of course, ski on water under your own power. In order to water-ski, you must grasp the rope and let the boat pull you. In faith you must obey the instructions of an expert, even if they seem silly or if you'd rather do it another way. Yet, after you get up, you can get scared or become distracted by the scenery and drop the rope. If you do that, you'll fall.

But falling doesn't alter the fact that there is a way for you to water-ski. And it doesn't mean that you can't ski again after falling. You can, of course, get a psychological hang-up and tell yourself, "I'll never water-ski again because I fell." But your feelings don't make that the truth. Later, if you continue water-skiing, your falls will be caused by pride and trying things you aren't yet ready for. But none of your failures will change the fact that there's a wonderful world of water-skiing that you can experience.

And the life of victory is the same way. Crucified with Jesus, you no longer must live a sinful, defeated life. Theodore Epp says of this: "God does not make it impossible for men to sin but He always makes it possible for them not to sin."[3] Believing that and deciding to live it is like crossing the Jordan into the Promised Land of victory.

But you will always need the stones of remembrance to remind you that you can live in faith and victory. Satan will lie, saying, "This case is different. You just can't help yourself." He will try using fear to make you

---

[3] *Ibid.*, p. 196.

fall. He'll try to distract you or make you proud. But always remember that dying to self and living to Christ is completely possible. And if you fail and sin, confess it, get back on your skiis and by faith claim victory.

"I have been crucified with Christ and I no longer live, but Christ lives in me. The life I live in the body, I live by faith in the Son of God, who loved me and gave himself for me" (Gal. 2:20).

"We always carry around in our body the death of Jesus, so that the life of Jesus may also be revealed in our body" (2 Cor. 4:10).

"He himself bore our sins in his body on the tree, so that we might die to sin and live for righteousness; by his wounds you have been healed" (1 Pet. 2:24).

"Since you died with Christ to the basic principles of this world, why, as though you still belonged to it, do you submit to its rules" (Col. 2:20).

1. Why must you die to your self-life in order to live a victorious Christian life?
2. How can the life of Jesus live in you?
3. Why is it possible to act on your death and resurrection with Jesus, then return to a life of defeat? Even if defeat is possible, is it necessary?
4. Have you died to your selfish self or do you still want your own way?

Brick Walls, Boring Days and Breakthroughs

"So on the second day they marched around the city once and returned to the camp. They did this for six days. On the seventh day they circled the city seven times. The seventh time around, when the priests sounded the trumpet blast, Joshua commanded the people, 'Shout! For the Lord has given you the city!' When the trumpets sounded, the people shouted, and at the sound of the trumpet, when the people gave a loud shout, the wall collapsed; so every man charged straight in, and they took the city" (Josh. 6:14–16, 20).

It's easier to fight one enemy than a bunch. You need to learn that many of the battles you face in your Christian life are unnecessary. Your enemies are self, the world and the devil. By eliminating the first two, you have only one enemy left.

Let's say you want to start a Bible study for your friends at school. If you've decided to follow Jesus no matter what other people think, the taunting from some classmates won't matter. You won't really have to fight the world, because it's not a threat.

There is, however, a more subtle enemy—self—which gets offended when people don't listen to what you say, which wants to watch basketball on TV rather than prepare the Bible study, and which gets discouraged by the criticism some students offer free of charge. This old sinful self was crucified with Jesus and you can enjoy that fact by realizing, *My old self is dead. Its desires are dead. I rose with Jesus and now I want only what Jesus wants.* (See Romans 6:11.)

If you really don't care what other people think of you, if you've died to the selfishness in you that always wants its own way, the only enemy left is the devil. He will always be there with his Jerichos to block your way, but God has given you authority over Satan. The Bible says, "Submit yourselves, then, to God. Resist the devil, and he will flee from you" (James 4:7). You can win the victory by applying this verse to your life. You can have victory over the devil.

The battle of Jericho shows how a war can be won with only one battle. By marching around the city wall, day after day, with spectators jeering from the towers, the Israelites proved they no longer cared what other people thought of them. If every citizen of Jericho thought they had lost their sanity, it was okay with the Israelites. They were dead to self. Under orders to march around in silence every day, they obeyed even though they were not told why they were doing such a seemingly senseless thing. As Theodore Epp explains, faith can't question God since He rarely interprets His commands in advance.[4] Nobody could complain about the unorthodox battle plan and offer his superior ideas. Nobody could gripe that marching was getting boring and that it didn't do any good anyway. Nobody could even jog to get some decent exercise. Each person had to be dead to his selfish desires and obedient to God.

The walls of Jericho fell down by faith. It's always the same. Only in faith can you defeat the devil. Walking around that great fortress with its tall, thick walls made every person realize defeating Jericho was humanly impossible. The battle had to be the Lord's. No one tried to use human tactics. That's why the walls of Jericho fell.

You'll never run out of Jerichos to conquer. The devil will see to that. But you can see all the walls crumble—if you'll obey God even when everybody else thinks you're dumb, even when His instructions cut across the grain of your personal desires, and even when you must admit total helplessness. (Actually, if you think you have things completely under control and can do it all by yourself, God can't really help you.) Don't get discouraged by your present Jericho. So what if you've hit a brick wall? Unpack your faith and obey God's instructions. Watching walls fall down is really fun!

"Do not love the world or anything in the world" (1 John 2:15).
"For we know that our old self was crucified with him so that the body of sin might be rendered powerless, that we should no longer be slaves to sin—because anyone who has died has been freed from sin" (Rom. 6:6, 7).

---

[4]*Ibid.*, p. 183.

"Be self-controlled and alert. Your enemy the devil prowls around like a roaring lion looking for someone to devour. Resist him, standing firm in the faith, because you know that your brothers throughout the world are undergoing the same kind of sufferings" (1 Pet. 5:8, 9).
"And do not give the devil a foothold" (Eph. 4:27).

1. How can you get rid of the obstacles caused by worldly opinions? Should ridicule ever stop you?
2. What has God done about the selfishness inside you? What is your part in making this real in your life?
3. How are you to deal with the devil?
4. Have you been nice to the devil lately? Don't waste any time before you kick him out.

Losing the Game but Winning the Championship

"When they returned to Joshua, they said, 'Not all the people will have to go up against Ai. Send two or three thousand men to take it and do not weary all the people, for only a few men are there.' So about three thousand men went up; but they were routed by the men of Ai, who killed about thirty-six of them. . . . Then Joshua tore his clothes and fell facedown to the ground before the ark of the Lord. . . . The Lord said to Joshua, 'Stand up! What are you doing down on your face? Israel has sinned. . . .' Then Joshua said to Achan, 'My son, give glory to the Lord, the God of Israel, and give him the praise. Tell me what you have done; do not hide it from me.' Achan replied, 'It is true! I have sinned against the Lord, the God of Israel.' Then the Lord said to Joshua, 'Do not be afraid; do not be discouraged. Take the whole army with you, and go up and attack Ai. For I have delivered into your hands the king of Ai, his people, his city and his land' " (Josh. 7:3-6, 10, 11, 19, 20; 8:1).

Does the following problem sound familiar? You rededicated your life to Jesus at camp or at some meeting, and during the next week you had a great time witnessing to some friends at school. Then disaster struck. Your mother yelled at you for not cleaning your room, for forgetting to buy milk on the way home from school, and for not remembering your aunt's birthday. Then you lost your cool, and with a B.C. display of temper lashed back at your mother with a torrent of vicious vocabulary. After it was over, you felt completely defeated and wondered how you could have experienced such great victory and defeat in one week.

The same thing happened to the Israelites. After watching the walls of the strongest city in the country fall down flat, they were defeated by the defenders of the little hick town of Ai. Why? First of all, they were self-confident. They acted as though they had destroyed Jericho when God had done it all by a miracle. Therefore they decided Ai was so weak that only two or three thousand soldiers could easily take the town. They forgot that God doesn't use the same strategy for each problem. He did not plan the same kind of defeat for Ai as He used for Jericho. And the Israelites never bothered to ask God about His method for capturing Ai.

There is a tremendous difference between self-confidence and Christ-confidence. There is never a reason to feel self-confidence after a victory in the Christian life because you didn't win the battle. God did. Such pride always leads to defeat (Prov. 16:18). Yesterday's faith or yesterday's strategy won't work for today's battle. You must keep in constant contact with Jesus.

The other reason for Israel's defeat was Achan's sin: He had kept some of the loot from Jericho that was to be set aside for God's work. This sin had to be confessed and punished before Israel could have another victory. Any sin that is not confessed and squarely dealt with will cause defeat.

What if you, like the Israelites, blow it completely? You can recover lost ground, even as Israel finally defeated Ai and again lived in victory. But that return to victory was not easy; Israel had more difficulty conquering Ai than Jericho. As Alan Redpath remarks: "Recovery of lost ground in the Christian experience is the most difficult problem of all."[5] But God can do anything and He can show you what to do after you have failed. Confess your pride and independence, your disobedience and lack of prayer. Then ask God what to do next. Sometimes apologizing to your mother can straighten out the problem immediately, but more often you'll have to regain the confidence of the person you've sinned against by living consistently before him for weeks—even months. Although God forgives immediately, a minute of disobedience may require hours, days or months of obedience before the wrong is wiped clean from the mind of the person you offended.

Don't let pride, prayerlessness or sin create an Ai for you. But if you do suffer a defeat, remember there is a road back to victory. That road may require drastic action, and it will mean sticking closer to God than ever before, but victory will come, no matter how bloody the defeat. So don't let the devil tell you differently. You may have lost a game but Christ in you can still win the championship.

"If we confess our sins, he is faithful and just and will forgive us our sins and purify us from all unrighteousness" (1 John 1:9).

"Wash and make yourselves clean. Take your evil deeds out of my sight! Stop doing wrong" (Isa. 1:16).

"Let the wicked forsake his way and the evil man his thoughts. Let him

---

[5]Alan Redpath, *Victorious Christian Living, Studies in the Book of Joshua.* Old Tappan, N.J.: Fleming H. Revell, 1955, p. 123.

turn to the Lord, and he will have mercy on him, and to our God, for he will freely pardon" (Isa. 55:7).

"Through love and faithfulness sin is atoned for; through the fear of the Lord a man avoids evil" (Prov. 16:6).

1. Using the above four verses, write down four steps for getting back on the road of victory after a defeat.
2. Verbal (spoken) confession of sin is the first step. Why is that not enough?
3. Jesus died for your sins and only He, not your good deeds, can forgive you. In what sense, then, do love and faithfulness atone (make up for) for your wrong?
4. If you have just experienced a defeat, prayerfully ask God for the specific steps you must take to get on the road to victory.

The First Masquerade Party

" 'We are your servants,' they said to Joshua. But Joshua asked, 'Who are you and where do you come from?' They answered: 'Your servants have come from a very distant country because of the fame of the Lord your God. For we have heard reports of him: all that he did in Egypt, and all that he did to the two kings of the Amorites east of the Jordan—Sihon king of Heshbon, and Og king of Bashan, who reigned in Ashtaroth. And our elders and all those living in our country said to us, "Take provisions for your journey; go and meet them and say to them, 'We are your servants; make a treaty with us.' " This bread of ours was warm when we packed it at home on the day we left to come to you. But now see how dry and moldy it is. And these wineskins that we filled were new, but see how cracked they are. And our clothes and sandals are worn out by the very long journey.' The men of Israel sampled their provisions but did not inquire of the Lord. Then Joshua made a treaty of peace with them to let them live, and the leaders of the assembly ratified it by oath" (Josh. 9:8–15).

The devil is very sneaky. He tries to catch you off guard and deceive you. But you've no need to worry. If you've given your life to Jesus and are living by faith, you'll win the war even though you may lose some battles.

If you really want to do God's will, Satan won't attempt obvious tricks, such as making you say the Bible is not true, or telling you to steal money. Instead, he will present you with a decision that seems unimportant and will try to convince you to use your own judgment. He'll try to make you think praying isn't important and to pressure you into a quick decision.

The devil used these very tactics against Joshua and the leaders of the Israelites. The Gibeonites, as other nations in Canaan, were practicing gross immorality and satanic worship. Because of their sin God had com-

"The devil is very sneaky. He tries to catch you off guard and deceive you."

manded that all Canaanites be destroyed. The Israelites were not to make any agreements with these people. In desperation, the Gibeonites planned a masquerade party for the Israelites; they dressed as hoboes and then claimed they had traveled from a far land. Unfortunately, Joshua and the leaders were gullible. It was a good sob story and they may have been quite flattered that people would walk that far just to make peace with them. So they didn't take time to pray about the matter. In making a snap judgment they didn't even consider that nations don't bother making a peace treaty with people whom they have no intention of fighting, or that bread gets moldy long before shoes wear out. They instead made an emotional response based on pride. Within three days they discovered their dreadful mistake: the Gibeonites were their neighbors.

Learn from Joshua's mistake and avoid spur of the moment decisions. "Sure, I'd be glad to," or, "No problem, I'll take care of it" is sometimes better unsaid. Beware of giving in to pressure for an immediate decision. The expensive watch which is drastically reduced (and which the clerk assures you will be gone in fifteen minutes if you don't buy it now) will still be there later if God wants you to have it. It's perfectly safe, sensible, and *necessary* to go home and pray about it before making the decision. Pray and think before accepting or making a date. Pray about what courses to sign up for, what books to read, what to do with your summer and whether or not to take tennis lessons. Lack of prayer will impair your judgment. If you just "let everything fall into place," you will do the falling!

But the story doesn't end here. Even though they had been tricked into the treaty, the Israelites kept their promise. They honored their treaty with the Gibeonites even though it meant fighting five kings who had attacked the Gibeonites. It was one of the greatest battles in history: God arranged the longest day on record so Joshua and the Israelites could finish destroying their enemies. After that the Gibeonites worked as servants for the Israelites, supplying the things necessary for the sacrifices used in worship. These tricksters remained loyal citizens and had a chance to learn about the God of Israel.

There's a beautiful truth here: Even if you've been tricked into a wrong decision, you can do the right things from now on. God can bring good out of evil and turn a curse into a blessing.

The world's first masquerade party has much to teach you, for the devil will try his trick-with-no-treat tactics on you, just as he did to the Israelites. So before you swallow what may be a bitter pill, ask God what's in the bottle. Before you cast your bait, ask God what you're going to catch. If you really believe that God is smarter than you are, you'll ask His opinion on everything.

"Trust in the Lord with all your heart and lean not on your own understanding; in all your ways acknowledge him, and he will make your paths straight. Do not be wise in your own eyes; fear the Lord and shun evil. This will bring health to your body and nourishment to your bones" (Prov. 3:5–8).

1. List the commands given in this passage.
2. What does God promise to those who consult Him about everything?
3. What mistakes have you made in the past because you didn't ask God what you should do? How can you avoid these mistakes in the future?
4. Make a list of your priorities—be honest. Now ask God about each item on your list, and change it if He tells you to.

Life with an Anti-boredom Guarantee

"When Joshua was old and well advanced in years, the Lord said to him, ' . . . there are still very large areas of land to be taken over. . . . all the inhabitants of the mountain regions from Lebanon to Misrephoth Maim, that is, all the Sidonians and Caleb said. . . . 'Now then, just as the Lord promised, he has kept me alive for forty-five years since the time he said this to Moses, while Israel moved about in the desert. So here I am today, eighty-five years old! I am still as strong today as the day Moses sent me out; I'm just as vigorous to go out to battle now as I was then. Now give me this hill country that the Lord promised me that day. You yourself heard then that the Anakites were there and their cities were large and fortified, but, the Lord helping me, I will drive them out just as he said.' The people of Joseph said to Joshua, 'Why have you given us only one allotment and one portion for an inheritance? We are a numerous people and the Lord has blessed us abundantly.' 'If you are so numerous,' Joshua answered, 'and if the hill country of Ephraim is too small for you, go up into the forest and clear land for yourselves there in the land of the Perizzites and Rephaites.' The people of Joseph replied, 'The hill country is not enough for us, and all the Canaanites who live in the plain have iron chariots, both those in Beth Shan and its settlements and those in the Valley of Jezreel' " (Josh. 13:1, 6; 14:6, 10-12; 17:14–16).

When you try to live above the circumstances, it's the little things that get you down. If you've committed your life to Jesus, you're not going to wreck your mind and body with drugs. You're not going to move in with your boyfriend or girlfriend, or flunk out of school to get even with your parents. Because Jesus has won victory for you, you want to follow His plan for your life, expecting Him to handle the "big things" in your life and give you victory.

But do you have faith to trust God if, through no fault of your own, you arrive late to the choir concert—in which you sing a solo? If your friend accidently spills a bottle of permanent ink on your new suit? If you lose your paycheck or have a car accident?

And what about those sensitive issues in your life? Do you have the faith to trust God if someone nags, "Aren't you ever going to get any taller? You're still a little shrimp"? If a person says, "Your sister is so outgoing and vivacious. Why are you so shy?" Little things can break us.

The Israelites found themselves in a situation where the little things would determine their entire future. They had conquered all the major kings. The only remaining fighting would consist of mopping-up operations. The leaders had assigned each tribe a portion of land, and each tribe was to drive out the enemies in its territory. God had given His promise of victory. Now the people needed only to act on these promises in faith.

But notice in the above verses the vast difference between the attitude of Caleb and the attitude of the people of Joseph. Caleb's clan conquered all the land assigned to them because they acted in faith. Others, however, cowered in fear and missed the blessing.

As the Israelites, you have tremendous promises from God. For instance: "He who did not spare his own Son but gave him up for us all—how will he not also, along with him, graciously give us *all things*?" (Rom. 8:32). What a promise! "All things" includes peace and poise when everything goes wrong. "All things" includes power to overcome personality defects and to handle the ridicule. God's power *can* touch every area of your life.

The reasons for not cashing in on God's promises never change. One reason is laziness. Instead of studying every verse in the Bible that speaks about peace, and then aligning your life with God's truth, you just let the problem slide, figuring your tendency to panic easily is something everyone else will have to tolerate. So you never get rid of the problem. Some Israelites also preferred taking it easy. Rather than fighting any more battles, they let the Canaanites stay in their territory.

Another reason for missing out on God's blessings is lack of faith, as demonstrated by the descendants of Joseph. They doubted an all-powerful God could do anything about iron chariots. (You probably do the same. Instead of putting your faith in the Creator of the universe, you prefer to keep your complex.) Other Israelite tribes didn't annihilate the pagans as God had commanded because they wanted the pagans' tax money. Maybe you also sometimes prefer to compensate for your weaknesses instead of letting God get rid of them.

But Caleb was different. According to God, Caleb's secret of success was: "Caleb has a different spirit and follows me wholeheartedly" (Num. 14:24). In the same manner, if you follow God with all your heart, your life will not be full of loose ends. Your victory isn't complete because you've been easygoing and slipshod instead of following God wholeheartedly. But you can change and live a life as exciting as Caleb's.

Just as He said to Joshua, God is saying to you, "There remains yet very much land to be possessed." Do you realize you could live to be 100 and still not exhaust God's power to change you and to change your circumstances? God always has more good things in store. His plans for your life come with an anti-boredom guarantee.

" 'Ask and it will be given to you; seek and you will find; knock and the door will be opened to you. For everyone who asks receives; he who seeks finds; and to him who knocks, the door will be opened. Which of you, if his son asks for bread, will give him a stone? Or if he asks for a fish, will give him a snake? If you, then, though you are evil, know how to give good gifts to your children, how much more will your Father in heaven give good gifts to those who ask him!' " (Matt. 7:7–11).

1. List the areas of your life that still need to be conquered.
2. Is power to conquer the problems on your list one of the good gifts God would like to give you? Yield yourself to Him and let Him give you that power.

Week Six

RUTH: FROM LOSER'S LANE TO THE WINNER'S CIRCLE

Introduction

When Everything Goes Wrong

Do you feel as if you come from "the wrong side of the tracks"? As if your life is filled with tragedy and misery? As if there is no way to better your situation? Then the story of Ruth is for you. From her you can learn principles which will help you deal with prejudice and disaster.

Ruth lived in Moab, a country of idol worshipers next to Israel. She met and married a young man from Israel who had moved to Moab with his family because of a food shortage in Israel. From this family she learned about the true God. But tragedy struck. First, Ruth's father-in-law, Elimelech, died. Next, both her husband and his brother (who had also married a Moabite woman) died. This left three widows: Ruth, her sister-in-law Orpah, and their mother-in-law Naomi. In those days, there were no good jobs for women, so a woman (such as Ruth) not under the protection of a father, husband, or son was poverty-stricken. The three women had to do something.

Naomi, Ruth's mother-in-law, decided to return to Bethlehem, her hometown, so she told her daughters-in-law to stay with their parents. If they returned home, their fathers would provide for them and arrange marriages with new husbands. Orpah chose to go home. Ruth, however, chose to follow Naomi, and thus follow the God of Israel. Because the law of Israel prohibited intermarriage with pagans, Ruth gave up the chance for remarriage by going with Naomi. She had to leave her family, her friends, and her country with its familiar ways. She risked everything to follow God.

Ruth and Naomi arrived in Bethlehem at harvest time. Because the law allowed poor people and foreigners to enter the grain fields and pick up, or "glean," the leftovers, Ruth went out to gather grain for herself and Naomi. Ruth soon found herself in the field of Boaz, a rich and prominent man of Bethlehem who happened to be a relative of her dead husband. Boaz noticed Ruth and took a special interest in her. He treated her very kindly and told his reapers to drop grain on purpose so she could gather more. He also invited her to lunch and asked her to stay in his field where she would be well-protected.

93

Risking Rejection

Naomi knew the laws of Israel, so with great interest she watched the friendship developing between Ruth and Boaz. In Israel land could not be permanently sold because property remained in a family. (This prevented the rich from owning all the land.) A piece of property could be leased until the Year of Jubilee which came every fifty years. At that time all the land was automatically returned to the descendants of the original owner. Of course, if all members of the original family had died, the land could be sold.

Maintaining the family line was considered so important that a childless widow could ask an unmarried brother-in-law (or nearest living male relative of the dead husband) to marry her. The first son of that marriage would bear the name of the woman's dead husband and thus continue the family line. In fact, a childless widow was expected to seek such a marriage. The man could refuse her proposal but he would suffer disgrace for not fulfilling his duty to his dead relative. The man in a position to marry a widow, buy back her late husband's land, and provide a son bearing the late husband's name was called a kinsman-redeemer.

Naomi hoped that through Ruth her family line could continue. Thus the friendship between Ruth and Boaz encouraged her—Boaz was showing Ruth great kindness and giving her special attention. Naomi realized, of course, that Boaz might be unwilling to buck public prejudice to marry a woman of foreign birth. Nonetheless, Naomi also realized that because Ruth was a follower of God and no longer an idol worshiper, the ban against intermarriage with foreigners did not necessarily apply in this case. By her virtuous character Ruth had broken down the prejudice of many. Naomi, therefore, had reason to hope that Boaz would marry Ruth.

Legally, Naomi could have taken the matter to court, but she didn't want to subject Boaz to public pressure. Instead, she sent Ruth at night to the place where the harvested grain had been piled, where Boaz and the families of his workers would be camping for the night. Ruth was to wait until Boaz was asleep, then lie down at his feet. According to Oriental tradition, this gesture meant, "I want to love and obey you. I'm willing to be your faithful wife, but if you reject me because I'm a foreigner, I'll understand." Boaz immediately understood what Ruth was doing, even though he had just awakened from a deep sleep. She had proposed marriage. But she was allowing Boaz to reject her offer without the whole world finding out.

Naomi's plan, which seems very strange to Western minds, must be understood in the light of the customs and ideas of the ancient Middle East. Ruth was not being immoral or flirtatious by lying at the feet of Boaz. She was simply following an accepted custom.

At the end of the harvest, the owner of the land, and his workers and their families would gather for the final job, winnowing, which included a big celebration. They had already completed the hard work of threshing—

breaking the husk from the kernel of grain, so now came the fun part. To winnow the grain they would throw it into the air and let the wind blow the husks away. The harvesters often did this job at night to take advantage of the stronger breeze. When the job was done, they would feast. By that time it was so late that all the families would sleep outdoors, on or near the threshing floor. J. Vernon McGee, recognized Bible scholar, comments "that the threshing floor was a public place and that these incidents all took place in the open. Both men and women were lying about the threshing floor. Entire families were gathered there."[1]

After her silent proposal, Boaz told Ruth he would love to marry her. There was, however, a man related more closely to Ruth's dead husband than Boaz was; legally, that man had the first right to marry Ruth and to buy the property of the family. Boaz, therefore, had to give him the first chance before he could make any promises. Wisely, Boaz told Ruth to leave before anyone sleeping on the threshing floor woke up. After all, if everyone knew Ruth wanted to marry Boaz, and the other relative decided to become Ruth's husband, things could become very embarrassing. Boaz promised to ask the other man about the marriage, so Ruth didn't have to worry about doing anything. She had fulfilled her responsibility.

In the morning, Boaz went immediately to the city gate, and there gathered the elders of the city, and his "rival," for a court session. The other eligible relative refused the chance to buy the property and marry Ruth. Now Boaz was free to marry Ruth.

Almost as a fairy tale, this real-life love story ended in a happy marriage. Ruth eventually gave birth to a son, named Obed, who became the father of Jesse, who became the father of King David. Ruth, therefore, was David's great-grandmother and one of the ancestors of Mary, the mother of Jesus. Because Ruth followed God totally, her life changed. Instead of being a desolate widow she became the wife of a loving, prosperous husband, and the mother of a son whose descendants would bless the entire world.

When Hope Is Gone

"In the days when the judges ruled, there was a famine in the land, and a man from Bethlehem in Judah, together with his wife and two sons, went to live for a while in the country of Moab. The man's name was Elimelech, his wife's name Naomi, and the names of his two sons were Mahlon and Kilion. They were Ephrathites from Bethlehem, Judah. And they went to Moab and lived there. Now Elimelech, Naomi's husband, died, and she was left with her two sons. They married Moabite women, one named Orpah and the other Ruth. After they had lived there about ten years, both Mahlon

---

[1] J. Vernon McGee, *Ruth: The Romance of Redemption.* Nashville: Thomas Nelson, 1982, p. 92.

and Kilion also died, and Naomi was left without her two sons and her husband. 'Look,' said Naomi, 'your sister-in-law is going back to her people and her gods. Go back with her.' But Ruth replied, 'Don't urge me to leave you or turn back from you. Where you go I will go, and where you stay I will stay. Your people will be my people and your God my God. Where you die I will die, and there I will be buried. May the Lord deal with me, be it ever so severely, if anything but death separates you and me' " (Ruth 1:1–5, 15–17).

When you visit your friend's beautiful house and see that his parents really love each other and that the community respects them, do you feel a twinge of envy in your heart? Do you feel as if you come from the wrong side of the tracks? Do you wish you could be proud of your house and the job your father holds? Do you feel hurt that your parents are divorced? Do you have trouble coping with your father's drinking or your mother's nervous condition? Do you work hard to hide "skeletons" in your family's closet? Do you feel hopeless because your father died or your best friend was killed in a car accident? If you can lay claim to any of the above feelings, the story of the life of Ruth will inspire and help you.

Ruth grew up in the pagan country of Moab. In Moab, perversions such as child sacrifice, immorality, and slave-like status for women were normal. Happily, she learned about the true God and a better way to live when she married a man from Israel. And she grew to love his mother, Naomi, a very kind person. But when Ruth's father-in-law, her husband, and her brother-in-law all died, life suddenly seemed hopeless.

When Naomi started going back to Bethlehem in Israel, her two daughters-in-law walked with her. But Naomi, aware of the hard life a widow in a strange country could face, urged Orpah and Ruth to return to their homes. At this, Orpah kissed her mother-in-law good-bye and left for home, but Ruth would not go back. She decided to follow the God of Naomi—no matter the cost—and the cost was very great.

In choosing to follow the true God, Jehovah, Ruth could never go home again, for she could no longer join in the Moabite's pagan worship. She had to leave her family and her friends forever. She had to face new and strange customs.

In choosing to follow Jehovah, Ruth gave up the idea of marriage and a home, the cherished dream of every woman. Jewish law forbade marriage to a pagan woman because God wanted to keep His people from idol worship. (Naomi's son had defied the law of Israel by marrying Ruth.) No husband would mean no income, because there were no paying jobs for women. Ruth therefore faced the possibility of a life of poverty and loneliness.

In choosing to follow Jehovah, Ruth gave up the right to make her own decisions. Because she was going to her mother-in-law's country and would be living with her, Ruth would be at Naomi's mercy. But worse, if something happened to Naomi, Ruth would be alone in a foreign land.

When Ruth said to Naomi, "Your God will be my God," she gave up everything. But look again. Once Ruth gave God her life, God gave back to her more than she ever could have dreamed. The same can be true for you.

Make this promise yours: " 'Surely God is my salvation; I will trust and not be afraid. The Lord, the Lord, is my strength and my song; he has become my salvation.' With joy you will draw water from the wells of salvation" (Isa. 12:2, 3). God wants to be your complete salvation—not just the One who saves you from hell, but the One who saves you from fear, who saves you from depression and despair, who gives you joy and gladness. If you completely give your life to God, He can turn things around—even if you see no hope. God can make something beautiful out of your mixed-up life if you let Him.

"The Spirit of the Sovereign Lord is on me, because the Lord has anointed me to preach good news to the poor. He has sent me to bind up the brokenhearted, to proclaim freedom for the captives and release for the prisoners, to proclaim the year of the Lord's favor and the day of vengeance of your God, to comfort all who mourn, and provide for those who grieve in Zion—to bestow on them a crown of beauty instead of ashes, the oil of gladness instead of mourning, and a garment of praise instead of a spirit of despair. They will be called oaks of righteousness, a planting of the Lord for the display of his splendor" (Isa. 61:1–3).

1. Jesus is the One who can do all these things (read Luke 4:17–19). Make a list of all the things Jesus can do for you.
2. Which of the blessings on your list do you need right now? Receive from Jesus what you need.
3. According to the passage from Isaiah 61, God wants to make the poor and the brokenhearted into advertisements of what God's love and power can do—"oaks of righteousness . . . for the display of his splendor."

The Fate of the Make-Believe Birthday Party

"Boaz asked the foreman of his harvesters, 'Whose young woman is that?' The foreman replied, 'She is the Moabitess who came back from Moab with Naomi. She said, 'Please let me glean and gather among the sheaves behind the harvesters.' She went into the field and has worked steadily from morning till now, except for a short rest in the shelter.' [Boaz said to Ruth,] 'May the Lord repay you for what you have done. May you be richly rewarded by the Lord, the God of Israel, under whose wings you have come to take refuge.' 'May I continue to find favor in your eyes, my lord,' she said. 'You have given me comfort and have spoken kindly to your servant—though I

do not have the standing of one of your servant girls' " (Ruth 2:5–7, 12, 13).

The parents of a boy with whom I attended grade school never let him bring friends home or plan anything special for his birthday. One day at school he announced it was his birthday. By the end of the day he had convinced himself that he was having a party, so he invited all of us. But the guests found no cake or Koolaid—only an angry mother telling eager children there was no party. That boy could not change his situation either by wishing or by forcing the issue.

You may think that boy was very foolish. However, you probably do the same kind of thing—create a new situation by attitudes and actions which deny the truth. In fact, you probably know a bunch of kids like that in your school. Lizzie Leach, Paul the Proud, and Pitiful Patty will probably seem too familiar.

Lizzie Leech does everything possible to get attention. She wears bizarre clothes. She chatters non-stop to anyone who will listen. She lays traps for all the guys. She stays after class trying out for teacher's pet. She cons kindhearted people into helping her with everything. With bitter determination she seeks acceptance, but instead drives everyone away.

Paul the Proud pretends he knows everything, acts as if he's loaded with money, and considers it beneath his dignity to speak to underclassmen. He brags constantly about the great things he has done, the prizes he's won, and the important people he knows. He never admits defeat or discouragement. Instead of drawing people to himself, he continues to build a brick wall around himself. People who know the truth would like to help Paul the Proud but he won't let them.

Pitiful Patty's life is one misfortune after another and, with the regularity of the morning news, she announces each misfortune to the public. (What a shame if someone were uninformed about the tough life she's had.) She could never give up her horrible plight, however, because then no one would feel sorry for her. She dreams of a world in which she'll have plenty of friends to feel sorry for her—but at the moment, fewer and fewer are listening to her woes.

Lizzie, Paul and Patty—each employs methods of making a bad situation worse, trying to force people to change their attitudes, or just pretending not to need help from anyone. No one will deny that these three, as many people, have been deeply hurt and carry the scars of those hurts. But there is a way out. And Ruth found it.

Ruth made the best of her circumstances. Because of her pagan background the Israelites would despise her, but she was willing to endure the prejudice. The law of the land allowed poor people and foreigners to enter the fields at harvest time and glean the leftovers. Ruth worked diligently at this back-breaking job, the only work she could get. She expected no favors. And when Boaz noticed her, she didn't make herself a pest by maneuvering for attention, but graciously received his kind words. Neither did she seek his sympathy by telling him the sad story of her life, hoping for a handout. Although she didn't beg for pity, she did not show arrogance, trying to give an impression that she could handle life without help from anyone. When he complimented her, there was none of Lizzie Leech or Pitiful Patty in Ruth.

As Ruth accepted her circumstances, she also believed God would take care of her no matter what. She knew that an all-powerful God had a plan, even for her life. This attitude gave her a humble, sweet spirit which won the hearts of Boaz and everyone in Bethlehem.

The Bible says, "But godliness with contentment is great gain" (1 Tim. 6:6). How can you gain anything if you're contented with what you've got? Well, it works like this. Your contentment will make other people accept you and want to be your friends. And your lack of rebellion will enable God to give you great things. But trying to solve your problem by forcing people to change and directing your circumstances is like trying to create a birthday party that doesn't exist. Your manipulations will suffer the same fate as the make-believe birthday party.

"I thank Christ Jesus our Lord, who has given me strength, that he considered me faithful, appointing me to his service. Even though I was once a blasphemer and a persecutor and a violent man, I was shown mercy because I acted in ignorance and unbelief. The grace of our Lord was poured out on me abundantly, along with the faith and love that are in Christ Jesus. Here is a trustworthy saying that deserves full acceptance: Christ Jesus came into the world to save sinners—of whom I am the worst. But for that very reason I was shown mercy so that in me, the worst of sinners, Christ Jesus might display his unlimited patience as an example for those who would believe on him and receive eternal life" (1 Tim. 1:12–16).

1. Which is more important: what you were in the past, or what Christ can make you in the future?
2. On which are you concentrating: your problems and your past, or what Jesus can do to change you?
3. Are you guilty of forcing people or circumstances in order to improve your situation? What can you do today to change this habit?

Jesus Says, "Take Two Giant Steps."

"Her mother-in-law asked her, 'Where did you glean today? Where did you work? Blessed be the man who took notice of you!' Then Ruth told her mother-in-law about the one at whose place she had been working. 'The name of the man I worked with today is Boaz,' she said. Naomi said to Ruth her daughter-in-law, 'It will be good for you, my daughter, to go with his girls, because in someone else's field you might be harmed.' So Ruth stayed close to the servant girls of Boaz to glean until the barley and wheat

harvests were finished. And she lived with her mother-in-law" (Ruth 2:19, 22, 23).

You must decide whether to keep your job or go out for volleyball. Whom should you ask for advice? Your non-Christian friends? Your boyfriend or girlfriend? Or anyone who will listen? The answer to this question is important, because your life is largely shaped by the people from whom you take advice. And if you face some extraordinarily difficult choices, good advice is critical. So take some pointers from Ruth.

Notice the steps Ruth took to get out of her tragic situation. First she decided to follow God, no matter what the cost. Second, she accepted her situation and didn't try to push people or manipulate circumstances to fulfill her needs. Instead, she trusted God. Finally, she took the advice of a godly person who cared about her—she obeyed Naomi. Ruth talked things over with Naomi and accepted her guidance. And because Ruth took advice from the right person, she made wise decisions.

The Bible says a great deal about getting advice from the right person. For example: "The plans of the righteous are just; the advice of the wicked is deceitful" (Prov. 12:5); and, "Blessed is the man who does not walk in the counsel of the wicked, or stand in the way of sinners, or sit in the seat of mockers" (Ps. 1:1). In other words, "Happy is the person who takes no advice from people who don't follow God."

Are you following the advice of non-Christians? If you are, that may be the reason you have so many problems. In fact, even the advice of half-committed Christians can be bad. (For example, the girl engaged to a non-Christian guy will tell you it's okay to date or marry a non-Christian—even though the Bible says "Do not be yoked together with unbelievers" (2 Corinthians 6:14).

Ask God to show you a wise, committed, strong Christian (who knows the Bible and is following God totally) from whom you can get good advice. This might be your pastor, an older Christian whom you admire, or a Christian friend. Maybe it will be someone you can write to. Even if you can't think of such a person right now, keep praying until God shows you one, because you need sound, spiritual advice.

You should not only follow godly advice, but you, like Ruth, should obey people in authority over you. Because Naomi was Ruth's mother-in-law and Naomi was providing her a home, Ruth had a responsibility to obey Naomi. And because Ruth obeyed Naomi's plan, even when she could have raised some logical objections, she was delivered from her miserable state. If you obey authority, God will also give you deliverance.

You make two kinds of decisions. One kind of decision is a matter of wisdom, such as deciding what to do with the money you've saved, or whether to study Zephaniah or Philippians in your quiet time. Wise, godly advice can help you make the right decision. The other kind of decision is a matter of submission—whether or not to obey authority. The Bible says a great deal about obeying authority, especially parents. Think about these verses: "Children, obey your parents in the Lord, for this is right" (Eph. 6:1); "The eye that mocks a father, that scorns obedience to a mother will be pecked out by the ravens of the valley, will be eaten by the vultures" (Prov. 30:17)—startling! If you want to follow God, you must obey authority. You have no choice. (The only exception is that extreme case in which obedience would require you to disobey God's Word—and even then you must be respectful.)

If you're in a tough situation, obeying authority can be difficult. The devil always tempts the girl from the ghetto, the boy from the broken home, or anyone with special problems, to become proud and independent, refusing to obey or take advice. The devil tries so hard to break down respect for authority because taking godly advice and obeying authority are two giant steps toward a new and better life.

"Pride only breeds quarrels, but wisdom is found in those who take advice" (Prov. 13:10).

"But Samuel replied: 'Does the Lord delight in burnt offerings and sacrifices as much as in obeying the voice of the Lord? To obey is better than sacrifice, and to heed is better than the fat of rams. For rebellion is like the sin of divination, and arrogance like the evil of idolatry. Because you have rejected the word of the Lord, he has rejected you as king' " (1 Sam. 15:22).

1. What are your reasons for not taking advice or obeying authority?
2. What are the dangers of refusing to take advice or obey authority?
3. Why is it sometimes easier to make great sacrifices than to be humble enough to seek godly advice and obey authority?
4. Are you refusing to obey an authority in your life? Is there some decision you must make for which you need sound, spiritual advice? Talk this over with God.

Rejects Recycled

"One day Naomi her mother-in-law said to her, 'My daughter, should I not try to find a home for you, where you will be well provided for? Is not Boaz, with whose servant girls you have been, a kinsman of ours? Tonight he will be winnowing barley on the threshing floor. Wash and perfume yourself, and put on your best clothes. Then go down to the threshing floor, but don't let him know you are there until he has finished eating and drinking. When he lies down, note the place where he is lying. Then go and uncover his feet and lie down. He will tell you what to do.' 'I will do whatever you say,' Ruth answered" (Ruth 3:1–5).

Do you avoid certain people just because you're afraid you might say the wrong thing and give them a bad impression of you? Have you decided not to try out for the volleyball team because you might not qualify? Do you avoid parties because you're afraid you don't have the right outfit to wear and someone might make a snide remark? Do you continue to be a loner because you fear that your attempt at friendliness might be rejected? Fear of rejection can paralyze you.

Ruth could have let fear of rejection ruin her life, because Israelite custom put her under obligation to find a husband—but the law required that she make the first move. This law of Israel must have seemed very strange to her. It stated that the closest, unmarried relative of a dead man should marry the childless widow, and thus continue the family line— but the widow was supposed to start the process. How scarey! Being in love with Boaz, an eligible relative of her late husband, must have made the whole affair even more frightening. What if he rejected her? Although Boaz, as a relative of her deceased husband, was obliged to marry Ruth, another law forbade intermarriage with foreigners. This was a complicated situation, to say the least, and no one could predict how things would turn out.

Naomi's plan must have seemed dreadful to Ruth at first. Ruth was to hide by the threshing floor where all the workers of Boaz and their families were having a feast. Later, as they each found a place to sleep on the threshing floor, Ruth was to watch where Boaz lay down to sleep. Then silently, so no one would waken, she was to lie down by his feet. This was not immoral or flirtatious. It was a Middle Eastern way of saying, "I want to be your wife," because by law the widow had to propose the marriage which could carry on her dead husband's family line. She could have done this in public court but Naomi did not want Ruth and Boaz to be the subjects of gossip, should Boaz decide not to marry a woman of pagan birth. Ruth bravely obeyed Naomi's plan.

Ruth found courage to carry out Naomi's plan because she was doing God's will. First, she was doing God's will by obeying His law. (God had instituted the seemingly strange law which told a childless widow to propose a marriage that would prolong the family line.) Second, Ruth was doing God's will by obeying her mother-in-law. (The Bible has much to say about obeying people in authority.) Because she was doing God's will, she knew she was accepted by God, even if she were rejected by Boaz. God would take care of her. This love story has a happy ending, but Ruth didn't know that. When she lay down at the feet of Boaz, she willingly risked rejection, because she knew she was doing God's will.

You have complexes because you do things not based in God's will. You tried to be the main attraction of the evening but got laughed at? Your motive was not based in God's will. You blew your soccer team tryout and feel humiliated because you didn't live up to your self-made standard? Your standard wasn't one that God set for you. You wanted friends that would make you feel important and popular, but instead they only had needs of their own. Your standards for friendship weren't based on God's Word, which says "A friend loves at all times" (Prov. 17:17).

God wants you to have good things but He wants your motives to be pure. Psalm 67:7 says, "God will bless us. And all the ends of the earth will fear him!" In other words, God wants to work in your life so others will be drawn to Him because of the good things He is doing in your life. He wants others to be favorably impressed by you, not so you can be named Miss Personality Plus, but so you can win other people into His kingdom. But God doesn't construct no-fail humans. Instead, He teaches you how to deal with mistakes and face rejection.

If you feel rejected, take comfort in this thought: God loves to recycle rejects so they can bring glory to Him. He is making you into a person who can take some risks, who isn't afraid to fail. The secret is to base your actions on God's Word and God's will. Then you won't care if someone else thinks you're unsuccessful. If he rejects you, that's his problem. Jesus faced that kind of rejection and He never let it stop Him. God can free you from the fear of failure so you can take the risks of faith.

"The Lord delights in the way of the man whose steps he has made firm; though he stumble, he will not fall, for the Lord upholds him with his hand" (Ps. 37:23, 24).

"For though a righteous man falls seven times, he rises again, but the wicked are brought down by calamity" (Prov. 24:16).

1. What does God think of someone who is following His path? Does it really matter if others don't think you're successful when you're following God's plan for you?
2. Why should you be unafraid to risk failure in something?
3. Does the Bible guarantee you'll never make a mistake, an error in judgment, or a social slip? Should you expect to never fail at anything or to never be rejected by anyone?
4. If you are following God and you fail at something, what is God's promise for you?

Your Prince Has Already Come

"Then Boaz announced to the elders and all the people, 'Today you are witnesses that I have bought from Naomi all the property of Elimelech, Kilion and Mahlon. I have also acquired Ruth the Moabitess, Mahlon's widow, as my wife, in order to maintain the name of the dead with his property, so that his name will not disappear from among his family or from the town records. Today you are witnesses!' " (Ruth 4:9, 10).

Ruth's life was transformed because she chose the true God, sought wise advice, obeyed authority, and stuck with doing what was right. But despite her own efforts, her obedience, she would never have experienced this complete transformation without Boaz her deliverer, her "prince charming," if you will. He was an eligible relative (kinsman-redeemer) of

"You don't have to sit around wishing someone would rescue you. . . ."

her dead husband, obliged to marry Ruth so the family line would not die out and lose the property. Boaz loved Ruth and willingly married her, even though she was a foreigner. He had the money to buy the inheritance because he had never gotten into debt himself. If Boaz had been unwilling or unable to buy (redeem) the land, Ruth could have never enjoyed her honored position in Hebrew history.

The story of Ruth and Boaz illustrates beautifully what Jesus did for you when He died on the cross. Just as Boaz was Ruth's kinsman-redeemer, Jesus is your redeemer, the One who has delivered your soul from sin. Just as Boaz was both willing and able to redeem Ruth's family property, Jesus is willing and able to save you if you come to Him. Just as Ruth lay down at the feet of Boaz to tell him she wanted to be redeemed, you must come to the foot of the cross in surrender to Jesus and ask for His salvation.

Boaz' payment to buy back the land and take Ruth as his wife transformed her total existence—past, present, and future. His marriage to her delivered her from the curse of being born a pagan. And the marriage not only wiped clean her past and gave her a honeymoon to enjoy at the present, but offered the promise of a lifetime with Boaz during which they could learn to love and understand each other. It offered a lifetime of sharing Boaz' wealth and prestige. It offered the joys of motherhood.

Jesus' salvation, His redemption, offers you an even greater transformation. He blots out all your past sins, no matter how gross. He offers you the joy of daily fellowship with himself. He can restore every part of your life which has been scarred or perverted by the world and the devil; as you cooperate with Him, He will renew your mind, give strength and health to your body, straighten out your finances, and improve your relationships with family and friends. His salvation can give joy and purpose to your life.

It is true that God will not save anyone who refuses to believe; and He will not change the life of anyone who won't permit Him to reign. But let's shift the emphasis from our response to God, who offers such great salvation. The only reason you, or anyone, can go from the wrong side of the tracks in the ghetto to a victorious and beautiful life is because Jesus died and rose again. The only reason you can have hope after tragedy and despair is because Jesus bought back and transformed every part of your life—ruined by the sin and selfishness of this world.

Jesus loves you much more than Boaz loved Ruth. It was this great love that sent Him to the cross. So you don't have to sit around wishing someone would rescue you, because your Prince has already come. His name is Jesus, and He loves you enough to promise you a bright, beautiful future. Jesus will be your Boaz, but like Ruth, you must begin to believe—*now.*

"This is how God showed his love among us: He sent his one and only Son into the world that we might live through him. This is love: not that we loved God, but that he loved us and sent his Son as an atoning sacrifice for our sins" (1 John 4:9, 10).

"In him we have redemption through his blood, the forgiveness of sins, in accordance with the riches of God's grace that he lavished on us with all wisdom and understanding" (Eph. 1:7, 8).

"He who did not spare his own Son, but gave him up for us all—how will he not also, along with him, graciously give us all things? No, in all

these things we are more than conquerors through him who loved us" (Rom. 8:32, 37).

1. Have you given your life to Jesus and accepted the salvation He offers?
2. What benefits are included in that salvation?
3. After Jesus has forgiven your sins and assured you of heaven, is that the end of what He wants to do for you?
4. If you've never received salvation, decide to stop sinning, then confess your sins (your acts of rebellion against God) to God, and receive the forgiveness of Jesus. Then ask Him what is included in the "all things" He has for you today.

How to Steer Clear of Loser's Lane, and Other Side Streets

"So Boaz took Ruth and she became his wife. And the Lord enabled her to conceive, and she gave birth to a son. The women said to Naomi: 'Praise be to the Lord, who this day has not left you without a kinsman-redeemer. May he become famous throughout Israel! He will renew your life and sustain you in your old age. For your daughter-in-law, who loves you and who is better to you than seven sons, has given him birth' " (Ruth 4:13–15).

The temptation to give up hits often. When geometry gets difficult, you drop the course rather than face hard work. When your parents seem even farther away from God than before, after your months of witnessing to them, you lose hope. When the job gets boring, you quit. When your friend lets you down, you dump him. When hardly anyone shows up for Bible study, you quit attending too.

Overcoming the effects of tragedy and the scars of life requires a hard-to-develop quality: loyalty—a willingness to stick with it no matter what. It's much easier to think the grass is greener on the other side of the fence and jump from one thing to another. If you've been badly hurt by people, fear keeps you from building loyalty. You fear getting hurt again, so the first time a friend disappoints you, you bail out. Your life becomes marked by instability. The Bible, however, shows how you can overcome instability and develop loyalty: "Let us not become weary in doing good, for at the proper time we will reap a harvest *if we do not give up*" (Gal. 6:9).

Ruth developed loyalty. She gave up everything to follow God, and even when she was lonely in a new country and exhausted from overwork, she didn't slip back into idol worship. Her loyalty to God was so well known that the first time Boaz spoke to Ruth he said, "May the Lord repay you for what you have done. May you be richly rewarded by the

Lord, the God of Israel, under whose wings you have come to take refuge" (Ruth 2:12). When going to the field to pick up grain day after day became tiring and boring, she didn't quit. Although living with an older lady—and a mother-in-law at that—couldn't have been very exciting, Ruth never complained. She worked hard to support Naomi, whom she respected and obeyed. And when Ruth married Boaz, and rose above the shame and the poverty of her background, she could easily have forgotten all about Naomi. But she didn't. In fact, her love for Naomi was so obvious that everyone in Bethlehem talked about it.

The life of Ruth is not just a Cinderella story in which everything turned out well in the end. It is a monument to the way God honors those who live by His commands—Ruth lived out the command, "Let us not become weary in doing good." She not only did the right thing, she stuck with it. And she reaped the benefits of one who doesn't give up.

The principles that worked for Ruth will work for you. First, *discover what is good and start doing it.* You find out what it is by studying the Bible. The following verses will do for starters: "Honor your father and your mother" (Ex. 20:12); "Whatever you do, work at it with all your heart, as working for the Lord, not for men" (Col. 3:23); "Therefore, as we have opportunity, let us do good to all people" (Gal. 6:10). Ask the Holy Spirit to apply these verses to specific situations in your life and then act on the insight He gives you.

Next (and most hard to do), *stick with it.* Honoring your mom is easy—until an acid test situation arises. Working with enthusiasm is easy during the first two months of school—but maintaining that attitude through two semesters is tough. Helping people is easy—until they take advantage of you or display some of their unlovable characteristics. But hanging in there and obeying by faith, when no results are showing, will make the difference.

The recipe for transforming tragedy and trouble doesn't include any here-today-gone-tomorrow ingredients. Once you've started down the main street which leads to your goal, you can't turn into every side street and expect to reach your destination. You must continually do what is right—stick with it—because the side streets all have names like Trouble Trail, Discouragement Drive, and Loser's Lane.

"Jesus entered Jericho and was passing through. A man was there by the name of Zacchaeus; he was a chief tax collector and was wealthy. He wanted to see who Jesus was, but being a short man he could not, because of the crowd. So he ran ahead and climbed a sycamore-fig tree to see him, since Jesus was coming that way. When Jesus reached the spot, he looked up and said to him, 'Zacchaeus, come down immediately. I must stay at your house today' " (Luke 19:1–5).

1. List all the things that could have kept Zacchaeus from seeing Jesus.
2. What risks did Zacchaeus take, and what extra effort did he expend to see Jesus?

3. When doing the right thing takes a lot more time and effort than you anticipated, are you willing to stick with it?
4. Pray about the tough challenges that are requiring you to "stick with it."

One of God's Billboards

"So Boaz took Ruth and she became his wife. And the Lord enabled her to conceive, and she gave birth to a son. The women living there said, 'Naomi has a son.' And they named him Obed. He was the father of Jesse, the father of David" (Ruth 4:13, 17).

Someone once wrote:

You're writing a gospel, a chapter each day,
By the things that you do and the words that you say.
Men read what you write whether faithless or true.
Say, what is the gospel according to you?

Paul wrote to his friends at Corinth, ". . . you are a letter from Christ," a letter "known and read by everyone" (2 Cor. 3:2, 3). The same is true for you. Your life either encourages someone to come closer to God or acts as a stumbling block to drive him further away. You know that others affect you this way. When Jim gave a great speech in English class about Jesus, and got an "A", you were encouraged. After you found out that a Christian you respected was caught cheating on his income tax, you were tempted to become discouraged.

Although you should keep your eyes only on Jesus, not on some other Christian, the Bible commands, "Let us encourage one another" (Heb. 10:25). This often occurs, not through words, but through action. For example, one day after school I went to witness to a fellow-teacher who was facing an operation and was afraid to die. She told me that two Christian students had come the night before and also told her about accepting Jesus. I was encouraged! Your following God can encourage someone else.

Biographies of great Christians make good reading. That's why God included stories of men and women of faith in the Bible—so you could learn from their mistakes and be encouraged by their victories. The story of Ruth, for example, teaches the value of obeying God and following His principles. As you read it you'll realize the love and mercy God showed to Ruth is also meant for you.

The story of Ruth also demonstrates the effect a faithful life has on other lives. For instance, Ruth was the great-grandmother of David, a great man of God. Ruth and Boaz lived during a time when few people were obeying God (the book of Judges tells all about it), but they put God first. Ruth trained her son in the ways of God and her faith was passed on for generations. Thus, God used her to bless the nation of Israel through King David. But that's not all. Mary, the mother of Jesus, was a direct descendant of David, as was Jesus' step-father Joseph. Ruth, therefore, was given the honor of being an ancestor of Jesus.

Even that isn't the end of the blessings of Ruth's life, because anyone born into a difficult situation, who has experienced great tragedy, can identify with Ruth. He can use her life as an example of how to face a hard situation. Ruth's life is a reminder that God wants to transform each life into something wonderful.

You can be a "Ruth" for someone else. In spite of your circumstances—misfortune, calamity, family problems, social status—you can choose to follow God. You can live by His principles. You can expect and receive His miracles. And God's blessings on your life will bring others to God. In a real sense you're one of God's billboards. What are you advertising?

"To this you were called, because Christ suffered for you, leaving you an example, that you should follow in his steps" (1 Pet. 2:21).

"Don't let anyone look down on you because you are young, but set an example for the believers in speech, in life, in love, in faith and in purity" (1 Tim. 4:12).

"In everything set them an example by doing what is good. In your teaching show integrity, seriousness and soundness of speech that cannot be condemned, so that those who oppose you may be ashamed because they have nothing bad to say about us" (Titus 2:7, 8).

1. Some people you know may never try to get to know Jesus, no matter how much they hear about Him. But if you truly follow in His steps, what will those people see?
2. In what ways are you to be an advertisement for Jesus?
3. When you make decisions, do you ever consider the effects your actions will have on others?
4. Are you willing to be a "Ruth," one of God's billboards?

Week Seven

SAUL: ANATOMY OF A FAILURE

Introduction

Do you ever imagine what your ten-year or fifteen-year class reunion will be like? Do you try to picture what you and your friends will look like then? Take it from those who have attended such reunions: Don't be surprised if some of the people who were the most popular in school and seemed most likely to succeed end up with nothing but problems. There is no guarantee against a messed-up life.

How do people wreck their lives? How can you keep it from happening to you? Jimmy Carter knew one secret of prevention: learn from others' mistakes. When he ran for President of the United States, he read biographies of all the presidents—because he didn't want to make the same mistakes they had made. You can do the same thing by studying the life of Saul.

In the 11th century, B.C., a tall, young, good-looking Hebrew man started from home to search for his father's donkeys. He had no idea that before he returned he would be anointed king over Israel. (It was the custom to pour oil over the head of the person chosen king.) His name was Saul. While searching he encountered the prophet Samuel, who gave him the royal oil treatment.

Soon, Samuel called all of the Israelites together at Mizpah to introduce Saul as king. When he called the new king forward, Saul didn't appear, so the men searched for him. He was hiding among the baggage. After publicly being proclaimed king, he returned home. But when one of the cities of Israel was threatened with invasion, he gathered an army and saved the city.

Impetuous and Impatient

Saul's first big mistake came in a tight spot while fighting against Israel's number-one enemy, the Philistines. Samuel, God's prophet, knew the people needed God's instructions if they were to win their battles, so when the Philistines came with their huge army to fight against Israel, Samuel told Saul to wait. Saul and his army were to camp at Gilgal for seven days until Samuel came to make a sacrifice to God and bless the army. Unfortunately, Samuel was late and the soldiers were deserting by droves. In fact, only six hundred men were left. In desperation, Saul finally offered the sacrifice himself, thus disobeying the law of Moses. (Only a priest, such as Samuel, was allowed to sacrifice.) Just as Saul was finishing the ceremony, Samuel appeared. He rebuked Saul, saying, "You acted foolishly. . . . You have not kept the command the Lord your God gave you" (1 Sam. 13:13).

Saul soon made his second mistake by issuing a rash order that almost forced him to execute his own son, Jonathan. A man of great faith, Jonathan and his armor-bearer boldly attacked a group of Philistines and threw them into great disorder. When the rest of the Israelite army (even the deserters) heard that the Philistines were fleeing, they returned to join the pursuit. Saul, under threat of death, rashly ordered his soldiers to eat nothing until sundown. The heroic Jonathan, however, didn't hear the order; so when he found some wild honey, he ate it. When Saul learned about this, he decided Jonathan should die. He preferred killing his son to admitting he was wrong and retracting his command. Although Jonathan was willing to die, the people argued that killing the hero of the battle wasn't fair, since he hadn't even heard the command.

The Way to a Hard Heart

Because he never repented, Saul sank deeper into sin and rebellion. Through Samuel, God ordered Saul to completely destroy the Amalekites, including everything they owned. (As we saw in the section on Joshua, when a group of people become so corrupt that they endanger many others, God may decide that group must be destroyed to save His world.) Instead of obeying, Saul and his soldiers saved King Agag and the best animals, then Saul went to erect a monument in his own honor for having won the battle. On the way he met Samuel. He lied, saying he had done everything God had commanded. Saul's heart was so hard that he had no conscience left.

Then Israel's old enemies, the Philistines, came to fight again. Their army stood on one hill, facing the Israelite army on another hill, waiting for the battle to start. Suddenly, a giant, about nine feet tall, swaggered into the valley and challenged any Israelite to a duel. The duel would decide the outcome of the battle. The Israelites were terror-stricken.

Into the scene walked David, probably only a teen-ager, coming to check on his brothers in the army. He was shocked that Goliath was being allowed to dishonor God and His armies. So David volunteered to fight the giant. Confident that God would honor his zeal, David slung a stone into Goliath's forehead, then proceeded to behead the nine-foot corpse.

To Saul's dismay, David instantly became a national hero, the subject of a women's folk song which elevated David above Saul. Saul became (literally) insane with jealousy. In the remaining years of his life, he spent much time with his army pursuing David, trying to kill him.

Far from God, Saul ended his life in defeat. While battling the Philistines, he was wounded by a sharpshooter's arrow; and dreading the thought of being finished off by his enemies, he asked his armor-bearer to kill him. The man refused. So Saul, in desperation, fell on his own sword, committing suicide.

You don't have to repeat Saul's mistakes. You don't have to disobey God's Word even if you're in a very tight spot. You don't have to make rash statements. You can admit when you're wrong and repent completely. You can obey God to the letter and avoid pride and jealousy at all costs. You can be closer to God at the end of your life than you are now. Let Saul be a reminder to you and don't follow in his footsteps.

Change the S to P and Add AUL

THE SAUL OF THE OLD TESTAMENT

His beginning:

"There was a Benjamite, a man of standing, whose name was Kish. . . . He had a son named Saul, an impressive young man without equal among the Israelites—a head taller than any of the others" (1 Sam. 9:1, 2).

His end:

"Surely I have acted like a fool and have erred greatly" (1 Sam. 26:21). "So Saul took his own sword and fell on it" (1 Sam. 31:4).

THE SAUL OF THE NEW TESTAMENT

His beginning:

"Meanwhile, Saul was still breathing out murderous threats against the Lord's disciples. He went to the high priest and asked him for letters to the synagogues in Damascus, so that if he found any there who belonged to the Way, whether men or women, he might take them as prisoners to Jerusalem" (Acts 9:1, 2).

His end:

"I have fought the good fight, I have finished the race, I have kept the faith" (2 Tim. 4:7).

You have just read the beginnings and the ends of the careers of two men who had the same name—Saul. King Saul of the Old Testament was an outstanding young man apparently headed for great success. Near the end of his life, however, he admitted to his archenemy, David, "I have played the fool . . ." Not long afterward, he killed himself. The Saul of the New Testament, because of Hebrew custom, changed his name to Paul following the greatest experience of his life. This Saul began his life "breathing threats and murder against the disciples of the Lord," determined to annihilate Christianity. But Jesus met him, and Saul's life changed drastically—he became a Christian. Near the end of his years spent preaching Jesus' gospel, Paul said with satisfaction, "I have fought the good fight, I have finished the race, I have kept the faith" (2 Tim. 4:7). What made the difference? You need to know.

You have great dreams and aspirations. You want to follow God and live a good life. Saul and Paul's lives show that the outcome of your life will depend on each decision you make along the way at each fork in the road—each chance to decide for or against God. Once he became a Christian, Paul chose God every time, and his life ended in triumph. In contrast, Saul repeatedly scorned God's ways, and his life ended in tragedy.

You will face many temptations that coax you to turn from God's path. You will be tempted to work too many hours to buy things you really don't need; tempted to make commitments without checking with God; tempted to waste your life in pursuits that don't matter. Warning about the danger of such temptations, Walter Hendricksen writes in *Many Aspire, Few Attain*: "You can climb on the shelf and render yourself ineffective for God in many ways. You can sign peace treaties with Satan and let him go his way while you go yours." Don't fall for such temptations.

Decide not to ride the fence, dividing your interests between God and the things of the world. Decide that God will own your heart, that you will hate sin, and that you will love God's Word. Trust Him, and be willing to admit when you're wrong.

Such a life will be demanding—you'll never be able to sit back and take it easy. Doing what is foolish and making your life a mess is easy, but following God and making your life count for Him requires combat—lots of it. The Apostle Paul called it a fight of faith. But someday you, as Paul did, will look back and evaluate your life. Will you have been a Saul or a Paul?

"Some people are like seed along the path, where the word is sown. As soon as they hear it, Satan comes and takes away the word that was sown in them. Others, like seed sown on rocky places, hear the word and at once receive it with joy. But since they have no root, they last only a short time. When trouble or persecution comes because of the word, they quickly fall away. Still others, like seed sown among thorns, hear the word; but the worries of this life, the deceitfulness of wealth and the desires for other things come in and choke the word, making it unfruitful. Others, like seed sown on good soil, hear the word, accept it, and produce a crop—thirty, sixty or even a hundred times what was sown" (Mark 4:15–20).

1. What you do with God's truth throughout your life will determine what you will become. What things can crowd God out of your life?
2. In the scripture passage above, what made the difference in the kind of crop produced?

3. What is going to be most important, the highest priority, in your life?
4. What can you start doing today to make sure you become a Paul, not a Saul?

Forgetting to Forgive and Flights of Fantasy

"Saul also went to his home in Gibeah, accompanied by valiant men whose hearts God had touched. But some troublemakers said, 'How can this fellow save us?' They despised him and brought him no gifts. But Saul kept silent" (1 Sam. 10:26, 27).

"The people then said to Samuel, 'Who was it that asked, "Shall Saul reign over us?" Bring these men to us and we will put them to death.' But Saul said, 'No one shall be put to death today, for this day the Lord has rescued Israel' " (1 Sam. 11:12, 13).

"After Saul returned from pursuing the Philistines, he was told, 'David is in the Desert of En Gedi' " (1 Sam. 24:1, 2).

When Saul became king he was tenderhearted, ready to forgive people who slighted him and refused to honor him as king. When men questioned his ability to lead, he kept silent. Even when some seemed ready to rebel against him, he forgave them. After his first military victory, instead of killing those who had not wanted him to be king, Saul gave God the credit for his victory: "No one shall be put to death today, for the Lord has rescued Israel" (1 Sam. 11:13).

The people of Israel responded enthusiastically, appreciating the sense of security such a king gave them. After Saul had forgiven his enemies, the citizens "went to Gilgal and confirmed Saul as king in the presence of the Lord. There they sacrificed fellowship offerings before the Lord, and Saul and all the Israelites held a great celebration" (1 Sam. 11:15). Saul began his reign with kindness, willing to overlook the sins of others.

The experiences of Saul and the teachings of Jesus show that a spirit of forgiveness isn't just a nice ornament, an optional extra for your personality. It's an absolute necessity. Jesus warned, "For if you forgive men when they sin against you, your heavenly Father will also forgive you. But if you do not forgive men their sins, your Father will not forgive your sins" (Matt. 6:14, 15).

When the disciple Peter heard Jesus say that, he probably thought there must be some limit to what God expected of a person. Later he asked, " 'Lord, how many times shall I forgive my brother when he sins against me? Up to seven times?' Jesus answered, 'I tell you, not seven times, but seventy-seven times' " (Matt. 18:21, 22). God expects you to forgive people over and over again, whether or not you feel like it, and no matter how unfair they have been. Impossible? Yes. Unless you're hooked up to God's power.

Somewhere along the line, Saul got tired of forgiving people—a temptation that strikes almost everyone. His life as king of the people of Israel, of course, was not an easy job. Their ancestors had murmured against Moses, and their fathers and grandfathers had not kept the laws God had given Moses. Therefore, it seems reasonable that once Saul's subjects began complaining they kept doing it. Saul finally became fed up. He decided to stop tolerating the griping, and he stopped forgiving.

When a person deliberately sins, as Saul did, he opens the door for Satan to fill his mind with lies. Soon Saul was not only refusing to forgive people who had offended him, but was imagining that everyone was against him. Eventually, plagued by fantasies, Saul could no longer think rationally. He even turned against David who had always shown him loyalty— he went after David with an army of three thousand men.

What happened to Saul could happen to you. You're not made of different stuff. If you stubbornly refuse to forgive, you'll become touchy. Little things will grow into mountains and you'll soon imagine no one is treating you justly. You'll make unreasonable demands of others and exaggerate your own sense of importance. You'll soon be against everyone, and everyone will be against you.

So do a little self-examination. If you've fallen into "saulish" thinking, forgiving others is the cure. Determine now that you will forgive everyone—no matter what—always.

"He who covers over an offense promotes love, but whoever repeats the matter separates close friends" (Prov. 17:9).

"Above all, love each other deeply, because love covers over a multitude of sins. Offer hospitality to one another without grumbling" (1 Pet. 4:8, 9).

"Bear with each other and forgive whatever grievances you may have against one another. Forgive as the Lord forgave you" (Col. 3:13).

1. If you refuse to forgive someone, why does that go against the Bible?
2. What attitude on your part will cover the faults and sins of others?
3. What does it mean to forgive others as God has forgiven you?
4. Is there someone you are unwilling to forgive? Talk to God about it now and find out what you should do to straighten out this problem.

No Exceptions, Please!

"Saul remained at Gilgal, and all the troops with him were quaking with fear. He waited seven days, the time set by Samuel; but Samuel did not come to Gilgal, and Saul's men began to scatter. So he said, 'Bring me the burnt offering and the fellowship offerings.' And Saul offered up the burnt offering. Just as he finished making the offering, Samuel arrived, and Saul went out to greet him. 'What have you done?' asked Samuel. Saul replied, 'When I saw that the men were scattering, and that you did not

*come at the set time, and that the Philistines were assembling at Micmash,
I thought, "Now the Philistines will come down against me at Gilgal, and
I have not sought the Lord's favor." So I felt compelled to offer the burnt
offering.' 'You acted foolishly,' Samuel said. 'You have not kept the command
the Lord your God gave you; if you had, he would have established your
kingdom over Israel for all time. But now your kingdom will not endure;
the Lord has sought out a man after his own heart and appointed him leader
of his people, because you have not kept the Lord's command' " (1 Sam.
13:7–14).*

Saul found himself in a tight spot. The Philistines, with their horses
and chariots, had come to attack the Israelites who didn't even have
swords for their soldiers. (The Philistines, who knew how to make iron,
had refused to sell their weapons or their manufacturing secrets to the
Israelites.) According to the Bible, the Philistines came with 30,000 chariots, six thousand cavalry, and footsoldiers as numerous as "the sand on
the seashore" (1 Sam. 13:5). Fear had struck the Israelites, including
King Saul, and soldiers began deserting. But Saul could do nothing until
the prophet Samuel arrived.

Samuel had instructed Saul to wait for seven days; at that time he
would come to offer a sacrifice to the Lord. God would then reveal His
strategy and give His blessing. Well, Samuel was late. And Saul knew his
soldiers would hesitate to fight without sacrificing to God first. But instead
of waiting his soldiers were leaving. Saul was getting desperate. So he
offered the sacrifice himself, thus disobeying the instructions of God's
prophet and the biblical command which stated only a priest should offer
special sacrifices (Num. 16:40). This was Saul's first major blunder.

When you get in a pinch, when things come down to the wire, your
relationship with God comes to the surface. When you're earning an *F* in
algebra, so everything depends on your grade for the final, and you get
that perfect chance to cheat, what you do will disclose your view of
obeying God. If you've let your car insurance lapse because you lost your
job, and you back into a car at midnight in the parking lot, what you do
will reveal how much you love God. When you've promised to pay your
friend for the stereo you got from him, then discover he gave you a raw
deal, what you do will show what place God has in your life. No matter
how spiritual you've made your "act," any hypocrisy will eventually be
uncovered—as Saul's was.

Saul's main problem was unbelief. He didn't believe the God of Abraham, Isaac and Jacob—with or without an army—could defeat the Philistines. Saul thought the age of miracles was past. He felt forced to take
things into his own hands, quite sure he knew better than God. Saul's
lack of true faith was the first big step toward his downfall.

The same principle holds for you. If you don't determine to obey God
always and to trust Him no matter how hopeless the outlook, soon every
problem will become a "special case," and another chance to disobey.

And you'll begin your downhill tumble.

Because God made you, none of His commandments are impossible to carry out—*if the Holy Spirit lives in you.* But you must trash the mentality which makes excuses for "special cases." Your life will not be ruined if you flunk the algebra final; God is more important than your report card. You won't go into bankruptcy and starve to death if you're honest and keep your promises—no matter what. God says, "Obey me, and I will be your God and you will be my people. Walk in all the ways I command you, that it may go well with you" (Jer. 7:23)—no exceptions, please.

"Blessed are they whose ways are blameless, who walk according to the law of the Lord. Blessed are they who keep his statutes and seek him with all their heart. They do nothing wrong; they walk in his ways" (Ps. 119:1–3).

"Teach me, O Lord, to follow your decrees; then I will keep them to the end. Give me understanding, and I will keep your law and obey it with all my heart. Direct me in the path of your commands, for there I find delight" (Ps. 119:33–35).

1. The best way to keep from sinning as Saul did is to develop the right attitude toward God's Word. List the attitudes mentioned in the above passages.
2. Do you delight in God's commands?
3. If there is some commandment of God which you are fighting against, ask God to change your heart. Then meditate on His Word until you can delight in it.
4. You cannot delight in God's commandments unless you realize that He is all-powerful and knows what is best for the people He created. Think about God's faithfulness and His power and learn to delight in His commandments.

Five-Page Assignments, Paper Airplanes, and Three Simple Words

"When all the Israelites who had hidden in the hill country of Ephraim heard that the Philistines were on the run, they joined the battle in hot pursuit. Now the men of Israel were in distress that day, because Saul had bound the people under an oath, saying, 'Cursed be any man who eats food before evening comes, before I have avenged myself on my enemies!' So none of the troops tasted food. But Jonathan had not heard that his father had bound the people with the oath, so he reached out the end of the staff that was in his hand and dipped it into the honeycomb. He raised his hand to his mouth, and his eyes brightened. Then Saul said to Jonathan, 'Tell me

what you have done.' So Jonathan told him, 'I merely tasted a little honey with the end of my staff. And now must I die?' Saul said, 'May God deal with me, be it ever so severely, if you do not die, Jonathan.' But the men said to Saul, 'Should Jonathan die—he who has brought about this great deliverance in Israel? Never! As surely as the Lord lives, not a hair of his head will fall to the ground, for he did this today with God's help.' So the men rescued Jonathan, and he was not put to death" (1 Sam. 14:22, 24, 27, 43–45).

You've probably encountered a similar scene in a classroom: The discipline is dreadful, so the exasperated teacher finally bellows, "If one more person throws a paper airplane, the whole class will get a five-page homework assignment—and the culprit will be suspended!" Soon after the pronouncement, Bobby Bookworm, armed with a green pass from the counselor's office, enters the room and quietly slips into his seat. The teacher doesn't see him enter. Absent-mindedly, Bob begins construction of a paper space shuttle, and as he tests its flightworthiness the teacher catches him. He immediately writes the five-page assignment on the board and prepares to escort Bob to the assistant principal's office. Suddenly, the classroom becomes a replay of the scene between King Saul and his soldiers as Bob's classmates desperately protest the unfair punishment.

It's quite easy to leave such a class complaining that "Mr. Talkathon" lectures nonstop, makes threats without thinking, and stubbornly refuses to admit his mistakes. However, these characteristics exist in most people—maybe in you. They are the fruit of pride, a subtle destroyer.

Pride begins with small stuff. You can easily brag about good grades, athletic success, or popularity. Then without thinking, you can slip into pretending you know all about the conflict in the Middle East, or the rock group currently at the the top of the charts. Soon, you find yourself defending the most ridiculous statements—just to protect your pride.

If you've helped with the Girl Scouts, or babysat for the neighbor kids, or coached Little League ball, you know that once you're in a position of authority, the temptation to make rash statements and to give impetuous orders increases greatly. And once you've said something in front of the whole group, it takes a lot of courage to admit that you're wrong and to back down. Sometimes, your stubbornness can make the situation even worse. Obviously, some caution would have avoided the mess in the first place.

Stubbornness that never says, "I'm sorry, I was mistaken," or, "I was wrong and I want to apologize," causes tremendous problems. First, it seals your downfall—"He who conceals his sins does not prosper" (Prov. 28:13). Second, it makes people lose respect for you and your word. Third, it causes great heartache for those who are close to you. It's not easy to live in the same family with someone who won't ever say, "It was my fault." It's hard to be a friend to an I'm-always-right person.

A big factor in Saul's first step to failure was stubbornness. He refused to choke his pride and admit that his ban on eating during the battle was a stupid decision. He began to lose the respect of his subjects. And more tragic, he began to lose the blessing of God.

Don't be a Saul. Pray with the Psalmist, "Set a guard over my mouth, O Lord, keep watch over the door of my lips" (Ps. 141:3). When you hastily say foolish things, correct your statements, revising every false remark. Three simple words, "I was wrong," can do wonders for your spiritual life.

"Therefore confess your sins to each other and pray for each other so that you may be healed" (James 5:16).

"But if we walk in the light, as he is in the light, we have fellowship with one another, and the blood of Jesus, his Son, purifies us from every sin" (1 John 1:7).

"Therefore, if you are offering your gift at the altar and there remember that your brother has something against you, leave your gift there in front of the altar. First go and be reconciled to your brother; and then come and offer your gift" (Matt. 5:23, 24).

"Be completely humble and gentle; be patient, bearing with one another in love. Make every effort to keep the unity of the Spirit through the bond of peace" (Eph. 4:2, 3).

1. If you have said or done something you shouldn't have to a person, what does God command you to do?
2. If you walk with Jesus "in the light," letting that light expose your defects, what is God's promise to you? What happens if you refuse to admit you are wrong?
3. List all the things you are supposed to do to get along with other people.
4. Is there someone to whom you must go and ask forgiveness? Do it right away.

Just a Bunch of Lions

"Early in the morning Samuel got up and went to meet Saul, but he was told, 'Saul has gone to Carmel. There he has set up a monument in his own honor and has turned and gone on down to Gilgal' " (1 Sam. 15:12).

You don't enjoy listening to bragging; and hypocrisy turns you off. You'd like to avoid them, but you definitely notice the "I'm the greatest" dude and the "You're lucky to have me around" chick—because you can't help it! You avoid at any price the course taught by the "Do as I say, not as I do" teacher. You ignore the speaker who flaunts himself as an archetype of virtue. But deep inside you feel the same pride about yourself.

It's a typical human problem. You hate pride in others but feel it is quite becoming in yourself. You scoff at the monuments others set up in their own honor, but erect your own and expect others to admire them. You quote "Pride goes before destruction" (Prov. 16:18) when you see the haughtiness of others, but fail to apply it to yourself. You even recognize pride was a chief ingredient in Saul's downfall—but think it's not so dangerous for you.

Pride raises its ugly head in a number of ways. You get offended and hurt when people don't notice and thank you for the great things you've done. You don't realize, however, that pride makes you think you're so important that the world should pay attention to you. You bristle against criticism, imagining you aren't an ordinary mortal who makes mistakes and has bad habits. (If it weren't for your arrogance, you'd be thankful for such an opportunity to improve yourself.) You tend to exaggerate— just a little—to make yourself look good, and you like to boast about your successes. You criticize others for the very things that you overlook in yourself. (You are so sure that the misunderstanding or the accident was the other guy's fault that you don't even bother to evaluate your own words and actions.)

Admit it. You're hooked on pride. But there is a way out.

In his letter to the Romans, Paul wrote by inspiration of the Holy Spirit, "For by the grace given me I say to every one of you: Do not think of yourself more highly than you ought, but rather think of yourself with sober judgment, in accordance with the measure of faith God has given you" (Rom. 12:3). Faith in God puts sense into this matter of self-concept. If your faith is in God, not in yourself, your reason for pride and ego-feeding disappears. You will realize that everything you have comes from God, so you can't take any credit. When you live by faith you will have no reason to brag in order to cover up feelings of inadequacy, because God's unlimited resources are yours to make you what God wants you to be.

How can you get such faith? According to the the Bible, "Faith comes from hearing the message, and the message is heard through the word" (Rom. 10:17). You'll get faith by digging into the Word of God. Read it, study it, memorize it, meditate on it. Make it the center of your thoughts. After all, you can never believe the truth unless you know it. The more of God's truth you know, the better your life will be.

One definition of "pride" is "group of lions." That is quite fitting for the kind of pride you deal with—just a bunch of lions. But these lions would like to get you. They have names, such as Hurt Feelings, Bragging, Defensiveness, and Criticism. True faith in God and His Word will shut the mouths of these lions. Only faith will defeat pride and keep you from being a Saul who starts well and ends in disaster.

"The Lord detests all the proud of heart. Be sure of this: They will not go unpunished" (Prov. 16:5).

"When pride comes, then comes disgrace; but with humility comes wisdom" (Prov. 11:2).
"And those who walk in pride he is able to humble" (Dan. 4:37).

1. What happens to proud people?
2. How can you get rid of pride?
3. What kinds of pride in your life is God showing you?
4. Are you willing to humble yourself, to study God's Word, and receive faith from God for each of those pride problems?

Having a Heart Check-up

"When Samuel reached him, Saul said, 'The Lord bless you! I have carried out the Lord's instructions.' Samuel said, 'Although you were once small in your own eyes, did you not become the head of the tribes of Israel? The Lord anointed you king over Israel. And he sent you on a mission, saying, "Go and completely destroy those wicked people, the Amalekites; make war on them until you have wiped them out." Why did you not obey the Lord? Why did you pounce on the plunder and do evil in the eyes of the Lord?' 'But I did obey the Lord,' Saul said. 'I went on the mission the Lord assigned me. I completely destroyed the Amalekites and brought back Agag their king. The soldiers took sheep and cattle from the plunder, the best of what was devoted to God, in order to sacrifice them to the Lord your God at Gilgal.' But Samuel replied: 'Does the Lord delight in burnt offerings and sacrifices as much as in obeying the voice of the Lord? To obey is better than sacrifice, and to heed is better than the fat of rams. For rebellion is like the sin of divination, and arrogance like the evil of idolatry. Because you have rejected the word of the Lord, he has rejected you as king' " (1 Sam. 15:13, 17–23).

You've seen it happen. First Christi Christian goes out with Agnostic Alan, and even feels a little guilty about accepting the date. After a couple of months, she's dating him steadily, but still wondering if she's doing the right thing. After a few more weeks she's thinking as he thinks and doing things she never used to even imagine doing. As time passes, she defends herself vehemently when asked about her actions, and even tries to arrange for her Christian girlfriends to date Alan's friends. The process is called hardening of the heart. As a person keeps ignoring God's voice, he goes deeper into disobeying the Lord, becoming almost immune to the Holy Spirit's nudgings, called conviction of sin. Hardening of the heart is dangerous. In fact, it's deadly. Saul is living—oops—*dead* proof.

Saul had a terrific start, depending on God's advice as he ruled Israel. Saul's heart, however, grew cold as he neglected to diligently study God's law and make it part of his life. He didn't trust God. Overly impressed by his royal authority, yet unduly worried about taking charge, he suc-

"Hardening of the heart is dangerous. In fact, it's deadly."

cumbed to the pressure of the moment and disregarded one of God's commandments—that only a priest could offer a special sacrifice. Later he gave the rash order that his soldiers were not to eat during battle, then he stubbornly refused to admit he was wrong. He never repented. Thus his heart became harder and harder, paving the way for premeditated, willful disobedience.

Then God gave Saul a job which included specific instructions: Attack the Amalekites, then totally destroy them and their possessions. (The chapter on Joshua showed that some groups of people were so corrupt that God had to destroy them for the good of the human race.) But Saul *purposely* disobeyed God's order, then made pious excuses to cover up his disobedience. God told Saul that his rebellion was as bad as witchcraft—and that's pretty bad!

Sin always harms others, and the result of Saul's sin almost wiped out God's people a few hundred years later. In the chapter on Esther you'll meet Haman, a descendant of an Amalekite who was not destroyed, and he almost succeeded in killing the entire Jewish nation—all because Saul had hardened his heart against God.

What would be the worst thing that could happen to you? Losing your entire family? Failing in your career? Being rejected by all your friends? No. The worst thing that could happen is hardening your heart against God—becoming so calloused that your conscience no longer registers guilt. That will ruin your life.

Give yourself a spiritual heart check-up, using the "Christian cardiogram" below. If you answer yes to any of the questions, get that matter straightened out with God before your heart gets any harder.

A CHRISTIAN CARDIOGRAM

1. Do you have a goal you are determined to reach, whether or not God wants you to have it?
2. Is there any Bible verse you are reluctant to read because it makes you feel guilty, or because you're not sure you want to obey it?
3. Is there anyone whose opinion you value more highly than God's?
4. Are you neglecting Bible reading and prayer because other things are more important to you?
5. Have you persisted so long in a sin that you no longer feel guilty about doing it?

"So I tell you this, and insist on it in the Lord, that you must no longer live as the Gentiles do, in the futility of their thinking. They are darkened in their understanding and separated from the life of God because of the ignorance that is in them due to the hardening of their hearts. Having lost all sensitivity, they have given themselves over to sensuality so as to indulge in every kind of impurity, with a continual lust for more. You, however, did not come to know Christ that way. Surely you heard of him and were taught in him in accordance with the truth that is in Jesus. You were taught, with regard to your former way of life, to put off your old self, which is being corrupted by its deceitful desires; to be made new in the attitude of your minds; and to put on the new self, created to be like God in true righteousness and holiness" (Eph. 4:17–24).

1. List all the things that cause a hard heart or are symptoms of a hard heart.
2. What must you do with the old self?
3. What things can keep you from being "renewed in the spirit of your mind"?
4. Ask God for a soft heart and do anything necessary to get it.

Playing with Poison

"When the men were returning home after David had killed the Philistine, the women came out from all the towns of Israel to meet King Saul

with singing and dancing, with joyful songs and with tambourines and lutes. As they danced, they sang: 'Saul has slain his thousands, and David his tens of thousands.' Saul was very angry; this refrain galled him. 'They have credited David with tens of thousands,' he thought, 'but me with only thousands. What more can he get but the kingdom?' And from that time on Saul kept a jealous eye on David. The next day an evil spirit from God came forcefully upon Saul. He was prophesying in his house, while David was playing the harp, as he usually did. Saul had a spear in his hand and he hurled it, saying to himself, 'I'll pin David to the wall.' But David eluded him twice" (1 Sam. 18:6–11).

The people of Israel rejoiced when they heard David had killed Goliath, for now the Philistines would not occupy their country. It was a great day! The women came out to meet the soldiers with singing and dancing. Wishing to honor David for winning this great victory, some woman composed a song: "Saul has slain his thousands and David his tens of thousands." Saul hated the lyrics. Instead of being grateful that David had saved his kingdom for him, he became super jealous. His one aim was to kill David.

Jealousy is unbelievably dangerous stuff. It's poison. Jealousy ruled and helped destroy Saul's life. First, jealousy inspired murder in his heart. Rather than respecting David's bravery and loyalty, he wanted to kill David. Eventually, jealously destroyed Saul's reason and emotions. He had been quite rational until he became consumed with jealousy. From the sequence of events, it appears that Saul's insane jealousy made him mentally ill. After that Saul suffered greatly. His life revolved around trying to kill David, the object of his jealousy, and he would mobilize an entire army to pursue David in the hill country of Judea. There was no peace for Saul.

Jealousy is one of the most effective weapons in the devil's arsenal. If he wants to get you off balance, just a little jealousy will do the trick. He tries to insert it in your mind in many situations: if you meet someone more attractive and more talented than you; if your friend finds school easy and you don't; if others own things you wish you had. God considers jealousy so terrible that He put in the Ten Commandments: "You shall not covet [long for, crave] your neighbor's house . . . or anything that belongs to your neighbor" (Ex. 20:17).

You can personalize that commandment this way: "It's wrong for me to be jealous of Vicki's good looks, her boyfriend, her clothes, or her good grades"; or, "It's wrong for me to be jealous of Eddie's Camaro, his charming personality, his muscular build, or his leadership ability." In other words, jealousy is breaking one of God's commandments.

When the devil tries to tell you jealousy is okay because it's natural, don't listen. Sin might appear natural, but it is not okay. Jesus Christ is supernatural, so the new life He gives to a Christian is supernatural. Jesus died to break the power of all sin, including jealousy. Through the

Holy Spirit He gives you power to reject jealousy. You can therefore thank God for everything you have and are. More than that, you can thank God for everything you will be because of what He will do for you.

Because God owns everything and gives His children what they need, it's foolish to covet, to be jealous. Instead of poisoning yourself with jealousy, you can simply ask God for what you need. He can transform your personality and make you attractive to others (if you cooperate with Him), so why be jealous of others?

Jealousy about attitudes can be more subtle than jealousy about possessions and status. For instance, you may be a sitting duck for jealousy if little brother is your mother's pet and gets more attention than you; or if you're so shy that teachers and classmates ignore you; or if you think members of the opposite sex don't notice you because you're not very good-looking. It's easy to think you're not very important to anyone, and when you think that, the poison of jealousy starts seeping in.

You wouldn't drink poison, even if it came in a pretty bottle and looked harmless, so why drink the poison of jealousy? It's sin. It will ruin your life. Therefore, you can't afford to have any of it around. Jesus has the power to deliver you, but the first step is realizing how bad jealousy really is. Saul swallowed jealousy in big gulps—and it destroyed him. If you don't stop putting up with the poison of jealousy, you, too, will be a victim.

"The acts of the sinful nature are obvious: sexual immorality, impurity and debauchery; idolatry and witchcraft; hatred, discord, jealousy, fits of rage, selfish ambition, dissensions, factions and envy; drunkenness, orgies, and the like. I warn you, as I did before, that those who live like this will not inherit the kingdom of God. But the fruit of the Spirit is love, joy, peace, patience, kindness, goodness, faithfulness, gentleness and self-control. Against such things there is no law" (Gal. 5:19–23).

1. Considering the sins it is listed with, how bad is jealousy?
2. What sins can result from jealousy?
3. If you put off the old nature and let the Holy Spirit take control, what characteristics will automatically develop in you?
4. Why can't the Holy Spirit be in control if you, even for a minute, defend sins in your life, such as jealousy, hatred, or immorality? If you are harboring any jealousy, be willing to do anything to eradicate it.

Week Eight

DAVID: HONORING GOD, IN SPITE OF BIG MISTAKES

Introduction

What should be the main goal of your life? How do you get back on the track after you've sinned? By studying the life of David you'll find the answers to these two important questions. The Bible devotes much space to David, who ruled the nation of Israel at the height of its power. In the midst of such great success he made some dismal failures, but the life of David will teach you how to honor God. It also will show you the value of true repentance for sin.

Waiting a Long Time for His Ship to Come In

David, a son of Jesse (a grandson of Ruth), grew up as a shepherd in Bethlehem. When David was young, the prophet Samuel visited Jesse's family and poured oil on David's head in a ceremony, indicating that David would be the next king of Israel. David, unlike most people, did not get bigheaded or try to take things into his own hands. He simply went back to care for Jesse's sheep.

Soon the Philistines came to invade Israel, and David's older brothers joined the army. Jesse sent the teen-aged David to visit them and take them some food. When David arrived at the army camp, he saw the giant Goliath challenging any one of the Israelites to a duel, and David remarked that nobody should get by with ridiculing the armies of the living God. Someone told King Saul what David had said. In desperation the king sent David to fight Goliath. And to everyone's surprise, David killed him.

Defeating the giant, and thus delivering Israel, made David a hero, so the women composed a song about him which undoubtedly made the top ten. Before long David was living at the palace, playing his harp to sooth Saul's frazzled nerves. But Saul was jealous of David's popularity.

Feeling threatened by David's popularity, Saul became downright nasty to David. He did not fulfill his promise to give his daughter in marriage to the man who killed Goliath, and instead had her marry somebody else. Saul then offered David the chance to marry his younger daughter—if David would kill one hundred Philistines. Saul, of course, was hoping David would die in the process. But, to Saul's dismay, David fulfilled his part of the bargain and became the king's son-in-law.

David soon realized that Saul wished to kill him, so he ran away. The first time he found safety with Samuel the prophet. The second time he made his own plans; having no food and no weapon, he paid a visit to a priest, Ahimelech. David knew no man would dare help him escape from the king, so he lied, saying he was on a secret mission for King Saul and needed bread and a weapon. When Saul found out that Ahimelech had helped David, he ordered the priest and his family killed.

David lived for years as a fugitive from the king, hiding in the barren hills of Judah and in the land of the Philistines. Saul frequently led his best troops out to capture David. During these years David twice had the opportunity to kill Saul, but didn't because Saul had been appointed king by God. Honoring God was more important to David than gaining his rightful place on the throne. He trusted that God would fulfill His promise without any human "help." And, of course, it happened just that way. When Saul and his son Jonathan were killed in battle, the men from David's tribe made David their king. Later, Saul's last son was killed and all Israel crowned David king.

After David became king, he captured the fortress of Jerusalem and made it the capital city. He then systematically defeated the enemies of Israel, bringing peace and prosperity to the land. But he did not forget his last promise to his best friend—Jonathan the son of Saul, a promise to show kindness to Jonathan's descendants. David found one son of Jonathan still alive, a lame man named Mephibosheth, and David invited him to live in his palace and eat at his table.

Just When Everything Is Going Well, He Blows It

After reaching the pinnacle of success, David fell deep into sin. He had decided, one spring, to stay home and relax while General Joab took the army out to fight the enemy. One evening while strolling on his roof to relieve his boredom, David saw something that intrigued him: a beautiful woman bathing in a neighboring house. Even though she—and he— was married, he slept with her, and she became pregnant. So David arranged that her soldier husband be sent to the most dangerous spot in the battle where he was sure to be killed—allowing David to marry the widow. David had now committed both adultery and murder.

In his pride, David tried to keep his sin secret. God, however, because of His great love for David, sent the prophet Nathan to accuse him. David repented fully and came back to God. The consequences of that sin, however, stayed around to haunt David. The child of that love affair died and another son rebelled against him. David showed himself to be a man of humility and tenderness as he passed through these trials.

David soon realized that, although he lived in a sumptuous palace, God was still being worshiped in a tent, so he decided to build a great temple for the Lord. The prophet Nathan, however, said the temple would be constructed by David's son, Solomon. Instead of feeling hurt that his idea was rejected, David went ahead and gathered all the materials he could to make Solomon's job easier. Here again, David showed that his highest desire was to honor God.

David is remembered not only as the best king Israel ever had, but as the writer of dozens of psalms which have blessed millions of people. He wrote these psalms as he experienced both mountain peaks of glory and deep valleys of suffering and despair. Troubled people who read his psalms recognize the words of someone who has suffered as they have, and has seen God's deliverance.

But David is remembered best as a man who loved God intensely, even though he sometimes disobeyed God in horrendous ways. God therefore called him "a man after my own heart; he will do everything I want him to do" (Acts 13:22). Would you like God to say the same of you? Learn from David.

A Goal Worth More Than Six Points

"The Lord said to Samuel, 'How long will you mourn for Saul, since I have rejected him as king over Israel? Fill your horn with oil and be on your way; I am sending you to Jesse of Bethlehem. I have chosen one of his sons to be king.' Samuel did what the Lord said. When he arrived at Bethlehem, the elders of the town trembled when they met him. They asked, 'Do you come in peace?' Samuel replied, 'Yes, in peace; I have come to sacrifice to the Lord. Consecrate yourselves and come to the sacrifice with me.' Then he consecrated Jesse and his sons and invited them to the sacrifice. When they arrived, Samuel saw Eliab and thought, 'Surely the Lord's anointed stands here before the Lord.' But the Lord said to Samuel, 'Do not consider his appearance or his height, for I have rejected him. The Lord does not look at the things man looks at. Man looks at the outward appearance, but the Lord looks at the heart.' Jesse had seven of his sons pass before Samuel, but Samuel said to him, 'The Lord has not chosen these.' So he asked Jesse, 'Are these all the sons you have? There is still the youngest,' Jesse answered. So he sent and had him brought in. He was ruddy, with a fine appearance and handsome features. Then the Lord said, 'Rise and anoint him; he is the one.' So Samuel took the horn of oil and anointed him in the presence of his brothers, and from that day on the Spirit of the Lord came upon David in power" (1 Sam. 16:1, 4–7, 10, 12, 13).

The real motive comes out sooner or later. It shows up immediately in little kids. If you have a younger brother or sister, or have babysat, you understand this. The spilled milk or the poorly drawn tree or the grimy face aren't important. The attitude (the motive) is. Selfishness is shown by the kid who intentionally spills his milk because he wants Coke, or who purposely smears chocolate all over his face. On the other hand, a desire to please and win the parent's heart is shown by the child who tries to follow instructions but, due to lack of coordination does the same things as the insolent brat.

God feels the same way about His children—He has a special place in His heart for those who really want to do His will. He says about David, "I have found David son of Jesse a man after my own heart; he will do everything I want him to do" (Acts 13:22). What a vote of confidence! Yet David was far from perfect. He sinned terribly and made serious mistakes. But in spite of his gross imperfections, his ultimate desire was to honor God and do His will. And this pleased God.

Maybe you avoid living the Christian life by making excuses such as, "I can't be a goody-goody; I like to goof around and have fun," or, "No saint ever started out with an explosive temper like mine," or, "Other people can give thanks for everything, but grumbling is more my style." Rather than drowning in such details, however, get to the central issue: reaching a goal—one worth more than the six points you get for reaching the end zone in football. If you, like David, decide your goal is to do God's will instead of your own, God will start to change you.

Doing God's will requires admitting your sin, repenting (turning away from sin), receiving forgiveness, and continuing to follow God. Sometimes, by deceiving you or exploiting your ignorance, Satan can get you off the track. He can lay some clever snares, often by using your well-developed skill of self-justification. But if you do sin, hope isn't gone. The key to recovery is repentance. David knew the value of true repentance and practiced it. That made all the difference in his life.

Once you realize that you have sinned, the goal of living to do God's will can save you. Instead of planning a clever cover-up, you'll admit it, confess it, and turn around and go the right way. You'll realize that you deserve the consequences of your actions and face them squarely. You'll do everything possible to keep from falling into the same trap again.

Doing God's will also means receiving His forgiveness. If you've sinned or made a bad mistake, wallowing in self-condemnation will not help God's cause. For example, suppose your friend Jim comes over, and, while demonstrating his karate chops, accidentally kills your favorite pet, Henrietta Hamster, who didn't know enough to stay out of the way. Jim begs your forgiveness and tells you he's sorry, so you pardon him totally. Jim, however, never accepts your forgiveness and mentions Henrietta every time you get together. He calls himself a murderer and never acts at ease in your presence. You would feel very hurt that Jim refused to accept your forgiveness, and his attitude would put a strain on your friendship.

It's the same with God. When God says He will forgive you, He means it. If you fall into sin, be a David. Confess it, forsake it, receive God's forgiveness and go on living for Him. Determine to be a person after God's own heart, a person whose goal is to do God's will.

"Have mercy on me, O God, according to your unfailing love; according to your great compassion blot out my transgressions. Wash away all my

iniquity and cleanse me from my sin. Cleanse me with hyssop, and I will be clean; wash me, and I will be whiter than snow. Let me hear joy and gladness; let the bones you have crushed rejoice. Hide your face from my sins and blot out all my iniquity. Create in me a pure heart, O God, and renew a steadfast spirit within me. Do not cast me from your presence or take your Holy Spirit from me. Restore to me the joy of your salvation and grant me a willing spirit, to sustain me. Then I will teach transgressors your ways, and sinners will turn back to you" (Ps. 51:1, 2, 7–13).

1. List all the things David prayed for.
2. Did David expect to do penance (self-punishment) or to go around for a while condemning himself so God could forgive him and use him again?
3. Which part of this prayer shows that David was primarily concerned with doing God's will?
4. Do you know how to receive God's forgiveness? Do you live as a forgiven person?

God's Honor Society

"Then he took his staff in his hand, chose five smooth stones from the stream, put them in the pouch of his shepherd's bag and, with his sling in his hand, approached the Philistine. Meanwhile, the Philistine, with his shield bearer in front of him, kept coming closer to David. He looked David over. David said to the Philistine, 'You come against me with sword and spear and javelin, but I come against you in the name of the Lord Almighty, the God of the armies of Israel, whom you have defied. This day the Lord will hand you over to me. . . . and the whole world will know that there is a God in Israel. All those gathered here will know that it is not by sword or spear that the Lord saves; for the battle is the Lord's, and he will give all of you into our hands.' So David triumphed over the Philistine with a sling and a stone; without a sword in his hand he struck down the Philistine and killed him" (1 Sam. 17:40, 41, 45–47, 50).

You probably were just a little tyke when you first heard the exciting story of David, the shepherd boy, killing big, bad Goliath, the giant. You may even recall the pictures in your Bible story book. As a child, however, you probably missed the point of the incident. David was not trying to play hero by showing off his bravery; rather, he was applying a spiritual principle: God defends His honor.

Despite their failures, the Israelites were God's people, and everybody knew it. But that didn't bother Goliath. He had no respect for the God of Israel. His boldness and size had the Israelites shaking in their sandals, and this spurred him to further mock God—the God who had divided the Red Sea, leveled the walls of Jericho, and used Gideon's 300 men to defeat an entire army. The Israelites had forgotten the God of miracles; and their lack of faith prevented God from acting. But then Goliath met David, who believed God could do anything and who believed God's reputation was not a laughing matter.

It happened this way: David, taking food from his father to his older brothers in the army, overheard soldiers saying that the man who killed Goliath would marry the king's daughter and free his own family from paying taxes. Desiring to make conversation, David asked a question about these rewards. He then immediately changed the subject to the disgrace Israel was suffering and the dishonor God was receiving from big-mouthed Goliath. David knew God wanted Goliath dead; the Law of Moses commanded, "When you go to war against your enemies and see horses and chariots and an army greater than yours, do not be afraid of them, because the Lord your God, who brought you up out of Egypt, will be with you. When you are about to go into battle, the priest shall come forward and address the army. He shall say: 'Hear, O Israel, today you are going into battle against your enemies. Do not be faint-hearted or afraid; do not be terrified or give way to panic before them. For the Lord your God is the one who goes with you to fight for you against your enemies to give you victory' " (Deut. 20:1–4). David knew he could depend on God's power if he did God's work in God's way. Therefore, he boldly told the giant he would kill him so "the whole world will know that there is a God in Israel" (1 Sam. 17:46).

David's attitude after killing the giant further proves that the honoring of God was his true motive. Even when he became famous in Israel— the women even made up a song about David's amazing feat—he remained humble. When Saul gave to someone else the daughter he had promised to David, David said nothing. When Saul exploited his younger daughter's crush on David by offering David her hand in marriage if David killed 100 Philistines, David only said, "Do you think it is a small matter to become the king's son-in-law? I'm only a poor man and little known" (1 Sam. 18:23). David never got bigheaded about his accomplishments.

Because God's honor was so important to him, David had no time to think about himself. He had no time to get scared of Goliath who was much larger than he was. He had no time to bask in the glory of being a national hero. He had no time to nurse a grudge against Saul who would not reward him. Instead, he contentedly waited for God's reward—something well worth waiting for.

God doesn't forget those who put Him first. He promises, "Humility and the fear of the Lord bring wealth and honor and life" (Prov. 22:4). God honors those who honor Him. It's worth the effort to become a member of God's Honor Society.

"A son honors his father, and a servant his master. If I am a father, where is the honor due me? If I am a master, where is the respect due me? says the Lord Almighty. . ." (Mal. 1:6).

"Honor the Lord with your wealth, with the firstfruits of all your crops; then your barns will be filled to overflowing, and your vats will brim over with new wine" (Prov. 3:9, 10).

". . . Those who honor me I will honor, but those who despise me will be disdained" (1 Sam. 2:30).

"Whoever serves me must follow me; and where I am, my servant also will be. My Father will honor the one who serves me" (John 12:26).

1. Why does God deserve to be honored?
2. How can you honor God?
3. What promises are given to those who honor God?
4. Has honoring God been your top priority? Ask God to point out areas in your life where changes need to be made.

Bomb the Fib Factory

"David answered Ahimelech the priest, 'The king charged me with a certain matter and said to me, "No one is to know anything about your mission and your instructions." As for my men, I have told them to meet me at a certain place. Now then, what do you have on hand? Give me five loaves of bread, or whatever you can find.' So the priest gave him the con-secrated bread. . . . David asked Ahimelech, 'Don't you have a spear or a sword here? I haven't brought my sword or any other weapon, because the king's business was urgent.' The priest replied, 'The sword of Goliath the Philistine . . . is here . . . take it.' . . . Then the king sent for the priest Ahimelech. . . . Saul said to him, 'Why have you conspired against me, you and the son of Jesse, giving him bread and a sword and inquiring of God for him, so that he has rebelled against me and lies in wait for me, as he does today? . . . You will surely die, Ahimelech, you and your father's whole family' " (1 Sam. 21:2, 3, 6, 8, 9; 22:11, 13, 16).

It escapes from your lips too quickly—that "No, I didn't" when Mom scolds you for not double-locking the front door when you came home last night, or when your teacher accuses you of passing a note to the kid across the aisle. You know you've lied, but exaggeration creeps into your speech just to make a better impression. The big lie that seemingly could get you off the hook in a tough situation tempts you fiercely.

Lying, unfortunately, dishonors God in several ways: First, it defies His commandments. Second, it implies God can't be trusted to get you out of a tight spot, or to guard your reputation. So you try to lie your way out. Rather than being content with what God has given, you ex-aggerate so others will think your life is a little more exciting than it really is.

David fell into the lying trap. True, he was running away for his life and the pressure was on, but when the same thing had happened before,

"God's truth, like a B-52 bomber, will demolish the fib factory that's still operating in your life."

David had gone to the prophet Samuel for help. When Saul came to kill David, Samuel and the other prophets provided such an awesome display of God's power that Saul and his men forgot all about chasing David. If David had again sought safety with Samuel, the lying could have been avoided. David ignored the first principle of bombing his fib factory: Get direction from God in the first place so you don't get yourself into a how-will-I-ever-get-out-of-this-one situation.

Because David hadn't asked God what to do, he found himself fleeing from an army, with no food to eat and no weapon to defend himself. So he stopped to ask a priest for food. The priest was suspicious because David was traveling alone. His skepticism gave David another chance to tell the truth but he blew it. David knew it was treason to help someone escape from the king, so he lied.

A lie eventually backfires. David's lie caused the deaths of an innocent priest and his family. What dreadful consequences a few words can cause! The Christian student who lies to his non-Christian teacher will raise one more barrier between that teacher and God. The boy who lies to his parents widens the "generation gap." The girl who lies to her friends loses their respect. Lies hurt other people and you. Do something about your fib factory.

Some of the most harmful lies are the ones you tell yourself. God's Word says you can do everything through Christ who gives you the strength (Phil. 4:13); so when you say, "I can't ever do anything right," you're lying to yourself. God's Word says, "He who hates correction will die" (Prov. 15:10); so when you say, "Nobody's going to tell me what to do," or, "I don't need any advice, thank you," you are hurting yourself. God's Word says, "Overcome evil with good" (Rom. 12:21); so when you say, "I've got a right to get even with him," you are convincing yourself to disobey God's command.

Lies dishonor God, hurt other people, and destroy you. But how can you break the habit? By replacing each lie with the truth—God's Word. God's truth, like a B-52 bomber, will demolish the fib factory that's still operating in your life.

"Do not lie to each another, since you have taken off your old self with its practices. . ." (Col. 3:9).

"Therefore each of you must put off falsehood and speak truthfully to his neighbor, for we are all members of one body" (Eph. 4:25).

1. What does God say about liars?
2. Will lying benefit you in the long run?
3. Have you been under the impression that a little lying isn't such a big deal? Have you changed your opinion?
4. In what situation have you found lying especially easy? Ask God to help you change the next time you face that temptation.

Racing Without a Reason

"So Saul went down to the Desert of Ziph, with his three thousand chosen men of Israel, to search there for David. Then David set out and went to the place where Saul had camped. He saw where Saul and Abner son of Ner, the commander of the army, had lain down. . . . So David and Abishai went to the army by night, and there was Saul, lying asleep inside the camp with his spear stuck in the ground near his head. Abner and the soldiers were lying around him. Abishai said to David, 'Today God has delivered your enemy into your hands. Now let me pin him to the ground with one thrust of my spear; I won't strike him twice.' But David said to Abishai, 'Don't destroy him! Who can lay a hand on the Lord's anointed and be guiltless? As surely as the Lord lives,' he said, 'the Lord himself will strike him; either his time will come and he will die, or he will go into battle and perish. But the Lord forbid that I should lay a hand on the Lord's anointed. Now get the spear and water jug that are near his head, and let's go' " (1 Sam. 26:2, 5, 7–11).

Before the invention of the telegraph or telephone, messages were often carried by runners. In 2 Samuel 18, after a battle, the commander ordered a runner to tell King David what had happened. Another man, Ahimaaz, asked if he could run too. The commander tried to discourage him, because he had nothing to report. But Ahimaaz insisted on running—and he won the race. His message to the king was less than enlightening; when David asked specifically how his son Absalom was, the runner blurted out between gasps, "I saw a great confusion . . . but I don't know what it was" (2 Sam. 18:29). No wonder the king asked him to step aside, and waited for the second messenger.

Before you laugh at this race without a reason, look at yourself. Are you running aimlessly without specific instructions from God? Does "lots of commotion, little progress" sum up your life? Are you, as Ahimaaz did, covering lots of miles but actually getting nowhere?

Ahimaaz, the marathon man of our story, was the faster runner; he won the race even though the other guy had a head start. And when King David heard who was running toward him, he remarked, "He's a good man." No doubt Ahimaaz had faithfully delivered messages before. But he had one weakness: He hated to wait. By acting before he had clear instructions, he wasted time and energy.

Maybe you should stop and get instructions from God before rushing into a new job or joining every club on campus. Even if you know something is God's will, wait to discover God's timing and God's method before going ahead. After all, God has done a great job of running the universe for who-knows-how-many years; it is rather logical that He not only can tell you what to do, but can arrange the perfect timing as well. And by letting Him plan the details of your life you honor Him.

David waited for God's direction amazingly well. Because he made honoring God his top priority, he handled a long, difficult time of waiting for God to fulfill His promise. As a teen-ager (the Bible doesn't tell his age, so he may have been even older), he had been anointed the next king of Israel. (The Israelites had a ceremony of pouring oil on the head of the person who was to be king.) Then he returned to caring for his father's sheep. After he killed Goliath, and later when he married Saul's daughter, the goal seemed within reach at last. Because of Saul's jealousy, however, David had to flee for his life, and then hide in the barren hills of Judah for years. During this time he had two chances to kill King Saul easily. David could have reasoned that having a madman for a king was bad for the country, that Saul was a terrible spiritual leader, and that God had promised the throne to David anyway. But he didn't think that way. He knew God had anointed Saul as king, so David waited for God's timing to remove Saul from office. Even after Saul's death he waited until all the people decided to make him king (the ten northern tribes took seven years to decide), but the long wait was worth it. David could reign knowing this was God's will and timing.

Because God's blessing was on his reign, David accomplished more than any other king of Israel. He captured Jerusalem and made it the capital. He defeated the enemies of Israel and brought peace and prosperity. He organized musicians to sing and play for worship services in the temple. He wrote many of the psalms in your Bible.

If God gives you a glimpse of His plan for your life, as He did to David, don't get in a rush. Let God fulfill that plan in His way in His time. I once read the letter of a young couple who had gone out as missionaries before they were ready. They had to come back. Many people could tell you of heartaches they've had from rushing into marriage or going ahead of God in another area. Learn to wait for God. Nobody wins great prizes for racing without a reason.

"I am still confident of this: I will see the goodness of the Lord in the land of the living. Wait for the Lord; be strong and take heart and wait for the Lord" (Ps. 27:13, 14).

"But you must return to your God; maintain love and justice, and wait for your God always" (Hos. 12:6).

"Do not say, 'I'll pay you back for this wrong!' Wait for the Lord, and he will deliver you" (Prov. 20:22).

1. Why is it easy to go ahead with your own solutions instead of waiting for God to act?
2. What promises are given, in the above verses, to those who wait for God?
3. What are you rushing into right now? Take some time to find out what God thinks about it.

The Price of a Promise

"[David] asked, 'Is there no one still left of the house of Saul to whom I can show God's kindness?' Ziba answered the king, 'There is still a son of Jonathan; he is crippled in both feet.' When Mephibosheth son of Jonathan, the son of Saul, came to David, he bowed down to pay him honor. David said, 'Mephibosheth!' 'Your servant,' he replied. 'Don't be afraid,' David said to him, 'for I will surely show you kindness for the sake of your father Jonathan. I will restore to you all the land that belonged to your grandfather Saul, and you will always eat at my table'" (2 Sam. 9:1, 3, 6, 7).

You make promises every day:
"I'll be there at 8:00 o'clock sharp."
"I'll send you a picture later."
"I'll pay you back at the end of the month."
"I'll do all the assignments tonight and hand them in tomorrow."
"I'll do the dishes every night for a month if you'll let me go on the camping trip."

How much are your promises worth? Is the price of your promises going up or down? Do you consider keeping your promises important, or are you in the same category as Willie Wishwash and Sandy Semi-Reliable? Maybe you never realized that sticking by your word is an important part of honoring God.

David went to great lengths to fulfill a promise he had made years before to Jonathan, son of King Saul. Although Saul was very jealous of David's popularity and success, Jonathan considered David his best friend. Jonathan didn't care if David became king instead of him; he told David, "You will be king over Israel, and I will be second to you" (1 Sam. 23:17). Then they promised each other lasting friendship and kindness to each other's descendants. (This was quite a pledge because in ancient times a new king customarily killed all members of the former royal family.)

David was hiding from Saul when he learned Jonathan had been killed in battle. Seven years later he became king over all of Israel. He then had to defeat the enemies of his nation, capture Jerusalem, and set up his capital city there. But David did not forget his promise. As soon as he had a little rest, he went all-out to find any living relatives of Jonathan. When he found Mephibosheth, the son of Jonathan, he gave him all the land that had belonged to his grandfather Saul, and invited him to live at the palace and eat at his table. In keeping his promise, David wasn't just doing a good deed in memory of his best friend; he was honoring God.

You see, God always keeps His promises; He says, "But I the Lord will speak what I will speak, and it shall be fulfilled without delay" (Ezek. 12:25). God's children should resemble Him in faithfully keeping promises. Parents are honored when their children are complimented for reflecting some of their good characteristics. God is honored when His children reflect His character.

If you don't keep your promises, you make a mockery of the God who based His entire revelation to man on His promises. Consider this: "Have we not all one father? Has not one God created us? Why then are we faithless to one another, profaning the covenant [pact, promise] of our fathers?" (Mal. 2:10). Breaking promises cheapens the whole idea of a covenant being a permanent promise. If you are sloppy about keeping your word, you'll have difficulty putting your faith in the promises of God and living by them. You'll tend to value God's promises as you value your own.

What's the price of a promise? If your perspective is right, a promise should be your most valued possession.

"Lord, who may dwell in your sanctuary? Who may live on your holy hill? He . . . who despises a vile man but honors those who fear the Lord, who keeps his oath even when it hurts" (Ps. 15:1-4).

"Do not be quick with your mouth, do not be hasty in your heart to utter anything before God. God is in heaven and you are on earth, so let your words be few. When you make a vow to God, do not delay in fulfilling it.

He has no pleasure in fools; fulfill your vow. It is better not to vow than to make a vow and not fulfill it" (Eccles. 5:2, 4, 5).

1. Do you make every promise as if in the presence of God?
2. Why should you be very careful before making any kind of a promise?
3. What must you do, even if you have made a promise which is very hard for you to fulfill?
4. Are you too quick to make promises? Have you made some promises that you have not kept? Ask God to show you how to make right (today) one of those unkept promises.

A Secret Sin That Everyone Knows About

"In the spring, at the time when kings go off to war, David sent Joab out with the king's men and the whole Israelite army. They destroyed the Ammonites and besieged Rabbah. But David remained in Jerusalem. One evening David got up from his bed and walked around on the roof of the palace. From the roof he saw a woman bathing. The woman was very beautiful, and David sent someone to find out about her. The man said, 'Isn't this Bathsheba, the daughter of Eliam and the wife of Uriah the Hittite?' Then David sent messengers to get her. She came to him, and he slept with her . . . Then she went back home. The woman conceived and sent word to David, saying, 'I am pregnant' " (2 Sam. 11:1–5).

Do you realize how important your actions are? Each brings either honor or dishonor to God. David's adultery with Bathsheba shows this clearly. Because of what David had done, his subjects could excuse their sins with, "Well, even the king doesn't obey the Ten Commandments." David's sons could justify their disrespect for their father with, "Who are you to tell me what to do? Look what you did." Even people today use David's sin to absolve themselves; it's the old argument that says, "See, people who claim to be religious don't live any differently than anyone else."

God will forgive if you sin, but He can't dissolve the dishonor you've brought to God and His kingdom. How sad if your gossip or sarcasm or anger causes someone to say, "If that's Christianity, I don't want it." How heartbreaking when people observe that a young adult who says he knows Jesus acts no differently than others. God has given you His Holy Spirit to provide all the power necessary to live above sin. Your job is to co-operate with the Holy Spirit.

Apart from your depending on Jesus, you are capable of terrible things. The Apostle Paul wrote, "I know that nothing good lives in me, that is, in my sinful nature" (Rom. 7:18). You are to live, not according to the desires of your old self-centeredness (which was crucified with Jesus on the cross), but by the power of the Holy Spirit (Rom. 8:4). God has planned for you to be victorious over sin by letting the Holy Spirit live through you. Beware, however, for any pride or yielding to the self-life will lead to a David-like disaster.

David fell into sin because of spiritual laxness, and God included David's blunder in the Bible so you can learn from David's mistakes. Several areas of laxness led to his downfall. First, he became careless about his work and his spiritual life. Jesus warned His disciples, "Watch and pray so that you will not fall into temptation. . ." (Matt. 26:41), but David dropped his guard. He deserted his responsibilities (by handing over command of the army to Joab), then became so bored that he was pacing back and forth on the palace roof—where temptation struck.

Idleness and boredom have sent many teen-agers looking for excitement in all the wrong places. Ask God each day what work you should do and what useful projects you should tackle in your free time. Don't let the devil find you with nothing to do and out of communication with God.

Second, David had been disregarding one of God's commands for a long time. The law of Moses stipulated that the king of God's people "must not take many wives, or his heart will be led astray" (Deut. 17:17), but David had married several women, just as the kings in surrounding countries did. This disobedience paved the way for his great sin with Bathsheba.

You'll often be tempted to ignore one or more of God's commands, simply because no one else seems concerned about it. Don't be fooled. One sin always leads to more. Strictly obey the Bible, even if everyone around you seems to be going against it.

Third, David didn't guard his eyes. He didn't have to look a second time when he saw Bathsheba bathing. Although he couldn't help the first look, the second look was sin. Rather than taking another peek, he should have gone downstairs.

You can't avoid some temptation. When you drive or shop you'll inevitably see billboards or magazine covers that will tempt you—but you don't have to look twice. God expects you to guard your eyes. Temptation is often unavoidable, but sin is never accidental. As someone once wisely said, "You can't keep a bird from flying overhead but you can keep it from building a nest in your hair."

Fourth, David misused his power in order to cover up his sin—he had Bathsheba's soldier husband positioned in the battle so he would be killed. Then David could legally marry the widow carrying his child.

You probably are thinking that was a terrible thing to do, but there may have been times when only your lack of power kept you from doing something equally bad. Do you take advantage of being older and smarter than your little brother, or are you always fair to him? Do you exploit your seniority at work by joining the plot to make the new employee do all the dirty work? Do you speak loud and long in your own defense every time you're cornered? Consider carefully how you use the power entrusted to you.

When David finally came to his senses, he repented fully and God forgave him. But his secret sin became world news—people are still reading about it in their Bibles. And David, whose heart's desire was to honor God, realized what a terrible example he had been.

Learn from David's mistakes. The story of David and Bathsheba doesn't need any modern reruns.

"See to it that no one misses the grace of God and that no bitter root grows up to cause trouble and defile many" (Heb. 12:15).

"Therefore, since we are surrounded by such a great cloud of witnesses, let us throw off everything that hinders and the sin that so easily entangles, and let us run with perseverance the race marked out for us. Let us fix our eyes on Jesus, the author and perfecter of our faith, who for the joy set before him endured the cross, scorning its shame, and sat down at the right hand of the throne of God" (Heb. 12:1, 2).

"Don't let anyone look down on you because you are young, but set an example for the believers in speech, in life, in love, in faith and in purity. Until I come, devote yourself to the public reading of Scripture, to preaching and to teaching" (1 Tim. 4:12).

"In everything set them an example by doing what is good. In your teaching show integrity, seriousness and soundness of speech that cannot be condemned, so that those who oppose you may be ashamed because they have nothing bad to say about us" (Titus 2:7, 8).

1. What can keep you from being a bad advertisement for Christ?
2. What can you do to be a good example to others?
3. From where does the power come to be a "model Christian"?
4. What kind of example have you been lately? What area of your life should you work on improving today?

Give the Gold Medal to the Coach

"David said, 'My son Solomon is young and inexperienced, and the house to be built for the Lord should be of great magnificence and fame and splendor in the sight of all the nations. Therefore I will make preparations for it.' So David made extensive preparations before his death. Then he called for his son Solomon and charged him to build a house for the Lord, the God of Israel. David said to Solomon: 'My son, I had it in my heart to build a house for the Name of the Lord my God. . . . Now . . . the Lord be with you, and may you have success and build the house of the Lord your God, as he said you would. May the Lord give you discretion and understanding when he puts you in command over Israel, so that you may keep the law of the Lord your God' " (1 Chron. 22:5, 7, 11, 12).

Someone has wisely observed that great things can be done for God if no one cares who gets the credit. You honor the Lord when you gladly do His work *whether or not anyone notices*. This sounds easy but beware of the subtle pitfalls: If no one says anything nice about your solo, are you content just because you sang to praise Jesus—or are you worried that everybody thought something was wrong with it? If you volunteered to help clean the church, and no one else who volunteered shows up, do you stay late to finish, even though you miss the NFC championship game on TV? But what if no one says the church looks nice, or commends you for missing the game to keep your promise? Face it: You like to see your name in print, but you're not very good at working without recognition.

When David got the idea of building a beautiful temple for God, the Lord told Nathan the prophet that David's son, not David, would construct it. Instead of being disappointed and asking why, David accepted God's answer. Then he proceeded to gather many of the materials Solomon would need to build it. David didn't say, "I need some time to relax. Let Solomon do the work for a change," or, "Solomon's going to get the credit. Let him do all the work." David wanted God's work to go forward. He wanted the God of Israel to have the most beautiful temple in the world. And he was willing to help make it a reality, without getting recognition.

You need to acquire David's attitude, to learn there are no big "I's" and no little "you's" in the kingdom of God. All believers are on the same team and the Coach is the only one who deserves any credit. After all, without God what could anybody do?

Once you get this straight, you'll eliminate many other problems. Since all the glory goes to God, from whom you got everything anyway, you'll see how ridiculous it is to be jealous of "spiritual giant" Christians. Instead, you'll pray for them and encourage them in their work. Also, you won't need to put down anybody to make yourself look good, because any credit goes to God, not you. In addition, such an attitude will save you from the pride that "goes before destruction" (Prov. 16:18).

When you want only to honor God, you won't be upset by those who try to be "big wheels" by acting super-important. You won't try to compete with them. You'll just go ahead and be an example of a person whose only goal is to further God's kingdom. And you won't get down on yourself for failures. You'll be trusting God for all you need, and He will provide. When you're a member of God's team, all the gold medals rightly go to the Coach.

"Such confidence as this is ours through Christ before God" (2 Cor. 3:5).

"I am the vine; you are the branches. If a man remains in me and I in him, he will bear much fruit; apart from me you can do nothing" (John 15:5).

"But by the grace of God I am what I am, and his grace to me was not without effect. No, I worked harder than all of them—yet not I, but the

grace of God that was with me" (1 Cor. 15:10).

"I became a servant of this gospel by the gift of God's grace given me through the working of his power. Although I am less than the least of all God's people, this grace was given me: to preach to the Gentiles the unsearchable riches of Christ . . ." (Eph. 3:7, 8).

1. Where does every ability you have come from?
2. Where does the strength to serve God come from?
3. Where does the vision and wisdom to do something out of the ordinary come from?
4. Is there any place for comparing yourself with others, trying to be better than others, or feeling jealous of others?

ELIJAH: STANDING ALONE AGAINST THE WORLD

Introduction

Do you ever feel that following Jesus gets a little lonely? That nobody else seems to take Christianity seriously? That when the chips are down you're the only one willing to take a stand? If you're tempted to become discouraged, the life of Elijah will inspire you.

Enter Elijah

TIME: About 864 B.C.

PLACE: The Northern Kingdom of Israel (capital city: Samaria).

SCENE: Jezebel, a sinful swinger from Phoenicia, had married Ahab, the king of Israel. She hated God and had decided the people of Israel were to worship the idol Baal, which she imported from her homeland. Sadly, the people of Israel, who possessed God's law—the Ten Commandments—did not resist her.

Elijah, however, obeyed God's law and, of course, got into trouble. He had prayed the people would turn back to God and God answered that prayer by sending no rain for three and a half years—this would give them good reason to pray to God and change their ways. (People tend to forget rain and sunshine come from the Creator, until the supply is cut off.) God then sent Elijah to tell Ahab there would be no rain until Elijah's next weather forecast. Of course, Ahab was angry, but the Lord protected the now unpopular Elijah, first by hiding him near a brook where ravens delivered Elijah's food, then by sending him to a widow's home in which God miraculously multiplied her supply of shortening and flour to feed herself and her son, and Elijah as well.

Elijah's next assignment was to confront Ahab and challenge him to a contest which would show the people who was the true God, Baal or Jehovah. So atop Mount Carmel, overlooking the Mediterranean Sea, Elijah took on 450 prophets of Baal. Amidst excitement greater than at a Super Bowl, Baal's prophets built an altar and placed upon it the pieces of an ox as a sacrifice. Then they danced, screamed and cut themselves for hours, trying to gain their god's attention. But he sent no fire. Then Elijah gathered 12 stones for a simple altar and placed upon it the pieces of his ox. Then he had 12 barrels of water poured over the pile—so no one would accuse him of cheating. Then he bowed his head and prayed. Fire roared down from heaven, devoured the meat, and even burned up the stones and water. The audience was impressed. The people immediately fell on their faces and admitted Jehovah, not Baal, was God. And at Elijah's command they executed the prophets of Baal. This was the first time they had obeyed God's laws in years.

Elijah declared to the awestruck Ahab that God would now send rain, though he could not see a single cloud. Then Elijah climbed to Carmel's peak and began praying until a tiny cloud was sighted. Soon came a downpour—and more trouble. As soon as Ahab arrived at home he told Jezebel what had happened. She became more angry than Ahab ever had seen, and promised to kill Elijah.

Exhausted, Disappointed and Depressed

This time, rather than trusting God to protect him, Elijah turned chicken and ran. In the middle of the Sinai desert, exhausted, Elijah fell beneath a bush and begged God to let him die. Instead, God sent an angel to give him water and bake him a cake. He ate two meals—and their nourishment lasted forty days! Elijah then headed for Mount Horeb where Moses had received the Ten Commandments. There God spoke quietly to him, renewed his faith, and gave him a fresh assignment.

Elijah apparently spent most of his remaining years training his successor, Elisha, and directing "schools of the prophets." God kept Ahab out of Elijah's hair by sending the Syrian army to invade Israel.

A Dangerous Assignment from God

Ahab later threw a tantrum because his neighbor, Naboth, wouldn't sell his grape field (the law of Moses didn't allow a man to sell his land and thus leave his children without property). So crafty Jezebel arranged to have Naboth sentenced to death by a kangaroo court, thus allowing Ahab to confiscate the field. God could tolerate no more; He sent Elijah to tell Ahab the entire royal family was doomed. Soon after, Ahab was killed in battle.

Just to make sure Elijah's life would be remembered for its uniqueness, God didn't let him die. Instead, the prophet who had called down fire from heaven was whisked away by a flaming chariot.

Although Elijah often had to stand alone for God, he was not a man to be pitied. Because Elijah's God was all-powerful, it would be easier to feel sorry for Elijah's enemies! But just as Elijah was never really alone, you need never be alone. The God of Elijah goes with you to school, to work, and to parties. That should give you confidence.

Facing the Big Bad World Alone

"Now Elijah the Tishbite, from Tishbe in Gilead, said to Ahab, 'As the Lord, the God of Israel, lives, whom I serve, there will be neither dew nor rain in the next few years except at my word' " (1 Kings 17:1).

Would the "I-know-what-the-world-is-all-about" seniors in your Social Problems class laugh if you raised your hand and explained the Bible teaches that sex before marriage is wrong? What reaction would you get if you told your lunchroom gang you always come in at the hour your parents request and never try to sneak out without permission? Would you lose all your friends if you reminded your geometry classmates you all deserved the punishment homework and that you planned to complete it? Do you feel like the only one in the whole school who really wants to know God and obey Him? Does it seem that being good is old-fashioned and out-of-style? Are you afraid that some day you'll just give in and follow the crowd?

Well, the Bible tells us about a guy who faced your problem: Elijah. Because Jezebel had made idol worship the state religion of Israel, very few people were following Jehovah—the true God. As Elijah looked around him, he felt very much alone. Following God had meant risking his life to deliver a message from Jehovah to the king. Would you like to know where he got his courage? You might be able to use some of it in the locker room, or in Mr. Cellular's biology class.

The Bible reveals Elijah's secret. We read in James that Elijah prayed earnestly from a righteous heart (5:17). Those weren't emergency, push-button, pit-stop requests, but deep communication with God. Not only did Elijah pray, he knew God and was conscious of God's constant presence with him.

His opening words to King Ahab were, "As the Lord, the God of Israel lives, before whom I stand. . . ."

Elijah knew God as He really is—alive, all-powerful, never bummed-out, always ready with an answer to each problem.

This he hadn't learned from his grandmother, but from daily depending on the almighty God. And that's the way which you too can learn to receive strength from God.

God is never overwhelmed when evil surrounds you. He knows a light shows up best in a very dark place, so He intends to give you the power to be that light. You may be facing a big bad world but you don't have to face it alone.

"For the Lord loves the just and will not forsake his faithful ones" (Ps. 37:28).

"Be strong and courageous. Do not be afraid or terrified because of them, for the Lord your God goes with you; he will never leave you nor forsake you" (Deut. 31:6).

"The Lord is with me; I will not be afraid. What can man do to me?" (Ps. 118:6).

1. Why are you afraid of other people and what they will think of you?
2. Why does God command us not to be afraid of what people think? (See Deut. 31:6.)
3. If you stick with God and are faithful to Him, what does He promise you?
4. Who are the people who scare you? How could praying about your fear and believing God's truth in the above verses make this week different?

Popularity, Self-confidence, a Bulletproof Vest, and Money in the Bank

"Then the word of the Lord came to Elijah: 'Leave here, turn eastward and hide in the ravine of Kerith, east of the Jordan. You will drink from the brook, and I have ordered the ravens to feed you there.' So he did what the Lord had told him. . . . Some time later the brook dried up because there had been no rain in the land. Then the word of the Lord came to him: 'Go at once to Zarephath of Sidon and stay there. I have commanded a widow in that place to supply you with food.' So he went to Zarephath. . . . After a long time, in the third year, the word of the Lord came to Elijah: 'Go and present yourself to Ahab, and I will send rain on the land.' So Elijah went to present himself to Ahab" (1 Kings 17:2–5, 7–10; 18:1, 2).

Does the constant criticism from your parents and big sister give you a complex? Do you feel like going into hiding because you missed the critical free throw or flubbed the clarinet solo? Does the first day at a different school or a new job petrify you? Then you have a disease: insecurity. And there's an epidemic going around.

Most cases are the "common chronic variety," but some are acute. For instance, the fear that rises when you read about the stabbing in the school across town, or when you hear the rumor of a neighbor girl being raped, or when you remember the guy who tried to break into your house last month, can cripple you, preventing your doing God's will.

Psalm 37:3 has the antidote for paralyzing insecurity: "Trust in the Lord and do good; dwell in the land, and enjoy safe pasture." That may sound too simplistic for real life, but the Bible tells of someone who proved it true—under circumstances probably a lot worse than yours: His name was Elijah.

Gutsy Elijah had told wicked King Ahab there would be no rain for three years. Elijah's popularity rating soon slipped 75 points as the land dried up, and he found himself ripe for a case of acute insecurity: Ahab's henchmen were ready to kill him on sight, supplies of food and water were withering, and no one seemed willing to trust and obey God.

But Elijah had a secret for coping with immense problems: unquestioning obedience to God's instructions. And those instructions sounded a bit strange. First he was to camp by a brook and be fed by ravens; then he was to get food and lodging from a poor widow in a foreign country; finally he was to again—horrors!—confront Ahab. Strange orders, yes, but Elijah did not argue, "Hey, wait a minute, God. Hungry ravens don't feed people during a famine. This brook can't last a week. A penniless widow can't even feed her family—let alone me. And besides, there's a price on my head; the moment Ahab's hit-men spot me, I'll be vulture-bait." Instead, Elijah assumed God knew what He was doing.

God honored Elijah's trust. The ravens daily delivered meat and bread. God miraculously supplied the widow with flour and shortening to make bread. And Ahab ended up obeying Elijah.

As you trust God, He cares for you in the same way He cared for Elijah. A. W. Pink, a famous theologian, once observed that God often puts you by a "brook" on the verge of drying up, rather than beside a river flowing from an endless supply—just so you'll trust *Him* to provide the money, love, or security you need. He will send His "ravens"—a Christian friend with a word of encouragement, a book that's just what you need, or even a squadron of angels. All power in the universe is His—and it's available to you.

God has all the power in the world, so if He calls you to be the Elijah of Central High, don't run away. Just stick around and watch for miracles. The security He provides is a lot better than popularity, self-confidence, a bullet-proof vest, or money in the bank.

"Do not let your heart envy sinners, but always be zealous for the fear of the Lord. There is surely a future hope for you, and your hope will not be cut off" (Prov. 23:17, 18).

"Find rest, O my soul, in God alone; my hope comes from him. He alone is my rock and my salvation; he is my fortress, I will not be shaken. My salvation and my honor depend on God; he is my mighty rock, my refuge. Trust in him at all times, O people; pour out your hearts to him, for God is our refuge" (Ps. 62:5–8).

1. Why is it wrong to keep fussing about all the evil and danger facing you, and using them as excuses to not live wholly for God?
2. What actions on your part will insure God's protection and grace, regardless of your situation?
3. What have you been complaining and worrying about lately? Read again the preceding Bible verses and decide what God wants you to do about worrying and complaining.

Fire from Heaven Instruction Manual

> *"So Ahab sent word throughout all Israel and assembled the prophets on Mount Carmel. Elijah went before the people and said, 'How long will you waver between two opinions? If the Lord is God, follow him; but if Baal is God, follow him.' But the people said nothing. At the time of sacrifice, the prophet Elijah stepped forward and prayed: 'O Lord, God of Abraham, Isaac and Israel, let it be known today that you are God in Israel and that I am your servant and have done all these things at your command. Answer me, O Lord, answer me, so these people will know that you, O Lord, are God, and that you are turning their hearts back again.' Then the fire of the Lord fell and burned up the sacrifice, the wood, the stones and the soil, and also licked up the water in the trench. When all the people saw this, they fell prostrate and cried, 'The Lord, he is God! The Lord—he is God!' " (1 Kings 18:20, 21, 36–39).*

Do you ever imagine yourself in front of a school assembly telling all the students how they can know Jesus? Or giving the perfect speech in English class which will convert not only the teacher, but the entire class? Or being the hero of the football game and telling the news reporters God deserves the credit? Or becoming homecoming queen so people will pay attention to your testimony?

Hold it. Get back on the Reality Train and be logical.

It's easier to be a one-day hero than to follow God step by step, day by day, through algebra assignments, school lunches and parking tickets. So stop dreaming about the hero stuff. Fantasizing the glamour and excitement of a one-day spiritual blow-out will stop you from obeying God *right now*.

Elijah didn't spend his life preparing to stage a big show on Mount Carmel. If he had, there would have been no fire—and no rain afterward. Mount Carmel was simply the culmination of walking with God, obeying Him in the little things, day after day. He knew God's voice, so when the moment arrived, he knew exactly what Jehovah wanted. He was not afraid. He had the calm courage of one who was a friend of God. People could tell he had no experience acting and a lot of practice praying. Although he was number one on Ahab's "Ten Most Wanted" list, no one was trying to kill him. This was no "I've-got-to-do-something-so-here-goes" experiment.

Daydreaming aside, the Mount Carmel fireworks are a wonderful reminder that a lone servant of God can conquer 450—or a million for that matter—prophets of Baal. God gives power to stand alone, even if all the other kids who claim to be Christians compromise, and the non-Christians treat you as a visitor from another planet. Elijah's power and courage came from God and you can have it too. "One with God is a majority" is more than a nice-sounding platitude. It's the truth.

Let the God of Elijah be your God. Let Him make you the person who stands up for God without being afraid of what other people think or say. But like Elijah, get specific instructions from the Lord. Follow Him step by step. Don't try to be the Incredible Christian. Don't attempt Wonder Woman witnessing. Don't decide to write your own Fire from Heaven Manual. Your plans will fail. God's plans will not.

" 'Woe [big trouble] to the obstinate children,' declares the Lord, 'to those who carry out plans that are not mine, forming an alliance, but not by my Spirit, heaping sin upon sin.' This is what the Sovereign Lord, the Holy One of Israel, says: 'In repentance and rest is your salvation, in quietness and trust is your strength, but you would have none of it. You said, "No, we will flee on horses." Therefore you will flee! You said, "We will ride off on swift horses." Therefore your pursuers will be swift!' Yet the Lord longs to be gracious to you; he rises to show you compassion. For the Lord is a God of justice. Blessed are all who wait for him!" (Isa. 30:1, 15, 16, 18).

1. Why is doing God's work in your own way a form of rebellion?
2. From where does real inner strength come?
3. Are you guilty of not waiting for God's instructions? On what "horses" are you speeding ahead without consulting Him?
4. Why can you receive God's strength only when you follow His plans?
5. Are you willing to give your ideas to God? To scrap or revise them as He commands?

Get Out Your Sword!

"Then Elijah commanded them, 'Seize the prophets of Baal. Don't let anyone get away!' They seized them, and Elijah had them brought down to the Kishon Valley and slaughtered there" (1 King 18:40).

You may be shocked that Elijah ordered the execution of Baal's prophets after their defeat on Mount Carmel. But Elijah was simply carrying out the laws of Israel, whose government was based on God's decrees—those who didn't want to obey God could leave. The Law of Moses demanded that the person who spiritually misled the people should be put to death: "That prophet . . . must be put to death, because he preached rebellion against the Lord your God. . . . You must purge the evil from among you" (Deut. 13:5). Such an extreme law would be similar to requiring the death penalty for anyone advocating heroin for teen-agers (thus contributing to many early deaths). False prophets in Israel were engineering the spiritual death of fellow-citizens. Heaven and hell were at stake. Therefore, these prophets could not be allowed to live.

Now before you spearhead a bloody campaign to rid the land of today's false teachers, take stock of Romans 13:1: "Everyone must submit himself to the governing authorities. For there is no authority except from God, and those that exist have been instituted by God." God requires you to live by the laws of your government, and there is no death penalty in this country for leaders who spiritually deceive and harm their followers.

So what does killing false prophets have to do with you? It teaches a very practical principle: never compromise with sin. Totally eliminate it from your life.

When many around you are boldly doing wrong and few want to follow God, it's easy to rationalize God's standards of holiness. It's easy to conclude you're so much better than those around you that you don't have to strictly follow the Bible. But God's standards don't change because society is more wicked. He hasn't changed His mind about the sinfulness of lying, premarital sex, gossiping, or reading dirty magazines. He won't make an exception for you just because "everybody's doing it." Instead, disobeying God will rob you of spiritual strength, and the worse the world gets, the more you'll need that strength.

Make a clean break with anything pulling you away from God; don't try to gradually stop. Someone has observed if you must cut off a dog's tail, it is better to slice it all at once than to chop off an inch at a time! So treat temptation like that dog's tail. Turn off the TV the moment you realize that show will pollute your thought life. Change the subject the moment a conversation shifts to gossip and criticism. Have your parents write a note so you'll be excused from the class in which an occult game is being played. Don't listen when you're told selfishness and rebellion are normal adolescent behavior.

Execute the "prophets of Baal" in your life, the influences that deceive and lead you to rebel against God. Start swinging your sword—"the sword of the Spirit, which is the word of God" (Eph. 6:17).

"Avoid every kind of evil" (1 Thess. 5:22).

"Do not conform any longer to the pattern of this world, but be transformed by the renewing of your mind. Then you will be able to test and approve what God's will is—his good, pleasing and perfect will" (Rom. 12:2).

"Do not love the world or anything in the world. If anyone loves the world, the love of the Father is not in him" (1 John 2:15).

1. Have truth and standards for right and wrong changed? Why not?
2. Why is it easy to get your ideas about good and evil from the world around you instead of the Bible? Why is this method dangerous?
3. Ask God to show you if you are being deceived about any issue in your life. If you're simply confused, rather than deceived, do a Bible study on that subject by using a concordance or asking your spiritual leader for scripture passages that will clarify the matter for you.
4. The "things in the world" are temporary. Which things in your life are temporary? Which are permanent, eternal?

Look at the World Through Faith-Colored Glasses

"Now Ahab told Jezebel everything Elijah had done and how he had killed all the prophets with the sword. So Jezebel sent a messenger to Elijah to say, 'May the gods deal with me, be it ever so severely, if by this time tomorrow I do not make your life like that of one of them.' Elijah was afraid and ran for his life" (1 Kings 19:1–3).

For three years, Elijah had witnessed miracles every day. Ravens had fed him in the desert. A widow's oil and flour supplies had never run empty. A king bent on murder had instead carried out his commands. Elijah had prayed down fire and rain from heaven. People had repented of their idol worship. And certainly there would be wonderful opportunities to teach these people the ways of God.

And then it happened. Elijah fell apart and acted as though God didn't

"Actually, the situation is not the problem. Instead, it is the attitude you choose to adopt toward that problem that makes the difference."

even exist. Elijah panicked and ran when Queen Jezebel vowed she would kill him. Why? After all, he had been a hunted man for three years. Admittedly, he was physically and emotionally drained in a vulnerable condition. But why such paranoia after years of bold faith? It was as though, like Peter, he had suddenly realized he'd been walking on water, and instead of looking through eyes of faith, he looked at the physical realities: water + gravity = drowning; only in Elijah's case it was: queen + anger = death. But God hadn't changed. He had just as much power as ever. But Elijah short-circuited the powerline.

You've probably made the same mistake yourself. Perhaps last month you trusted God to give you power to live above the tension and chaos in your home, and things went remarkably well. But then your little sister borrowed your best blouse without permission and spilled sulfuric acid on it in chem lab—and your marvelous faith for your home situation went up in smoke. You started to look at the problems in human terms and saw no solution in sight.

Or maybe for a long time you had been trusting God for your dating life, but then Jody's smart remark spurred you to quit waiting for God's best; instead you decided to lay a trap for a Saturday night date. Or you may have told God it was okay if you weren't muscular and athletic, but one day in front of the mirror you started listening to Satan's whispers and now you feel ugly and unacceptable.

Actually, the situation is not the problem. Instead, it is the attitude you choose to adopt toward that problem that makes the difference. When Jesus healed two blind men, He told them, "According to your faith will it be done to you" (Matt. 9:29). It is a spiritual principle, a formula. The answer may not come instantly, but "[God] acts on behalf of those who wait for him" (Isa. 64:4). If you decide to face the problems of life without depending on an all-powerful God, nearly every problem will defy solution. You must look at the world through faith-colored glasses.

Evidently, Elijah learned his lesson from this incident and taught his successor, Elisha, the importance of facing each crisis with unwavering faith:

"When the servant of the man of God got up and went out early the next morning, an army with horses and chariots had surrounded the city. 'Oh, my lord, what shall we do?' the servant asked. 'Don't be afraid,' the prophet answered. 'Those who are with us are more than those who are with them.' And Elisha prayed, 'O Lord, open his eyes so he may see.' Then the Lord opened the servant's eyes, and he looked and saw the hills full of horses and chariots of fire all around Elisha" (2 Kings 6:15–17).

1. What do you think the servant would have done if Elisha had not prayed for him?
2. Do you constantly pray for God to help you see things through the eyes of faith? Or are you part of the "Alas, what shall we do" club?

3. What is true reality, everything we see around us, or God's power?
4. What problems are you looking at from a human viewpoint? Now ask God to open your eyes and put faith-colored glasses on you.

Panic and a Picnic

"Elijah was afraid and ran for his life. When he came to Beersheba in Judah, he left his servant there, while he himself went a day's journey into the desert. He came to a broom tree, sat down under it and prayed that he might die. 'I have had enough, Lord,' he said. 'Take my life; I am no better than my ancestors.' Then he lay down under the tree and fell asleep. All at once an angel touched him and said, 'Get up and eat.' He looked around, and there by his head was a cake of bread baked over hot coals, and a jar of water. He ate and drank and then lay down again. . . . Strengthened by that food, he traveled forty days and forty nights until he reached Horeb, the mountain of God. There he went into a cave and spent the night. And the word of the Lord came to him: 'What are you doing here, Elijah?' He replied, 'I have been very zealous for the Lord God Almighty. The Israelites have rejected your covenant, broken down your altars, and put your prophets to death with the sword. I am the only one left, and now they are trying to kill me too.' The Lord said, 'Go out and stand on the mountain in the presence of the Lord, for the Lord is about to pass by.' Then a great and powerful wind tore the mountains apart and shattered the rocks before the Lord, but the Lord was not in the wind. After the wind there was an earthquake, but the Lord was not in the earthquake. After the earthquake came a fire, but the Lord was not in the fire. And after the fire came a gentle whisper. When Elijah heard it, he pulled his cloak over his face and went out and stood at the mouth of the cave. Then a voice said to him, 'What are you doing here, Elijah?' He replied, 'I have been very zealous for the Lord God Almighty. The Israelites have rejected your covenant, broken down your altars, and put your prophets to death with the sword. I am the only one left, and now they are trying to kill me too.' The Lord said to him, 'Go back the way you came, and go to the Desert of Damascus. When you get there, anoint Hazael king over Aram. Also, anoint Jehu son of Nimshi king over Israel, and anoint Elisha son of Shaphat from Abel Meholah to succeed you as prophet' " (1 Kings 19:3–6, 8–16).

Have you ever come home from school completely discouraged, feeling as if all your teachers yell at you, your friends ignore you, and your parents don't understand you, even though you're trying your hardest to do everything right?

Well, Elijah's day had been even worse although it had begun fabulously. After the fire from heaven had proven who was the true God and rain had fallen for the first time in three and a half years, he had expected the nation—even the king and queen—to turn to God. Instead, Jezebel was determined to kill him by the next morning.

After a panicked run into the desert, Elijah fell beneath a scrubby bush. He had no food or water. He begged God to let him die.

Although Elijah deserved it, God did not yell at him, or give him a long lecture, or write him off His list. Rather, he sent an angel to bake a cake for Elijah and give him water—a picnic in the desert! And then He spoke to Elijah with a still small voice. He understood how Elijah was feeling.

God also understands when the pressure on you is too great. He wants to meet your physical, emotional, and spiritual needs. He will do it, regardless of the circumstances. How does it happen?

First, you must realize it is never God's will to sit around and mope, endlessly mulling over your problems. When you're tempted to do this, ask God what you should do next. It usually will be something ordinary such as cleaning your room, tackling the hard biology assignment, apologizing to your father, or getting to bed at a decent time. God assigned Elijah several tasks. As he completed them, his depression vaporized. Ask God for your next assignment.

Second, stop trying to run away. Forget your plans for dropping out of school or moving to another city. God sent Elijah right back into Jezebel's territory. (He could have saved himself a trip by listening to God in the first place!) Don't panic or make rash decisions. Be willing to stay exactly where you are until God moves you, or changes the circumstance, or changes you. And usually God wants to change you.

Elijah could have eaten his picnic in much more pleasant surroundings if only he hadn't yielded to his fears. God has some picnics planned for you, too. If you'll trust Him even through tough times, you'll enjoy them much more than Elijah enjoyed his.

"So do not fear, for I am with you; do not be dismayed, for I am your God. I will strengthen you and help you; I will uphold you with my righteous right hand" (Isa. 41:10).

"Therefore, strengthen your feeble arms and weak knees. 'Make level paths for your feet,' so that the lame may not be disabled, but rather healed" (Heb. 12:12, 13).

"Let us not become weary in doing good, for at the proper time we will reap a harvest if we do not give up" (Gal. 6:9).

"Whatever you do, work at it with all your heart, as working for the Lord, not for men. . . ." (Col. 3:23).

1. Using the above verses, write a prescription to cure discouragement.
2. Hebrews 12:12, 13 teaches if you baby yourself and engage in self-pity, God cannot heal your hurts and heartaches. List the problems about which you will now stop feeling sorry for yourself, and for which you will now trust God. Ask Him to heal the raw edges of your emotions.

3. Do you study "heartily, as serving the Lord"? Do you work with the strength which God can supply, or are you prone to give up? Ask Him to teach you to conquer discouragement by obeying in these things.
4. According to Galatians 6:9, what is the reward for sticking with a task?

Survival Kit for the Lonely, Outnumbered Christian

"Now Ben-Hadad king of Aram mustered his entire army. Accompanied by thirty-two kings with their horses and chariots, he went up and besieged Samaria and attacked it. Meanwhile a prophet came to Ahab king of Israel and announced, 'This is what the Lord says: "Do you see this vast army? I will give it into your hand today, and then you will know that I am the Lord."' Afterward, the prophet came to the king of Israel and said, 'Strengthen your position and see what must be done, because next spring the king of Aram will attack you again.' The next spring Ben-Hadad mustered the Arameans and went up to Aphek to fight against Israel. The man of God came up and told the king of Israel, 'This is what the Lord says: "Because the Arameans think the Lord is a god of the hills and not a god of the valleys, I will deliver this vast army into your hands, and you will know that I am the Lord"'" (1 Kings 20:1, 13, 22, 26, 28).

If you're the only Christian on the football team, or the only person who comes faithfully to youth group meetings at your church, or the only person at work who refused the invitation to a wild party last weekend, you're probably ripe for the "They're-out-to-get-me" mentality. But before you fall for it, memorize this verse: "When a man's ways are pleasing to the Lord, he makes even his enemies live at peace with him" (Prov. 16:7).

Elijah saw the principle of that verse in action as God went to great lengths to provide him with some peace and quiet. God protected him from Jezebel; He sent the whole Syrian army to keep Ahab occupied; He even made Ahab want to hear Elijah's student prophets prophesy about upcoming battles. All these were miracles. But Elijah would never have seen miracles without first obeying God in the midst of crises.

If you consider yourself Miss Persecuted and Picked-On Christian, ask God what you are doing that doesn't please Him. If your attitude toward your "enemies" is, "I'm better than you because I don't do dreadful, dirty, disgusting deeds," no wonder they don't respect you. Perhaps you're guilty of legalism—avoiding or denouncing things only because of tradition or your ungodly attitudes, not because of what the Bible or Holy Spirit has said. Perhaps it is hardness of heart, a self-centered unwillingness to care for other people. Perhaps you're touchy, easily offended, expecting others to be as understanding as God. Whatever your personality defect, if you ask God He will point it out and remake you so people will respect you.

But if you're looking for instant respect and peace, beware. God did not say, "If your life pleases me, your enemies will be at peace with you *today*." His promise has no time limit. For instance, Paul was an enemy of godly Stephen, even wholeheartedly approving stoning him, but he did not make peace with Stephen until long after Stephen's death. Instead of assuming your Christian testimony is causing people to hate you, ask God if your life pleases Him, and be willing to change. Then when your heart is pure, pray for your enemy until God changes his heart. This kind of attitude may be one of the most important items in the survival kit for the lonely, outnumbered Christian.

"The Lord was with Jehoshaphat because in his early years he walked in the ways his father David had followed. He did not consult the Baals but sought the God of his father and followed his commands rather than the practices of Israel. The Lord established the kingdom under his control; and all Judah brought gifts to Jehoshaphat, so that he had great wealth and honor. His heart was devoted to the ways of the Lord; furthermore, he removed the high places and the Asherah poles from Judah. In the third year of his reign he sent his officials Ben-Hail, Obadiah, Zechariah, Nethanel and Micaiah to teach in the towns of Judah. They taught throughout Judah, taking with them the Book of the Law of the Lord; they went around to all the towns of Judah and taught the people. The fear of the Lord fell on all the kingdoms of the lands surrounding Judah, so that they did not make war with Jehoshaphat. Some Philistines brought Jehoshaphat gifts and silver as tribute, and the Arabs brought him flocks . . ." (2 Chron. 17:3–7, 9–11).

1. List the things Jehoshaphat did which pleased the Lord. Mark with a check which ones you also do (be honest).
2. Jehoshaphat made certain everyone in his country was taught God's laws. Do you plead ignorance as an excuse for your disobedience, or do you diligently search God's Word for guidance and answers?
3. Have you ever used the persecuted Christian excuse to avoid dealing with your faults and sins?
4. Make a list of your enemies. Now, as you pray for them, what attitudes and actions should you take toward them?

Week Ten

JONAH: DOING GOD'S WILL THE HARD WAY

Introduction

Trying to Run Away from God

Maybe you think you're young only once, so you should live it up a little. After all, there'll be plenty of time to do God's will later. You may reason that if you go your own way for a while, you'll get the rebellion out of your system and you'll be more steady to serve God. All of this is a lie—straight from the devil. If you're tempted to believe it, you need to take a look at a man who tried this philosophy: Jonah, the son of Amittai.

The Bible makes it clear that Jonah was a real person, thus undermining the argument that the book of Jonah is only fiction with a nice moral lesson. First, he was recognized as a real prophet. 2 Kings 14:25 says he predicted the former boundaries of Israel would be restored. (Jonah was not a common name in Old Testament times, so no one can reasonably argue that Jonah the son of Amittai mentioned in 2 Kings was another person.)

Second, Jonah was from a real place. He came from Gath Hepher, which is the modern village of el Meshed, about five miles from Nazareth.

Third, Jesus twice told His listeners to consider the sign of Jonah (Matt. 12:39–41; 16:4), and predicted, "For as Jonah was three days and three nights in the belly of a huge fish, so the Son of Man will be three days and three nights in the heart of the earth" (Matt. 12:40). Those who question the accuracy of the account of Jonah reject not only the integrity of the Old Testament, but the integrity of Jesus Christ as well!

God called Jonah to go to Nineveh to warn the people their city would be destroyed if they did not stop their wickedness. Jonah knew, however, that God would not destroy Nineveh if the people repented. But Jonah hated Nineveh and wanted the city destroyed—for good reason. Assyria, with its capital at Nineveh, was the superpower of the world, constantly conquering more territory; and "at this time the Assyrians were making forays down into the northern kingdom of Israel."[1] They would make surprise attacks on cities. After taking the women captive, they would kill all the men and children. So it's possible the Assyrians had murdered people Jonah knew personally. Modern historians rank the Assyrians

---

[1]J. Vernon McGee, *Jonah & Micah*. Pasadena: Through the Bible Books, 1982, p. 30.

among the cruelest oppressors of all times. Jonah felt justified in refusing to go to Nineveh.

Jonah hurried to Joppa, the nearest seaport, and boarded a ship headed for Tarshish, a city on the southern coast of Spain—as far away from Nineveh as he could travel. He couldn't, however, escape from God.

A huge storm came up and terrorized the men on the ship, so each began praying to his god. Jonah, however, was sleeping. The captain woke him and asked him to pray to his God as well. Then they cast lots (something like our throwing dice) to see who had caused the great disaster, and the lot fell on Jonah. As they quizzed him, Jonah admitted he was running away from the God who made heaven and earth. So the men asked Jonah what to do. He suggested they throw him overboard.

How Can a Man Live Inside a Fish?

The Bible says, "And the Lord appointed a great fish to swallow up Jonah; and Jonah was in the belly of the fish three days and three nights. And the Lord spoke to the fish, and it vomited out Jonah upon the dry land" (Jon. 1:17; 2:10). Many skeptics, of course, assert this never happened, that miracles are impossible. But if you know God and have seen Him change lives, you'll have no problem believing this "whale of a tale."

There are several ways of approaching the "Jonah in the whale" mystery. It is possible that God created a special fish (the Bible says fish, not whale) with custom features to keep Jonah safe for three days and three nights. And some recognized Bible scholars think Jonah died inside the whale, and was then raised from the dead to provide a picture of the resurrection of Jesus. Or it may be that Jonah simply survived in the belly of a whale.

There is strong evidence that Jonah could remain intact inside a whale. One writer reports that "entire sharks and seals have been found in the bellies of both sperm and killer whales."[2] In 1941, Eugene Maximillian Karl Geiling, a Chicago pharmacology professor, crawled through the gullet of a dead whale to prove it could be done. He noted, "It was a pretty slimy trip, but there was plenty of room."[3] These accounts don't prove a man could live within a whale for three days, but they do show he could fit.

There are quite a few old yarns about whalers swallowed by their prey, and even a few about men living through the ordeal. According to writer David Gunston, however, "In a long and close study of the subject I have discovered only one instance completely corroborated by reliable authorities, and its details are so remarkable that it is worth recounting." The victim was David Bartly.

In February, 1891, Bartly was aboard the *Star of the East*, an English

---

[2]Christopher Hallowell, "Research Report," *The Dial*, Dec. 1982, p. 15.

[3]Hy Gardner, "Glad You Asked About That," *The Star News*, Washington, D.C., January 10, 1974.

whaling ship searching near the Falkland Islands for oil-rich sperm whales about 60-70 ft. long. Upon spotting a whale, the crew gave chase in two small boats. One harpooner speared the whale in the side, and during the ensuing struggle, the other boat overturned. One man drowned, and a later check revealed that Bartly was missing.

After killing the whale, crewmen secured it to the side of their ship and began to cut the huge creature apart. The next morning as they prepared to cut open the stomach, it moved! Mystified, they opened it and found fellow-crewmember, David Bartly, "doubled up, drenched, but still alive though deeply unconscious." His face and hands had been bleached white by the whale's gastric juices. The men soaked him with sea water and put him to bed in the captain's cabin. At first delirious, within three weeks Bartly recovered. When recounting the experience, Bartly said breathing was no problem, but he found his "prison" terribly hot. (The body temperature of a whale is 104 degrees F.) Bartly continued his life as a sailor and apparently avoided publicity. [4]

David Bartly's experience has been authenticated by fellow crew members and investigated by others. Both the captain and another officer of *Star of the East* issued separate and detailed accounts of the incident. Later, the story was investigated by M. de Parville, a respected scholar who was scientific editor of the *Paris Journal des Debats*, and Sir Francis Fox, an esteemed British civil engineer; both scrutinized the details of the incident and concluded the story was accurate.

David Bartly's ordeal doesn't prove a man could live three days and three nights inside a whale without miraculous intervention. After all, Bartly was not inside the whale as long as Jonah was, and Bartly's whale was dead part of that time. Nonetheless, the incident should squelch people who categorize the account of Jonah and the whale with *Gulliver's Travels* and Little Red Riding Hood.

Having learned his lesson, Jonah went straight to Nineveh and found himself facing a huge task. Although the actual walled city (unearthed by modern archaeologists) was only about 2.5 miles long and 1.3 miles wide, it was surrounded by several large cities equivalent to today's suburbs. Experts estimate the area's population at several million. Jonah, therefore, had a large area to cover and a large audience to reach. [5] With God's help the message reached the people and they repented from their sins. Jonah should have been delighted with his success, but he wasn't.

After preaching to this metropolis, Jonah erected a small shelter and camped in it, waiting to see Nineveh destroyed. God even provided a vine to give shade from the hot sun, and to get Jonah's attention. But a worm chewed the stem and killed the vine. This made Jonah angry. He didn't hear God saying, "How can you be mad because a plant died, yet not

[4] David Gunston, "The Man Who Lived Inside a Whale and His Name Was Not Jonah," *Compass,* Spring, 1972, pp. 10, 11.
[5] J. Vernon McGee, *Jonah & Micah.* Pasadena: Through the Bible Books, 1982, pp. 56–59.

care at all about the people of Nineveh—including 120,000 children?" God wanted Jonah to see things from His perspective.

The Bible doesn't say if Jonah learned his lesson. In a sense, that doesn't matter, because the most important question is: Have *you* learned *your* lesson? Have you learned to do exactly what God says? To see things from His point of view? You probably have a ways to go in that department. And if you do, you can learn from Jonah.

God Always Means What He Says

"The word of the Lord came to Jonah son of Amittai: 'Go to the great city of Nineveh and preach against it, because its wickedness has come up before me.' But Jonah ran away from the Lord and headed for Tarshish. He went down to Joppa, where he found a ship bound for that port. After paying the fare, he went aboard and sailed for Tarshish to flee from the Lord" (Jon. 1:1–3).

"I'm praying about whether or not to steal the money."

"I'm seeking God's will about marrying a non-Christian."

"God wouldn't let me fall in love with Harry if it weren't His will for me to date him."

"I got the last ticket available for the heavy metal concert so I know it's God's will that I attend."

"My friend lent me the money to run away from home so I'm certain I'm doing to the right thing."

Wait a minute! Something is radically wrong with these statements. What is it?

Jonah may have used the same kind of reasoning to duck out of God's command to go to Nineveh and warn the people. Jonah had good reasons for not wanting to go there. The Assyrians were the cruelest people in the Middle East, and Nineveh was their capital. They skinned people alive. They buried men up to their necks in the hot desert sand, put holes in their tongues, and let them bake to death. They used men's heads as decorations for their garden parties. They had made raids into Israel, so they may have killed friends or relatives of Jonah. He had some very good excuses.

But quality of excuses wasn't the point. God had told Jonah to go. Period. Jonah wasn't supposed to say, "How unpatriotic to help Israel's enemies. Besides, no other prophet has ever been asked to do such a thing. And God should punish the Ninevites for being so cruel. It must not be God's will that I go. Oh, wow! I just heard there are no tickets for Nineveh until next month, but the last ticket for Tarshish is available. Now I know I'm not supposed to go to Nineveh." Does this kind of reasoning sound silly? Of course. When God told Jonah to head for Nineveh, that was God's will.

Sometimes your reasoning is just as ridiculous. You must, therefore, learn to take God's word at face value. God says, "Do not repay anyone evil for evil. Be careful to do what is right in the eyes of everybody" (Rom. 12:17), live with high standards. So if a voice tells you to do a little cheating or shoplifting, assume you're hearing the devil. When God says, "Do not be yoked together with unbelievers" (2 Cor. 6:14), consider the issue settled. It is not God's will that you marry a non-Christian. A desire is not necessarily a sign of God's will, for "each one is tempted when, by his own evil desire, he is dragged away and enticed" (James 1:14). Neither is an ideal circumstance a sign of God's will.

You understand the importance of obeying instructions. If your mom asks you to buy two loaves of bread at the store, you don't spend two hours trying to decide what your mother's will is. You buy two loaves of bread. If the store is out of bread, you don't conclude that your mother actually wants chocolate cake. Or if you're hungry for corn chips, you don't spend the money on a bag of Fritos.

Just as your mother clearly states her instructions, God clearly states His will in His Word; no amount of rationalizing about circumstances or desires will alter what God says in His Word. God means what He says—every time.

Once you get used to obeying God precisely, you'll develop an instinctive "feel" for God's will. It's a natural result of listening. If you've carefully listened to your mother, you can buy a gift that probably will please her—even if she has never said she'd like that item. A similar thing happens when you've carefully listened to God. By regularly studying God's Word, and asking the Holy Spirit to show you verses you need and to show you how to apply them to your life, you'll soon know God very well. So well, in fact, that sometimes you'll sense in your spirit what He wants, without even looking for a verse, because you'll be hearing His voice. Nothing is as important in finding God's will as the words He himself has spoken.

" 'What do you think? There was a man who had two sons. He went to the first and said, "Son, go and work today in the vineyard." "I will not," he answered, but later he changed his mind and went. Then the father went to the other son and said the same thing. He answered, "I will, sir," but he did not go. Which of the two did what his father wanted?' 'The first,' they answered" (Matt. 21:28–31).

1. What is more important, piously talking about doing God's will or obeying His Word?
2. According to Jesus, what does doing God's will actually mean?
3. Do you glibly talk about doing God's will without ever thinking about His Word?
4. When you must make a decision, do you *first* go to the Word of God or do you just do a lot of talking?

Whaling and Wailing

"But Jonah ran away from the Lord and headed for Tarshish. He went down to Joppa, where he found a ship bound for that port. After paying the fare, he went aboard and sailed for Tarshish to flee from the Lord. Then they took Jonah and threw him overboard, and the raging sea grew calm. But the Lord provided a great fish to swallow Jonah, and Jonah was inside the fish three days and three nights" (Jon. 1:3, 15, 17).

If Jonah had relied on circumstances and opinion polls to show him God's will, all of them would have indicated he should not go to Nineveh. (1) It was a long, hard trip. (2) The Assyrians of Nineveh were enemies of Israel. (3) The Assyrians were so cruel that everyone else in the world thought the destruction of Nineveh was a good idea. (4) None of Jonah's friends would have encouraged him to go. But God doesn't pay attention to such statistics.

If you wander through the maze of circumstances, looking for God's will without heeding the Bible and the voice of the Holy Spirit, you'll become a practicing atheist. Your attitude will be: If it looks easy, if everything works out, and if it's what I want, I'll go for it. God's Word says, however, you must "live by faith, not by sight" (2 Cor. 5:7).

Biblical examples of people receiving guidance show that often the circumstances fell in line after the person began following God's directions. The circumstances before Moses crossed the Red Sea, before Joshua conquered Jericho, and before David killed Goliath were terrible. But these men knew God well enough to discover His will from His Word and the voice of His Holy Spirit within.

If you're like most people, you probably tend to live as a pagan but piously stick God's name into conversations about guidance: "The sun is shining today so it must be God's will for us to go on a picnic"; "Tom invited me to the game so it must be God's will that I skip the algebra assignment"; "I lost the money I was going to give in the offering so God must not want me to give anything to the church this week." Such thinking is devoid of faith and renders to every breeze of fate rather than trusting God for guidance. Circumstances play only a small role in discovering God's will.

Some issues of God's will are cut and dried, because God has provided specific scripture on the topic. For example, you don't have to sit around wondering if you should love your enemies; the Scriptures say you must, so you obey—regardless of the circumstances. Other issues, though, are not as clear, so you need guidance from the Scriptures and from the Holy Spirit. These issues include decisions such as what subjects to take, whether or not to buy a motorcycle, which college to attend, what career to pursue, and where to live. And there are some issues which God may leave completely to your discretion, such as what color shirt to buy, what to eat for lunch, or which football team you cheer for. In every decision, however, you must be sensitive to the Holy Spirit.

Norman Grubb, a famous missionary leader, gives some useful guidelines for decision-making. First, you should not expect an audible voice because God almost always speaks to a person by making an impression on his heart. He says, ". . . guidance is the direct communication of the Spirit with our spirits." The Holy Spirit will apply a certain Bible verse to your situation or give you inner assurance that a certain course of action is correct. To receive such revelation from the Holy Spirit you must be willing to obey (no matter what); then you must use your mind in the right way—not to make the final decision, but to gather information. Grubb claims the mind's "function is to investigate, tabulate, theorize, memorize, but not to direct." You are responsible to examine your situation, gather facts, and study relevant scripture.

Next, you should deliberately stop thinking about the situation and trust God, believing that you, as God's servant, have a right to know what He wants you to do. With such an attitude you'll be free from worry and a sense of urgency. With such peace in yourself, you'll be able to hear the Holy Spirit. He will show you if a circumstance makes certain actions necessary or if a particular scripture clarifies God's will in your situation. However, it is always the Holy Spirit, not your outward circumstances, that determines God's will for us.[6]

Jonah knew God's will, but he didn't want to obey God. He rushed into action based solely on his view of the circumstances. He did not listen to God's clear guidance, so Jonah's stubbornness and resulting ignorance led to his experience of whaling and wailing! Willingness to obey, waiting for the voice of the Holy Spirit, and expecting God to show you His way will save you from a Jonah and the whale experience.

"I will instruct you and teach you in the way you should go; I will counsel you and watch over you. Do not be like the horse or the mule, which have no understanding but must be controlled by bit and bridle or they will not come to you. Many are the woes of the wicked, but the Lord's unfailing love surrounds the man who trusts in him" (Ps. 32:8–10).

"The Lord is my shepherd, I shall lack nothing. He makes me lie down in green pastures, he leads me beside quiet waters, he restores my soul. He guides me in paths of righteousness for his name's sake" (Ps. 23:1–3).

1. What promises do you have that God will guide you? Do you believe them and claim them or do you run around saying, "I just don't know which way to turn"?
2. What kind of attitude keeps God's instructions to you from sinking in?
3. In what kinds of paths does God lead you? In light of this fact, what can keep you from finding the right road?

---

[6]Norman Grubb, *Touching the Invisible*. Fort Washington, Pa.: CLC, 1960, pp. 22–25.

4. What is the promise for those who trust God? Are you trusting God to show you His will?

Choose the Easy Way and Enjoy the Trip

"Then the Lord sent a great wind on the sea, and such a violent storm arose that the ship threatened to break up. Then the sailors said to each other, 'Come, let us cast lots to find out who is responsible for this calamity.' They cast lots and the lot fell on Jonah. 'Pick me up and throw me into the sea,' he replied, 'and it will become calm. I know that it is my fault that this great storm has come upon you.' But the Lord provided a great fish to swallow Jonah, and Jonah was inside the fish three days and three nights" (Jon. 1:4, 7, 12, 17).

What's the most frightening experience you can think of? Nuclear

"All sorts of disasters can come from being out of God's will!"

war? Cancer? Losing your parents? Realizing you're married to the wrong person? It may surprise you to find out that there is a right answer to that question. The most frightening experience a person can have is being out of the will of God.

All sorts of disasters can come from being out of God's will. Take Jonah, for example. Because he didn't want to preach in Nineveh, he tried to run away from God, and the ship he was on encountered a dreadful storm. When the captain finally woke him, he saw the terror-stricken faces of the other men on board. How ashamed he must have felt when he realized that he was causing innocent people to suffer! But he felt even worse when he had to admit his guilt and be thrown overboard. Imagine sliding down the esophagus of a huge fish. He could do without such high adventure! Jonah found that being out of God's will was worse than any nightmare.

Don't think that you're different, that you can run away from God without suffering any consequences. God made it very clear to the Israelites that His people reap exactly what they sow: "All these blessings will come upon you and accompany you if you obey the Lord your God" (Deut. 28:2), and the list of blessings is a long one. On the other hand: "However, if you do not obey the Lord your God and do not carefully follow all his commands and decrees I am giving you today, all these curses will come upon you and overtake you" (Deut. 28:15), and the list of curses is longer than the list of blessings.

The consequences of obedience or disobedience are part of a spiritual principle Jesus illustrated this way: "Therefore everyone who hears these words of mine and puts them into practice is like a wise man who built his house on the rock" (Matt. 7:24). Even amidst violent storms the house stood firm. But Jesus continued, "But everyone who hears these words of mine and does not put them into practice is like a foolish man who built his house on sand" (Matt. 7:26). This house on the sand, of course, was ruined by the rains and the floods. Why? Because when you are out of God's will, when you are not obeying all His commands and practicing all His teachings, you lay yourself open to all kinds of trouble.

Following God does not assure you a problem-free life; Jesus said both houses would go through storms. After all, the greatness of the storm on the outside does not cause disaster; but if the storm gets inside of you, then you've got trouble. This is why the same troubles can be a blessing for one person and a curse for another. For example, if a man with a gun holds up two people in a subway, one may pray in faith and trust God so his fear disappears, and thus have a blessed experience to remind him of God's faithfulness. The other person, however, with no power except his own, may become so traumatized that he will be afraid to go out alone for the rest of his life.

If Jonah had obeyed God in the first place, his trip to Nineveh would have been much less eventful—and much less painful! He could have chosen the easy way and enjoyed the trip. You can avoid making the same mistake.

"The eyes of the Lord are on the righteous and his ears are attentive to their cry; the face of the Lord is against those who do evil, to cut off the memory of them from the earth. The righteous cry out, and the Lord hears them; he delivers them from all their troubles. A righteous man may have many troubles, but the Lord delivers him from them all . . ." (Ps. 34:15–17, 19).

"Who is going to harm you if you are eager to do good?" (1 Pet. 3:13).

"But the eyes of the Lord are on those who fear him, on those whose hope is in his unfailing love" (Ps. 33:18).

1. What promises of protection do those who follow God's will have?
2. What have those who do evil brought upon themselves?
3. Rather than offering the person who follows God a problem-free life, what does God promise him?
4. Is being in God's will more important to you than anything else? What are some reasons for making God's will the most important thing in your life?

Spread the Blessings Around

"Then the sailors said to each other, 'Come, let us cast lots to find out who is responsible for this calamity.' They cast lots and the lot fell on Jonah. This terrified them and they asked, 'What have you done?' (They knew he was running away from the Lord, because he had already told them so.) The sea was getting rougher and rougher. So they asked him, 'What should we do to you to make the sea calm down for us?' 'Pick me up and throw me into the sea,' he replied, 'and it will become calm. I know that it is my fault that this great storm has come upon you'" (Jon. 1:7, 10-12).

You've heard it. Maybe you've even said it: "It's my life and I can do what I want." It sounds logical. But is it true?

The Bible says, "For none of us lives to himself alone and none of us dies to himself alone" (Rom. 14:7). Whatever you say or do affects many other people. Your choice to do God's will or to act on your feelings will help or hurt those around you much more than you realize.

Jonah's disobedience harmed many people. The storm God used to bring runaway Jonah to his senses affected everyone on the ship—everyone faced the fear of drowning and the fear of having to throw Jonah overboard. Jonah's "detour" affected the people of Nineveh; because they had to wait longer to hear that repentance was possible and no doubt some died during the delay. And, of course, Jonah's slow obedience affected those who followed his example as a prophet of God. They may have decided, "If a prophet can run away from God, it's okay for me to disobey once in a while too."

You're no different than Jonah; your example is important to many people. (I still remember my feelings when a lady told me her nine-year-old daughter idolized me. I was completely taken by surprise. I had been unaware of how important my example was to that little girl.) You will never know how many people are being affected by your life. The way you live is noticed by your family, your friends, your teachers, your fellow-workers, your neighbors, and even casual acquaintances. But don't get burdened with the awesomeness of the responsibility, or get a guilt complex for not doing better. You don't need to paste on an artificial smile and take acting lessons so everyone will think you're a model Christian.

God does the perfecting work in you. The Bible assures that "if anyone is in Christ, he is a new creation; the old has gone, the new has come!" (2 Cor. 5:17). You must believe and act on this fact. God's new creations aren't inferior products. He stands by to give you the strength, the righteousness, the joy—everything you need to be what He wants you to be. Any self-consciousness comes from the devil who whispers, "Oh, dear, everyone's watching you. You'll probably fail and blow your testimony."

God wants you to see life as a wonderful challenge rather than as a threat. What a privilege to be a positive example of God's new creations, demonstrating that Jesus lives inside you. Knowing this, you can relax and let the Jesus inside you shine out for all to see. You can say with the Apostle Paul, "Christ lives in me" (Gal. 2:20), and Christ only wants to do God's will. And that's just what He will do if you don't stand in His way with unbelief or stubbornness. By living in God's will you'll enjoy great blessings—with plenty left over to spread around to others!

"Brothers loved by God, we know that he has chosen you, because our gospel came to you not simply with words, but also with power, with the Holy Spirit and with deep conviction. You know how we lived among you for your sake. You became imitators of us and of the Lord; in spite of severe suffering, you welcomed the message with the joy given by the Holy Spirit. And so you became a model to all the believers in Macedonia and Achaia. The Lord's message rang out from you not only in Macedonia and Achaia— your faith in God has become known everywhere. Therefore we do not need to say anything about it, for they themselves report what kind of reception you gave us. They tell how you turned to God from idols to serve the living and true God" (1 Thess. 1:4–9).

1. How do you know that Paul, who wrote the above letter to the Thessalonians, was letting Jesus inside him shine out to others?
2. How do you know that the Thessalonians, even though they were new Christians, were letting Jesus inside them spread to their neighbors?
3. What kind of things automatically happen when Jesus is allowed to live His life through a Christian?
4. Have you believed the devil's line that you must live the Christian life in your own strength and that it's a terrible burden? Decide not to believe this lie.

The God of the Second Chance

"From inside the fish Jonah prayed to the Lord his God. He said: 'In my distress I called to the Lord, and he answered me. From the depths of the grave I called for help, and you listened to my cry. Those who cling to worthless idols forfeit the grace that could be theirs. But I, with a song of thanksgiving, will sacrifice to you. What I have vowed I will make good. Salvation comes from the Lord.' And the Lord commanded the fish, and it vomited Jonah onto dry land" (Jon. 2:1, 2, 8–10).

As you're reading about God's will, your heart may be aching—you know you're out of God's will. Perhaps you're depending on drugs or alcohol to help you forget your problems; or you're involved in a dating relationship which has gotten out of control; or you've gotten into a habit of cheating, or shoplifting, or stealing little things from your employer. Perhaps you've become chained by laziness, procrastination, and lack of self-discipline, and are unable to do what you should. Perhaps you feel hopelessly out of God's will as the devil whispers, "It's no use, give up." If this is your predicament, the story of Jonah will be good news. It will give you hope.

No matter how bad you feel, Jonah felt even worse as he entered the mouth of the great fish. After all, he was a prophet and he should have known better than to run away from God. What a terrible testimony he had been to the men on the ship! As the fish gulped him down, Jonah didn't realize the storm had stopped, so he probably was feeling responsible for the certain deaths of the innocent men on the ship. He saw no possibility of making amends. But in this tough situation he repented and promised to go to Nineveh. He said, "What I have vowed [promised] I will make good." And God performed a complete miracle to give Jonah a second chance.

You, too, can know the God of the second chance. No matter what you've done, you can repent and get back into God's will. The only catch is that you have to go to Nineveh—stop taking drugs, or break off the relationship, or pay back the money you stole. That is real repentance.

When you repent you turn around. You have to retrace your steps. So where did you get off the track in the first place? What were you unwilling to do? God won't make any deals. He expects obedience on the very issue that kept you from God's will in the first place. Jonah had to go to Nineveh. You must go to your Nineveh. There is no other way to get right with God.

Don't wait as long as Jonah did to return to God. Don't ignore that uneasy feeling of guilt. Don't decide you'll keep sinning just a little longer. Don't buy a ticket to Tarshish. Don't get your conscience so hardened you can sleep soundly even if you're disobeying God. Don't become so insensitive that only a big shock will bring you around—three days in a whale's stomach is not a pleasant experience. Ask anyone who has persisted in disobeying God and he will tell you: It would have been a lot easier to obey God's will in the first place. If you are out of God's will, take the second chance that God offers. And take it now.

"Seek the Lord while he may be found; call on him while he is near. Let the wicked forsake his way and the evil man his thoughts. Let him turn to the Lord, and he will have mercy on him, and to our God, for he will freely pardon" (Isa. 55:6, 7).

"Therefore, O house of Israel, I will judge you, each one according to his ways, declares the Sovereign Lord. Repent! Turn away from all your offenses; then sin will not be your downfall. Rid yourselves of all the offenses you have committed, and get a new heart and a new spirit. Why will you die, O house of Israel? For I take no pleasure in the death of anyone, declares the Sovereign Lord. Repent and live!" (Ezek. 18:30–32).

1. What does God promise to those who repent, change their ways, and get back into the will of God?
2. What are the dangers of continuing in sin?
3. Ask God to search your heart. If you are out of His will, get right with God and get back on the track.
4. Thank God that He will give you all the strength and grace you need to walk in the right way.

The Supply Is Unlimited—Just Help Yourself

"Jonah obeyed the word of the Lord and went to Nineveh. Now Nineveh was a very large city; it took three days to go all through it. Jonah started into the city, going a day's journey, and he proclaimed: 'Forty more days and Nineveh will be destroyed.' The Ninevites believed God. They declared a fast, and all of them, from the greatest to the least, put on sackcloth. When God saw what they did and how they turned from their evil ways, he had compassion and did not bring upon them the destruction he had threatened" (Jon. 3:3–5, 10).

Do you ever think God asks the unreasonable? Do you wonder how a missionary can live with a jungle tribe in unsanitary conditions, endure ridicule for language mistakes, and eat monkey meat and toasted beetle grubs, yet survive without TV, pizza, and ski trips—just so the jungle dwellers can hear about Jesus? Do you ask how it could ever be God's will to give up a cherished dream to play in the big leagues or to sing professionally, in order to serve the Lord? Do you fear that God's will is something too hard for you to do?

Jonah certainly could have used that argument. Going to Nineveh must have seemed impossible. First of all, it was over five hundred miles away—straight across the desert, but much farther by common trade routes. The trip would be long and lonely. Second, the city proper was fortified with tall, thick walls and well-guarded gates, so Jonah couldn't be sure of entering even after traveling all that way. Third, as you've already read, the people of Nineveh were famous for cruelty. Certainly some foreigner prophesying the destruction of their city would be a prime candidate for torture and death. Fourth, if he did get to preach, why would these idol worshipers pay attention to anything the God of Israel had to say? Jonah probably thought God was asking too much of him.

Interestingly, once Jonah decided to obey, he was able to travel to Nineveh. He got inside the city and preached, and the people listened and repented! Nothing similar had happened when Jonah preached in Israel. This was a miracle.

If you think God's will is too difficult and you like Jonah have disobeyed, take heart. The power to carry out God's wishes is available if you decide to obey.

True obedience, however, comes from a heart of faith and love—not merely from a sense of obligation. You can obey either from fear or from faith! If you obey God because "God is a big meany, but I'd better do what He says anyway," you aren't in a position to receive the grace and power God has to give. You are believing a lie. On the other hand, if you obey in faith, knowing that what God asks of you is best for you and that He will give you the strength you need to carry out His instructions, doing God's will will not be a struggle, but a joy. The task that appeared hard will become a challenge, an adventure with God; you will expect miracles and a new depth of relationship with Him.

If you act in faith, you can break up with your non-Christian boyfriend or girlfriend, and God will fill your emotional needs in His way. If you act in faith, you can take a stand for Jesus in Social Problems class, and God will give supernatural courage and the right words to say. If you act in faith, you can obey your alcoholic father, and God will work in his heart—and yours—to heal your shattered relationship.

When you go out on a limb to obey God, you'll be in very good company. By faith, Abraham left Ur, Moses crossed the Red Sea, Joshua conquered Jericho, and David faced Goliath. Take the risk to join them—God has not changed.

Pray this way: "Lord, I'm willing to obey, but I have to depend on you for every ounce of wisdom and strength." Receive it from Him, and help yourself to God's never-ending supply of courage, grace, peace, wisdom, and strength.

"This is love for God: to obey his commands. And his commands are not burdensome, for everyone born of God has overcome the world. This is the victory that has overcome the world, even our faith" (1 John 5:3, 4).

"With my lips I recount all the laws that come from your mouth. I rejoice

in following your statutes as one rejoices in great riches. I meditate on your precepts and consider your ways. I delight in your decrees; I will not neglect your word" (Ps. 119:13–16).

"Open my eyes that I may see wonderful things in your law" (Ps. 119:18).

"Direct me in the path of your commands, for there I find delight. Turn my heart toward your statutes and not toward selfish gain. Turn my eyes away from worthless things; renew my life according to your word" (Ps. 119:35, 37).

1. What makes people think God's commandments are too strict and too difficult to obey?
2. Why should you rejoice in whatever God commands you to do?
3. Pray with the Psalmist that God will show you how wonderful obeying all of God's commands can be.
4. Are you afraid that God's will is too difficult for you? Talk this over with God.

Seeing Eye to Eye with God

"Jonah went out and sat down at a place east of the city. There he made himself a shelter, sat in its shade and waited to see what would happen to the city. Then the Lord God provided a vine and made it grow up over Jonah to give shade for his head to ease his discomfort, and Jonah was very happy about the vine. But at dawn the next day God provided a worm, which chewed the vine so that it withered. When the sun rose, God provided a scorching east wind, and the sun blazed on Jonah's head so that he grew faint. He wanted to die, and said, 'It would be better for me to die than to live.' But God said to Jonah, 'Do you have a right to be angry about the vine?' 'I do,' he said. 'I am angry enough to die.' But the Lord said, 'You have been concerned about this vine, though you did not tend it or make it grow. It sprang up overnight and died overnight. But Nineveh has more than a hundred and twenty thousand people who cannot tell their right hand from their left . . ." (Jon. 4: 5–11).

It's probably happened to you—a painful quarrel with someone you love because you didn't understand his or her priorities. On Saturday your father arrives to pick you up at the shopping center exactly at 11:30 a.m. as he had promised, but you are fifteen minutes late. As you climb into the car, you apologize as best you can for being late, then explain, "At five to eleven I discovered a sale on sweaters. They had my size—and even the colors I wanted! What a fantastic bargain!" Then you remember, "Oh, and Dad, I bought a bag of peanuts for you."

Instead of flashing his usual broad grin at your generosity, your father merely mutters something.

Then you exclaim, "Dad, we're only a block from Jennifer's house!

May we stop there? She promised me the biology notes from the two days I missed last week, and Monday's test will be a biggie. Please. It'll only be a minute."

Now your father explodes, "Can't you ever think of anyone except yourself?" Stunned, you wonder what you did wrong.

You had forgotten your father has a crucial business deal pending, and that he needed to reach the post office by noon, before it closed, to mail several important business letters. Now, because of your lateness and heavy traffic, he won't get those letters mailed. Your father's priorities are very different from yours. As you can see, it's important to understand what others consider important.

How can you discover what's important to another person? Start by listening very carefully to everything he says. Spend so much time with him that you can automatically sense what are his priorities. As you learn to love him more and more, you'll be willing to sacrifice your priorities for his.

You learn what is important to God by the same method. Much of doing God's will depends on getting to know Him so well that you automatically know how He thinks, and growing to love Him so much that for His sake you'll willingly sacrifice anything you want because God's priorities will be yours.

Jonah didn't share God's priorities. Why? Pay close attention so you don't allow yourself to commit the same errors. First, Jonah was caught up in running his own life, going where he wanted to go. Only a whack on the head, a personal tragedy, or a terrible storm and a tour of a whale's digestive tract could make him consider going where God wanted him to go.

Second, Jonah was prejudiced. He didn't like pagans. He thought the Ninevites were mean, cruel, and terrible (and some, of course, were). He didn't view them as equals, people created by God. He wouldn't let God give him love for the people of Nineveh. When Jonah did preach to them, he was disappointed that God didn't destroy their city. He didn't recognize God's purpose in the lives of others.

Third, Jonah had mixed-up priorities. He placed great importance on little things such as the plant that provided his shade. Therefore, when a worm destroyed the plant, he was angry. God explained to him that the people of Nineveh were much more important to Him than some plant. God was trying to give Jonah His eternal point of view. Sadly, the Bible doesn't say Jonah changed his attitude.

You're probably thinking Jonah was being very selfish and hardhearted, like a spoiled brat. But if you double-check the list, more than likely you'll find you're not very different than Jonah. Ask yourself these questions:

Am I too busy running my own life to find out what God wants me to do?

Do I hide a list of "I won'ts" some place deep in my heart?

Are there little comforts and joys in my life which I place above the will of God?

If you answered yes to any of these questions, you must take action. You must rid yourself of the things that keep you from seeing eye to eye with God, that keep you from sharing His priorities. Learn to let God's will become your will.

" 'My food,' said Jesus, 'is to do the will of him who sent me and to finish his work' " (John 4:34).

"For I have come down from heaven not to do my will but to do the will of him who sent me" (John 6:38).

"I eagerly expect and hope that I will in no way be ashamed, but will have sufficient courage so that now as always Christ will be exalted in my body, whether by life or by death. For to me, to live is Christ and to die is gain" (Phil. 1:20, 21).

1. Honestly fill in the blank: "For me to live is _____."
2. What should you start doing so you can begin to think as God thinks, and so His will is your top priority?
3. Tell God that you want to get to know Him better. Then study His Word and learn what His will is; surrender your "I won'ts" to God; decide you want to become the person who can say, "For me to live is Christ."

Week Eleven

JEREMIAH: HOW TO FACE THE END OF THE WORLD

Introduction

Do thoughts of the mushroom cloud, a real Star Wars disaster, or a worldwide financial crisis frighten you? Do you think you were born in the wrong generation, and thus resent having to think about the world blowing up at any moment? Do you feel uncertain about growing up in a world stockpiled with nuclear weapons, bulging from overpopulation, and queasing from unprecedented pollution—greater problems than those seen by any other generation? You need to meet Jeremiah. He can help you, because he lived through tough times that his parents and grandparents knew nothing about.

Jeremiah was born in a small town north of Jerusalem during the reign of perhaps the most wicked king the country of Judah had ever had. Jeremiah's father was a priest, so Jeremiah also became a priest. But while he was still a young man, Jeremiah was called by God to be a prophet, to warn the people of coming disaster.

Although Jeremiah was shy, self-conscious, and sensitive, God chose him for the most difficult of all jobs. And God knew what He was doing. Jeremiah was the best person to deliver, with love in his voice and compassion in his heart, a very harsh message. Through Jeremiah God could show love, even while giving the sternest warning. And through Jeremiah God could show His power, because people would realize how much a man such as Jeremiah needed to depend on God in order to deliver the message at all.

Even though Jeremiah is called "the weeping prophet," and even "God's crybaby," he is best known for courage and faithfulness. No man could have preached for forty years to an unresponsive audience, braved threats on his life, and watched his country fall further into sin, without moments of discouragement, yet Jeremiah did those things and never gave up. Remarkably, he never ran away or went into permanent hiding. Jeremiah's life was an adventure in obedience.

Losing the Popularity Contest

Jeremiah was not popular. When Jeremiah began his ministry, young King Josiah befriended the prophet—Josiah had tried to bring his nation back to God, so he understood the burden on Jeremiah's heart. After Josiah died, however, none of the succeeding kings appreciated Jeremiah's message. King Jehoiakim hated Jeremiah so much that he took his penknife, hacked up the scroll containing Jeremiah's message, and threw it on the fire. People ridiculed Jeremiah by asking, "What's the sad news from God today?" They ignored his warnings. Yet, because of his faithfulness and love for God, Jeremiah kept right on speaking God's truth. And God protected him from those who wanted to kill him, and brought him out of prison. God also gave him a best friend named Baruch who stuck with him through thick and thin.

When the World Seems to Be Falling Apart

Jeremiah repeatedly warned the people that if they didn't repent, Jerusalem would be destroyed by the Babylonians. His listeners ignored him. The proud, headstrong people of Judah prepared to fight Babylon and accused Jeremiah of treason. But Jerusalem was destroyed, just as Jeremiah had said. To a Jew, the destruction of Jerusalem was the end of the world.

Jeremiah faced the "end of the world" with God, and that made all the difference. The calamity he had prophesied so long came to pass, but even in the midst of disaster God protected him. The Babylonians treated Jeremiah kindly and let him choose whether to live in Babylon or stay in Judah. He chose to stay. The Jews who were left in Judah, however, still wouldn't listen to Jeremiah. In rebellion they moved to Egypt and forced Jeremiah and Baruch to go with them. This is the last record of Jeremiah, but you can be sure he continued to preach God's Word until he died.

Although Jeremiah was a failure by the world's standards, he was a tremendous success because he obeyed God. His life has been an inspiration to many. His example is especially significant in this age when the end of the world seems a real possibility. As a "last days Christian," a young person living in these times, you will profit greatly from the study of a great prophet, Jeremiah.

But That's Not the Future I've Planned

"The word of the Lord came to me, saying, 'Before I formed you in the womb I knew you, before you were born I set you apart; I appointed you as a prophet to the nations.' 'Ah, Sovereign Lord,' I said, 'I do not know how to speak; I am only a child.' But the Lord said to me, 'Do not say, "I am only a child." You must go to everyone I send you to and say whatever I command you. Do not be afraid of them, for I am with you and will rescue you,' declares the Lord" (Jer. 1:4–8).

You have dreams for your future—a happy marriage, attractive and well-adjusted children, a prestigious and high-paying job, skiing vacations, and Caribbean cruises. Will they come true? Actually, the realities of the world situation—crumbling economies, the danger of a superpower clash, and increasing terrorism—might create for you a future far different from the one you have been intending.

Jeremiah also had dreams, but he didn't get to live out the future he had planned. His fellow Israelites' hypocrisy, rebellion, and idol worship were about to bring God's judgment. And God wanted to use Jeremiah as His messenger. His life would not be at all what he had expected. But he was comforted by knowing God had figured it all out ahead of time, for before Jeremiah was even born, God had set him apart to be His special prophet.

God had designed Jeremiah to be a "tough times baby" who would grow up to be the man God needed for such a crisis. Yet, when Jeremiah learned God had chosen him to be a prophet, to give God's words to the country of Judah, he was surprised—for several reasons. First, he thought he was too young. (He was probably a teen-ager.) Second, he did not know how to speak in public, as prophets had to do. Third, he was very shy and tenderhearted, not a bold Elijah who could easily denounce sin. Jeremiah's personality didn't seem to fit the job description. But God promised to put His words in Jeremiah's mouth, and to put courage and strength in Jeremiah's heart. And that's exactly what He did. Although Jeremiah's message was unpopular, and his life was never easy, his days were filled with excitement and adventure.

Maybe you feel as Jeremiah did, not sure you have what it takes to be a "last days Christian." You need to realize that God made you exactly for that purpose. That is why you're living now, rather than a hundred years ago. Be assured He will give you what you need to accomplish His purpose. He wants you to depend on Him for strength and wisdom. That's why He gives assignments that seem too hard, work that you can't complete without depending on Him. He wants to make you a person who can cope with tension, danger, and uncertainty, a person who can thrive in challenging and difficult times. This kind of life may have many ups and downs, but it will give you marvelous opportunities to trust God.

Think about it. Do you really want the boring, predictable future you've planned? Who had a richer life—Hudson Taylor, who faced rejection, hardship, and sorrow in faraway China while helping thousands of Chinese to accept Christ? Or the man who stayed in England, married the girl next door, enjoyed a prosperous job, and retired in style? Wouldn't you rather be a Hudson Taylor?

There's something wonderful about living on the cutting edge, experiencing the agony and the ecstasy of being on the front lines. Maybe the future won't turn out the way you planned, but as a "last days Christian" you can live a thrilling, action-packed life.

" 'Do not be afraid of them, for I am with you and will rescue you,'

declares the Lord. Then the Lord reached out his hand and touched my mouth and said to me, 'Now, I have put my words in your mouth. See, today I appoint you over nations and kingdoms to uproot and tear down, to destroy and overthrow, to build and to plant. Get yourself ready! Stand up and say to them whatever I command you. Do not be terrified by them, or I will terrify you before them. Today I have made you a fortified city, an iron pillar and a bronze wall to stand against the whole land—against the kings of Judah, its officials, its priests and the people of the land. They will fight against you but will not overcome you, for I am with you and will rescue you,' declares the Lord" (Jer. 1:8–10, 17–19).

1. Make a list of all your fears about the future. Now, reread the above verses, cross out each fear on your list, and replace it with a promise from God.
2. Do you face the future with dread or with anticipation? What can you learn from the above passage which can erase the dread?
3. What are the "kings of Judah" which may fight against you this week? Pray about the situation, asking God for His courage and His protection?

Stamping Out Worldliness, Wickedness and Weeds

" *'Only acknowledge your guilt—you have rebelled against the Lord your God, you have scattered your favors to foreign gods under every spreading tree, and have not obeyed me,' declares the Lord. 'Return, faithless people,' declares the Lord, 'for I am your husband. I will choose one of you from every town and two from every clan and bring you to Zion. If you will return, O Israel, return to me,' declares the Lord. 'If you put your detestable idols out of my sight and no longer go astray, and if in a truthful, just and righteous way you swear, "As surely as the Lord lives," then the nations will be blessed by him and in him they will glory'* " (Jer. 3:13, 14; 4:1, 2).

Can you imagine a fast-spreading weed which would resist all insecticides? Which would fatally infect anyone who touched it? Which would cause slow death to any animal that ate it? Which would contaminate the milk and meat of that animal, thus infecting anyone who drank the milk or ate the meat?

If such a weed existed, would people just shrug their shoulders and concede, "There's nothing we can do"? Would they half-heartedly try to destroy this plant? Of course not. If a chemical for eradicating this weed were discovered, they would pay any amount, and travel anywhere to buy it. They would then search out every plant and systematically destroy it.

Sin is like that imaginary weed. It contaminates anyone who touches it. Although its effects cannot always be immediately seen, those who persist in sin suffer eternal death. Left unchecked, sin will destroy any person, society, or country.

God, of course, has a cure. He destroyed your sin and self-centeredness when Jesus died on the cross, and now He offers you the cure. But this cure can't be yours without complete repentance. Only repentance enables you to accept God's offer of a new life.

Repentance, however, isn't a casual, "Jesus, come into my heart, Amen," in response to your Sunday school teacher's suggestion. Repentance means completely turning from sin. It means ruthlessly hating and rejecting every sin in your life.

Genuine repentance depends on knowing God's character: His love, justice—and power. Do you know God in that way? Or do you resent His commanding you to obey your parents, or His prohibiting sex before marriage? Until you see God as loving and just, you won't repent; you'll instead defend yourself against an unreasonable God. Therefore, you must study God's character as revealed in the Bible, and let the Holy Spirit reveal to you what God is like.

So how can you apply all this to your life? First, realize that true repentance involves a complete change—turning around and going in the other direction. Second, you must see God as He really is: loving and just.

Finally, you must daily comform your life to these facts. For example, if you feel sorry for yourself because you're not as smart as your brother and sister, you must hate the sin of self-pity and believe that God was loving and just in making you the way you are. (He didn't want a world full of geniuses—and for good reason.) You also must believe that God is all-powerful, and will give you all the brains to do the things He wants you to do. Then thank Him.

You now have turned from self-pity to thanking God for making you just the way you are; you have performed a 180-degree reversal—that's repentance. This initial repentance, giving your whole life to Jesus, puts you on a new road. Now you must keep walking down the highway.

Maybe you already know that the breaking up world around you is infected by sin—which is the root cause of the whole mess. But you maybe don't know that you can be a Jeremiah, offering people a way out. Although the Israelites ignored Jeremiah, at other times in history entire regions, even countries, accepted the call to repent, and became islands of peace in a disintegrating world.

Every Christian, including you, is appointed to give people in his neighborhood the chance to repent and live a new life. You are to become an eradicator of weeds—stamping out worldliness and wickedness, offering hope even as the end of the world breathes down your neck. But if you don't practice repentance, you'll be part of the problem instead of part of the solution.

"... *God's kindness leads you toward repentance*" (Rom. 2:4).

"The kingdom of God is near. Repent and believe the good news!" (Mark 1:15).

". . . unless you repent, you too will all perish" (Luke 13:3).

"I [Paul] preached that they should repent and turn to God and prove their repentance by their deeds" (Acts 26:20).

"Therefore go and make disciples of all nations . . . teaching them to obey everything I have commanded you. And surely I will be with you always, to the very end of the age" (Matt. 28:19, 20).

"If my people, who are called by my name, will humble themselves and pray and seek my face and turn from their wicked ways, then will I hear from heaven and will forgive their sin and will heal their land" (2 Chron. 7:14).

1. Why does the kindness—love—of God lead people to repentance?
2. Why must you repent to receive salvation?
3. Why must your initial repentance be followed by a daily walking in that repentance?
4. Why is your repentance, and your teaching it to others, important to your community and your country?

A Bright Future and the End of the World

" 'Have you not brought this on yourselves by forsaking the Lord your God when he led you in the way? Now why go to Egypt to drink water from the Shihor? And why go to Assyria to drink water from the River? Your wickedness will punish you; your backsliding will rebuke you. Consider then and realize how evil and bitter it is for you when you forsake the Lord your God and have no awe of me,' declares the Lord, the Lord Almighty" (Jer. 2:17, 19).

You can see it on the screen—cities enveloped in flames, a world staggering with radioactivity, slow death, and suffering; life reduced to a daily struggle against a hostile environment. You can hear it in church—a stirring sermon proving you are living in the last days. You can read it in the newspaper—street violence, guerilla warfare, and terrorism. Everything seems to scream: "The end of all things is near" (1 Peter 4:7)! How can you, a teenager who has every right to look forward to a bright future, face such a world?

Jeremiah experienced the "end of the world" as he knew it. The Babylonians' knocking down the gates of Jerusalem frightened him as much as thoughts of a glowing mushroom cloud terrify you. Death from famine, disease, and sword seemed no more pleasant to him than death from fire and radioactivity seems to you. Life as a captive in a foreign land appeared just as hopeless to him as life without electricity, safe food, and automobiles appears to you. Either way, life would never be the same again. The experiences of Jeremiah, who lived in times as tough as today, are recorded in the Bible as a guide for "last days Christians."

You must understand, as Jeremiah did, that the evil in the world is a result of sin, and also the most effective way to show people they must change their ways. Each sin has a consequence—for example, greed causes war, dishonesty ruins economies of nations, and selfish actions create chaos. God uses these consequences to make people realize that there must be a higher way of life, that they should give their lives to God. Sometimes, only sin and its consequences exposed in the most extreme form will open people's spiritual eyes.

Today, as in Jeremiah's time, God gives prophecies (special messages) to His people, so they can know what to expect and how to prepare for what's coming. God not only used Jeremiah to prophesy impending doom—the fall of Jerusalem and the need to repent, but also to explain His total plan. God would use the destruction of Jerusalem and the captivity in Babylon to cure the survivors of idol worship, so they would return to their land. Then He would send them a Savior (Jesus) and bring them to a time when "I [God] will put my law in their minds and write it on their hearts. I will be their God, and they will be my people. . . . they will all know me, from the least of them to the greatest" (Jer. 31:33, 34). In the midst of despair, God was giving them hope!

We are living in difficult times. And that's what Jesus predicted over 1,950 years ago: "You will hear of wars and rumors of wars, but see to it that you are not alarmed. Such things must happen, but the end is still to come. Nation will rise against nation, and kingdom against kingdom. There will be famines and earthquakes in various places." But there's hope, a bright future: ". . . he who stands firm to the end will be saved" (Matt. 24:6, 7, 13). The New Testament tells clearly that Christ will return, and that true Christians will enjoy everlasting life in heaven!

God has everything planned. He has a pattern and purpose, even in this falling-apart world. And if you've given Jesus your life, the future couldn't be brighter, because it will be forever spent with Him.

"The Lord is not slow in keeping his promise, as some understand slowness. He is patient with you, not wanting anyone to perish, but everyone to come to repentance. But the day of the Lord will come like a thief. The heavens will disappear with a roar; the elements will be destroyed by fire, and the earth and everything in it will be laid bare. Since everything will be destroyed in this way, what kind of people ought you to be? You ought to live holy and godly lives as you look forward to the day of God and speed its coming. That day will bring about the destruction of the heavens by fire, and the elements will melt in the heat. But in keeping with his promise we are looking forward to a new heaven and a new earth, the home of righteousness" (2 Pet. 3:9–13).

1. What is God's purpose in all that happens? (See verse 9.)
2. What is going to happen in the future?
3. How should your knowledge of the future affect the way you live now?
4. Those who have given their lives to Jesus look forward to a great hope. What is that hope?

"Stop the World, I Want to Get Off"

"The Lord said, 'It is because they have forsaken my law, which I set before them; they have not obeyed me or followed my law. Instead, they have followed the stubbornness of their hearts; they have followed the Baals, as their fathers taught them.' Therefore, this is what the Lord Almighty, the God of Israel, says: 'See, I will make this people eat bitter food and drink poisoned water.' This is what the Lord says: 'Let not the wise man boast of his wisdom or the strong man boast of his strength or the rich man boast of his riches, but let him who boasts boast about this: that he understands and knows me, that I am the Lord, who exercises kindness, justice and righteousness on earth, for in these I delight,' declares the Lord" (Jer. 9:13–15, 23, 24).

Life seems overwhelming. School is a parade of locker-room jokes, swearing "seminars," anti-Bible opinions, wholesale cheating, and harassment of honest people; home is a hotbed of bickering and selfishness; and work is a snakepit of dishonesty and favoritism. Trying to stay clean and live for Jesus can, at times, seem impossible. If life were a bus, you'd probably ask the driver to let you off.

Jesus understands! He told His disciples before He left for heaven, "Because of the increase of wickedness, the love of most will grow cold, but he who stands firm to the end will be saved" (Matt. 24:12, 13). You can be one of those who stand firm to the end.

"Wait a minute," you're saying. "That's easier said than done."

But it can be done—Jeremiah proved it. He not only stayed close to God, he kept giving God's Word to a disrespectful, potentially dangerous audience. Often Baruch, his secretary, was the only one who stood with him. Wickedness was increasing rapidly, false religion was flourishing, and the international situation was dreadful. Does this sound just like today? It was. And the God of Jeremiah hasn't changed either. So, if you want to know how God can make you strong and keep you close to Him, keep reading.

Jeremiah realized that knowing the God of kindness, justice, and righteousness was more important than doing anything else, and he lived that way, in complete dependence on God. He couldn't count on his family or the people he preached to for comfort, so he got it directly from God. He didn't try to become a member of the ungodly "in group." He followed God—virtually alone. He never used the "everybody-else-is-doing-it" excuse. God's opinion was all that mattered to him. He told God, "When your words came, I ate them; they were my joy and my heart's delight, for I bear your name, O Lord God Almighty" (Jer. 15:16). God's presence and words were the joy of his life.

Such a life wasn't always easy. Jeremiah was often lonely and even heartbroken—some call him "the weeping prophet." He cared so much for his people that he could deliver even the harshest message with love. He didn't allow himself to become calloused or hard-boiled. Neither did he run away or try to hide.

What was his secret? A deep love relationship with God that went far beyond simple knowledge. Jesus said the real test of love is obedience, and Jeremiah's obedience proved he loved God more than anyone or anything.

If you truly love someone, you'll suffer anything for him. You'll let the rest of the world think you're a fool, because you're satisfied that you've given happiness to the person you love. That is the kind of love you must give Jesus. He loves you so much He went to the cross. He loves you so much that even though He knows everything about you, He still wants you in His family. His love will never end.

Respond to that love. Don't let your love for Jesus grow cold. Be willing even to suffer for Him in a sick, sad and sinful world, and be ready to receive from Him all you need to live above the mess.

"This is what the Lord says: 'Cursed is the one who trusts in man, who depends on flesh for his strength and whose heart turns away from the Lord. He will be like a bush in the wastelands; he will not see prosperity when it comes. He will dwell in the parched places of the desert, in a salt land where no one lives. But blessed is the man who trusts in the Lord, whose confidence is in him. He will be like a tree planted by the water that sends out its roots by the stream. It does not fear when heat comes; its leaves are always green. It has no worries in a year of drought and never fails to bear fruit' " (Jer. 17:5–8).

"[Jesus said,] 'O Jerusalem, Jerusalem, you who kill the prophets and stone those sent to you, how often I have longed to gather your children together, as a hen gathers her chicks under her wings, but you were not willing" (Matt. 23:37).

"This is what the Lord says: '. . . I have loved you with an everlasting love; I have drawn you with loving-kindness' " (Jer. 31:2, 3).

1. If you're concerned about what other people think, why will you lose the battle before it even starts?
2. Have you told God that you want to be a tree with roots in the river of His love and truth, rather than be a scrubby bush that gets love and opinions from those around you?
3. Can you recall times when you refused the love and guidance God wanted to give you?
4. How can God's great love help you face a sick and sinful world?

186

"I'd Like a Religion That Believes Selfishness Is a Virtue"

"Among my people are wicked men who lie in wait like men who snare birds and like those who set traps to catch men and have grown fat and sleek. Their evil deeds have no limit; they do not plead the case of the fatherless to win it, they do not defend the rights of the poor. A horrible and shocking thing has happened in the land: The prophets prophesy lies, the priests rule by their own authority, and my people love it this way. But what will you do in the end?" (Jer. 5:26, 28, 30, 31).

"But I said, 'Ah, Sovereign Lord, the prophets keep telling them, "You will not see the sword or suffer famine. In deed, I will give you lasting peace in this place." ' Then the Lord said to me, 'The prophets are prophesying lies in my name. I have not sent them or appointed them or spoken to them. They are prophesying to you false visions, divinations, idolatries and the delusions of their own minds' " (Jer. 14:13, 14).

Have you noticed how often people change their beliefs in order to avoid guilt? Ginny worships love because, she says, "Love will solve all the world's problems"; it also allows her to sleep with her boyfriend. Paul is "finding himself" through the martial arts; he'd rather practice karate than attend church, anyway. Jennifer thinks Eastern thought has the answer; at least it doesn't tell her she's a sinner. Dave doesn't advertise it, but he'd like to join any cult which teaches that selfishness is a virtue.

Believing in the true God requires accepting what He says and conforming your life to it, not making up a religion and a god that allow you to do as you please. There is only one way. With so many philosophies floating around, however, you may sometimes wonder if you're on the right track—as Jeremiah did. So how do you make sure you're staying on course? By understanding the basic reasons for false religions and thus discovering some ways to guard against error.

False religions appeal to two kinds of people. They appeal to people who wish to cover their sinful actions with outward piety—church attendance and well-publicized good deeds. They are attractive also to people who try to relieve their guilt by finding a religion which condones their actions. Such people hate to admit their sins and repent—even though they'll receive the forgiveness Jesus accomplished when He died on the cross. They believe it's more comfortable to "pay" their own way by performing prescribed rituals and doing good works.

People who haven't received God's forgiveness continually try to fill a big vacuum inside themselves. Therefore they easily fall for anything that sounds promising. Here is how Jeremiah described such people: "My people have committed two sins: They have forsaken me, the spring of living water, and have dug their own cisterns, [water-tight pits for storing rainwater] broken cisterns that cannot hold water" (Jer. 2:13).

On the other hand, those who sincerely desire God act differently. They are sensitive to what is true and what is false. Here is how Jesus described them: "He who belongs to God hears what God says. The reason you do not hear is that you do not belong to God" (John 8:47).

Even Christians must realize that if ever they turn away from God, they, too, will be building broken cisterns. It might be well to check yourself, to see if you're digging any cistern pits. So ask yourself these questions: Do I ever act religious or do good things to cover up a sin I should confess and forsake? Am I ever unwilling to admit I'm wrong? Am I too lazy to thoroughly study what the Bible says on a topic, and thus prone to accept what somebody else says? Am I unwilling to obey Jesus on every issue? If you answered yes to any of these questions, you've got trouble.

Hypocrisy, pride, ignorance, and disobedience to truth breed false religions. If you decide you can't live without your boyfriend—no matter what God thinks—you'll open yourself to all kinds of deception and wrong doctrine. If you insist on deciding what is true for you, you'll make up your own religion. And you'll undoubtedly find people who will tell you selfishness is okay. But whenever you run to be first in the dessert line so you'll get the biggest piece of pie, you'll still feel guilty; God's truth is built into the universe, and you can't avoid it.

Because people don't want to acknowledge God's truth, false religions will flourish in these last days, as the Bible says they will. Countries will disintegrate, empires will fall, and people will be nervous wrecks—because they disobey God. Hundreds of religious philosophies will claim truth, but, as always, "this is eternal life: that they may know you, the only true God, and Jesus Christ, whom you have sent" (John 17:3).

"She will give birth to a son, and you are to give him the name Jesus, because he will save his people from their sins" (Matt. 1:21).

"Salvation is found in no one else, for there is no other name under heaven given to men by which we must be saved" (Acts 4:12).

"Not at all! Let God be true, and every man a liar. As it is written: 'So that you may be proved right in your words and prevail in your judging' " (Rom. 3:4).

"For there is one God and one mediator between God and men, the man Christ Jesus, who gave himself as a ransom for all men—the testimony given in its proper time" (1 Tim. 2:5).

1. How would you answer this question: "Why are there so many religions if there's only one God?"
2. What's the answer to this question: "How can you be confident there's only one way to God?"
3. Are you going to follow your own logic and convenience, or God's truth as found in the Bible? Ask God to show you if you've gotten off the track. Then do what you must to get right with Him.

"But Lord, I Want to Get Married"

"Then the word of the Lord came to me: 'You must not marry and have sons or daughters in this place.' For this is what the Lord says about the sons and daughters born in this land and about the women who are their mothers and the men who are their fathers: 'They will die of deadly diseases. They will not be mourned or buried but will be like refuse lying on the ground. They will perish by sword and famine, and their dead bodies will become food for the birds of the air and the beasts of the earth' " (Jer. 16:1–4).

Are you already planning your wedding? If you're a girl, do you dream of a perfect June day, an elegant eggshell gown, four bridesmaids in lavender, and Mr. Wonderful waiting for you at the end of the aisle? If you're a guy, do you dream of marrying a breathtaking blonde who will make all the guys jealous of you? After all, you couldn't bear the thought of being an "old maid" or ending up as the guy that nobody would marry.

"Life's priority is following Jesus and building His kingdom, not getting married or having dates."

But before you get trapped into the "I'd-better-get-married-while-I-have-the-chance" syndrome, consider three important thoughts.

First, God intended that you get your fulfillment from Him, not from anyone else. In heaven, where every person will be completely fulfilled, there is no marriage, because Jesus will be the bridegroom, and His church will be the bride. God wants you to be able to say, "Whom have I in heaven but you? And being with you, I desire nothing on earth" (Ps. 73:25). When God becomes that important to you, you'll be able to give to others what God has given to you—unconditional love. You won't be a leech trying to get from another person what Christ alone can give you. Only then will you know how to treat a roommate, a boyfriend, a girlfriend, or even a husband or wife.

Second, life's priority is following Jesus and building His kingdom, not getting married or having dates. This attitude takes the pressure off you. If you're taken up with obeying Jesus, and He gives no go-ahead to pursue a relationship, you'll be single (or dateless), not because you're ugly and undesirable, but because Jesus has given you an important work which you can accomplish better single than married. Of course, the person who constantly bemoans being single will never discover that special assignment. This is not a cop-out for being anti-social and slovenly, or avoiding contact with those of the opposite sex. Nonetheless, you will have clear priorities; if God calls you to be single, He has something special for you to do.

On the other hand, if Jesus tells you to marry, He knows you can serve Him better with a partner. Because your marriage "orders" came from God, however, you'll have no reason to feel superior and look down on unmarried people. As a bonus, if you marry in obedience to God, you'll have a solid base from which to solve any marital problems that may crop up.

Third, God can better see the future, and therefore knows best how to protect you and enable you to work for Him. A book about Christians in Communist Bulgaria describes a man who endured terrible imprisonment, including brainwashing and torture. In spite of his suffering he did not break down. This man had a couple of advantages: he was physically strong and he was single. Why did singleness help him? The authorities could not break him by threatening his wife and children.

This is why God forbade Jeremiah to marry. When the prophet preached against the sins of Israel, no one could threaten his wife and children. When Jerusalem was destroyed, he would not be burdened by worry for a family. In the tough days ahead, God may need other single "Jeremiahs" to do His work.

God knows if ten years from now your being single will allow you the time or money or freedom to do something for His kingdom which no married person could accomplish. And you won't be miserable without marriage. God will provide all the emotional fulfillment and companionship you need. He gave Jeremiah a loyal and faithful companion, Baruch, who stuck with him all his life. Best of all, God will free you from anxiety about the future. Let Him change your prayer from "Lord, I want to get married," to, "Lord, I want to do your will."

"I would like you to be free from concern. An unmarried man is concerned about the Lord's affairs—how he can please the Lord. An unmarried woman or virgin is concerned about the Lord's affairs: Her aim is to be devoted to the Lord in both body and spirit" (1 Cor. 7:32–24).

"Wives, submit to your husbands as to the Lord. Husbands, love your wives, just as Christ loved the church and gave himself up for her . . . 'For this reason a man will leave his father and mother and be united to his wife, and the two will become one flesh.' This is a profound mystery—but I am talking about Christ and the church" (Eph. 5:22, 25, 31, 32).

1. What should be a person's main purpose, whether he is married or single?
2. What is wrong with saying, "I want to be single because I want freedom and fun"? or, "I want to get married so I'll be important to someone"?
3. Why can worrying about getting married keep you from serving Jesus right now?
4. Do you think of marriage as an opportunity to demonstrate the relationship that Christ has with His church, and to show Jesus to the world? Or is your idea of marriage status, sexual satisfaction, and security?

Where Does Courage Come From?

" 'I will make you a wall to this people, a fortified wall of bronze; they will fight against you but will not overcome you, for I am with you to rescue and save you,' declares the Lord. 'I will save you from the hands of the wicked and redeem you from the grasp of the cruel' " (Jer. 15:20, 21).

As you read in the papers about brainwashing, genetic engineering, heads of state encouraging "holy" war, and the possible death of our solar system, you may shudder a little with fear—realizing that if the world doesn't end soon, it may not be fit to live in. But fear can hit much closer to home—such as when you walk a few blocks alone at night, or when you meet a certain gang in the halls at school, or when you hear a teen-aged girl was murdered three blocks from your house. At those times you may wonder, "Where does courage come from?" Again, you can learn from Jeremiah, who was called by God to a dangerous, unpopular job.

Pretend, for a moment, that Jeremiah's Israel is today's United States: In fear of a Soviet invasion, the federal government has suspended all constitutional rights, allowing traitors to be immediately shot—so God commands you to announce that the US is losing the war with the USSR because of people's sin and their unwillingness to repent. And the solution He offers is that the US should surrender and allow the Soviets to punish the United States for God. If that isn't bad enough, God tells you to make your pronouncements from the front steps of the White House! Now you know how Jeremiah felt when he told Israel to repent, and when he predicted the fall of Jerusalem.

Jeremiah was in constant danger. People from his hometown wanted to kill him. Even his family turned against him. The government and religious leaders, and false prophets wanted him executed for treason. He endured verbal attack, house arrest, and even imprisonment in the mucky bottom of a cistern. Through all this Jeremiah displayed remarkable courage. What was his secret?

Jeremiah's secret was *faith*. God had promised to protect him, and Jeremiah believed Him. He realized confidence in God's promises was better than any sword, or bodyguard, or karate lesson. When the powerful, influential men of Judah wanted to kill him, he told them bluntly that God had sent him to give a message, so if they killed him they would be responsible to God—then he kept right on preaching. God kept His promise to protect Jeremiah.

God also provided people to help and protect Jeremiah. He used Baruch, an ever-loyal companion, to faithfully transcribe Jeremiah's sermons. He used Ebed-melech, an African servant in the palace (from modern-day Sudan), to convince the king that Jeremiah should be lifted out of the cistern where he was imprisoned; Ebed-melech risked his career to save Jeremiah (Jer. 38). God also used the Babylonian captain in charge of Jewish prisioners to give Jeremiah not only freedom, but food and a gift (Jer. 40).

God gave Jeremiah a super-hazardous job *and* perfect protection, so if He asks you to take a big risk, be assured God will take care of you. He knows you live in a dangerous world, and He may ask you to take a dangerous assignment. But you can have courage by placing complete confidence in God and His promises of protection—and there's a bunch. Study those promises. Memorize them. Make them part of you. Allow the God of promises to be your God, your friend, and your protector.

"Peter and the other apostles replied: 'We must obey God rather than men!' " (Acts 5:29).

"The wicked man flees though no one pursues, but the righteous are as bold as a lion" (Prov. 28:1).

"I sought the Lord, and he answered me; he delivered me from all my fears" (Ps. 34:4).

"The Lord is my strength and my shield; my heart trusts in him, and I am helped. My heart leaps for joy and I will give thanks to him in song" (Ps. 28:7).

1. God promises to protect you if He sends you on a dangerous assign-

ment. Can you expect God to protect you when you do something dangerous, just to show off? Why is there a difference?

2. Do you pray in faith, asking God for courage? What fears do you have that God would have you conquer?
3. Have you memorized any of God's promises to help you overcome fear? If you haven't, start now.

Week Twelve

ESTHER: A CRASH COURSE IN COURAGE

Introduction

If you feel that you've dug yourself into a hole and you're lonely and afraid, the story of the life of Esther will help you. She shows us that fear can be conquered and that there is a way to get back on the right track. Have you ever backed yourself into a corner and let fear keep you there? Fear can ruin your life, so you need to know how to overcome it. The life of Queen Esther can give you a crash course in courage.

What Happens If You Get Yourself into a Mess?

The events recorded in the book of Esther took place about 474 B.C. when the Persian Empire ruled most of the known world. The empire reached its height during the reign of King Xerxes. Except for Greece, which had repelled his powerful army, Xerxes' empire contained most of the land in the world worth having.

When Vashti, Queen of Persia, dared to disobey King Xerxes, he divorced her. And to find a suitable replacement, he sponsored an empire-wide beauty contest to choose a new queen. The winner was Esther, a Jewish orphan. Her people had been led as captives to that part of the world after the Babylonians had destroyed Jerusalem in 587 B.C. When the Persians had conquered Babylon, King Cyrus allowed the Jews to go back to the land God had promised Abraham, but many families chose to stay. Esther's family was one of these. Her parents died when she was young, so Mordecai, an older cousin, raised her. He advised her to keep her Jewish heritage secret.

Life as queen of the world's greatest empire was not necessarily easy. By concealing her identity, Esther was really denying God. Besides, in order to keep her Jewishness hidden, she may have had to participate in pagan worship. Hypocrisy is never fun. And you can be sure that being married to a temperamental king with a large harem was no fun.

But those soon became the least of Esther's troubles when Mordecai informed her that Haman, prime minister of Persia, had ordered that all Jews be killed. Mordecai begged her to confront the king and plead for the lives of the Jews. She hesitated, however, because anyone who dared enter the king's inner court without invitation was routinely executed—unless the king held out his scepter, his golden rod of authority.

What If You Need Some Extra Courage?

Esther was afraid to go before the king. Mordecai then reminded her that she'd die anyway if all the Jews were killed (someone would blow her cover) and that this was her chance to save God's people. He reminded her that God had things under control and that His master plan did not include the destruction of the Jews. And if she didn't do something to save God's people, her family would be destroyed and God would have to use someone else to do the job. She had become the queen for just such a time. She got the point.

Recognizing her need for God's power, she asked the Jews of the capital city of Susa to fast (go without food or drink) for three days while she and her servants did the same. Fasting would help them seek God. During this fast Esther must have prayed a lot for she found not only the courage to approach the king, but the best method of approaching him.

Dressed in her best royal robes, she took a deep breath and stepped into the king's inner court. Catching a glimpse of the king on the throne, she did not see the man who was her husband. She could only see the ruler who would shortly decide whether she would live or die. She walked closer and closer, each step seeming an eternity. Suddenly he held out his golden scepter and asked her what her request was. Phew! But she didn't tell him everything. She merely invited him and Haman to a banquet.

At the banquet she didn't make her request for the Jews. Instead, she promised to tell the king at a second banquet. The king was so anxious to hear what she wanted that he couldn't sleep that night. Finally, when Esther told him Haman had plotted to kill all the Jews, the king became furious and ordered Haman killed. He decreed that the Jews were free to defend themselves against any who tried to harm them. And he appointed Mordecai the new prime minister.

You will learn from the story of Queen Esther that even if you did wrong in the first place, God can supply the courage to do His will—if you earnestly seek Him and do what His Word says. He is the same God Esther had.

God's Magic Master Plan

"He also gave him a copy of the text of the edict for their annihilation, which had been published in Susa, to show to Esther and explain it to her, and he told him to urge her to go into the king's presence to beg for mercy and plead with him for her people. Hathach went back and reported to Esther what Mordecai had said. Then she instructed him to say to Mordecai, 'All the king's officials and the people of the royal provinces know that for any man or woman who approaches the king in the inner court without being summoned the king has but one law: that he be put to death. The only exception to this is for the king to extend the gold scepter to him and spare his life. But thirty days have passed since I was called to go to the king.' When Esther's words were reported to Mordecai, he sent back this answer: 'Do not think that because you are in the king's house you alone of all the Jews will escape. For if you remain silent at this time, relief and deliverance for the Jews will arise from another place, but you and your father's family will perish. And who knows but that you have come to royal position for such a time as this?' " (Esther 4:8–14).

Your sin and stubbornness got you into trouble. Now that you've had time to suffer the consequences of your actions, you feel completely trapped. And you feel it isn't fair to ask God to bail you out.

Or maybe it's the wrongdoing and pride of another person that created the circumstances that have imprisoned you. You feel crushed by the complex, tangled maze you must walk through. Well, it's time you learned about something called the providence of God.

"Our God is in heaven; he does whatever pleases him" (Ps. 115:3) wrote the Psalmist. Do you believe those words? Do you realize God has a master plan for running this world, and that plan includes you? The theological word for this, "providence," is defined by the dictionary as "preparation for the future" and "wisdom in management." In other words, God who is all-knowing has already decided how your problem will work out to His glory. The magic of God's master plan is that even if you or someone else messes it up, the moment you confess your sin and give the whole thing over to Him, He begins to unravel the mess.

Stories of kings and queens are fascinating. How romantic to have riches, power, and prestige! Well, life in ye olde palace isn't always so great, as Queen Esther discovered. She had been queen only a short time before realizing she had really ruined her life. Although she was queen of the huge Persian Empire, she was married to a king much older than she. As queen she had to share her husband with a large harem which meant that she didn't live "happily ever after." He was not known as an even-tempered man and hadn't even asked to see her for thirty days. Besides her marital problems she had spiritual problems, for even though her guardian had approved, she had broken God's law by marrying a pagan king. And she had denied God by telling no one she was Jewish, a woman of God's chosen people. So much for royal romances.

To make matters worse, the king's prime minister was plotting to kill all the Jews in the empire; and Esther knew she was the only person who could ask the king to save her people. Yet, the law stated if anyone approached the king without invitation, that person would quickly be killed—unless the king decided otherwise. And since the king had not called her for thirty days, she likely assumed he was angry with her. What was she to do?—she would probably die if she approached the king, or if she did nothing. No doubt she wished she could run away.

Then Mordecai, the cousin who loved her and had raised her, gave Esther the encouragement she needed: "And who knows whether you have not come to the kingdom for such a time as this?" In faith she accepted her responsibility.

No matter how badly you've messed up God's plan for your life— even if you've committed gross sin—if you will give the mess to God, He will give you a fresh start. He can work out His will from the midst of the worst of problems. He uses former drug addicts to spread the news about Jesus to people who might listen to no one else. He takes kids from broken, mixed-up families and gives those kids emotional stability and winsome personalities—so they can be great advertisements of His power. So whatever your situation, there is hope for you.

If you have sinned, ask for forgiveness. Then pray, "God, bless this mess"—and He will! That's God's magic master plan.

"Then the word of the Lord came to me: 'O house of Israel, can I not do with you as this potter does?' declares the Lord. 'Like clay in the hand of the potter, so are you in my hand, O house of Israel. If at any time I announce that a nation or kingdom is to be uprooted, torn down and destroyed, and if that nation I warned repents of its evil, then I will relent and not inflict on it the disaster I had planned'" (Jer. 18:5–8).

1. What are the consequences (for a nation or individual) of persisting in sin?
2. What will God do for the individual or nation who confesses and forsakes sin?
3. What can a potter do with soft clay if the vase isn't turning out right? What can God do with a messed-up life that is given to Him?
4. What areas of your life have you messed up? Are you willing to hand the complete mess over to God, believing He will entirely remake your life?

Fear Is a Liar

"Then she instructed him to say to Mordecai, 'All the king's officials and the people of the royal provinces know that for any man or woman who

approaches the king in the inner court without being summoned the king has but one law: that he be put to death. The only exception to this is for the king to extend the gold scepter to him and spare his life. But thirty days have passed since I was called to go to the king.' When Esther's words were reported to Mordecai, he sent back this answer: 'Do not think that because you are in the king's house you alone of all the Jews will escape. For if you remain silent at this time, relief and deliverance for the Jews will arise from another place, but you and your father's family will perish. And who knows but that you have come to royal position for such a time as this?' " (Esther 4:10–14).

You've had thoughts like these:

"Maybe I'd better not drive to work. What if I have an accident and the doctors have to amputate my leg? I'd never run another race."

"What if the plane I take gets highjacked to Cuba and an international crisis develops so I'll have to stay there all my life?"

"What if after all this work Mr. Footnote still gives me an *F* on my term paper so I'll flunk English, and thus fail to graduate?"

"Maybe this bridge will collapse and all of us will drown within five minutes."

"Now that I've bought a new stereo maybe the house will burn down and I'll never get to listen to it again!"

Crazy? Exactly. Fear is irrational—if you know God. And a good dose of truth will dissolve most fears immediately. Others may take a little longer, but they all will go.

When Esther said, "I can't go before the king because I'll get killed," Mordecai reminded her that she'd die anyway if the Jews were all murdered. He also convinced her that God was running the universe—not exactly new information. He suggested that maybe God wanted to use her to protect His people, and she could expect punishment if she disobeyed Him. Facts tend to change a person's viewpoint. They changed Esther's.

Esther had fallen into a common trap: she had allowed fear to paralyze her and make her thinking fuzzy. Maybe she'd listened to people around her who were afraid of the king—the advice of ungodly people is often based on fear. But when Mordecai sent her the message, she listened to the truth and acted accordingly. This was step one in conquering her fear.

Like Esther, you must defeat fear with fact. You must learn to tell yourself the truth. If God sends you a Mordecai to set you straight, listen to him, take his advice, and thank him. If He doesn't send you a Mordecai, you must learn to use truth yourself—the truth that God is all-powerful.

Here's how to use truth against the fearful thoughts voiced in paragraph one. If such ideas go through your mind, talk to yourself like this:

"God is all-powerful and He can prevent any accident. Besides, He could heal my leg so it wouldn't have to be amputated. And God certainly could make me happy even if I couldn't run in any more track meets."

"If I got stranded in Cuba, God could make me such an effective missionary that the Communists would send me home."

"If I received an *F* on my term paper, God could show me how to appeal to the teacher for a chance to do some extra credit work to make up for it. And if I didn't graduate, I could always come back for another year. School's free and my time is God's, so if He wants me to spend another year in school that's His problem."

"If the bridge fell down, God could bring a boat to rescue me. If He didn't I would go straight to heaven and what could be better than that?"

"If the house burned down, I could live very well without my stereo and other junk. God has promised to provide me with everything I need."

The passive (inactive, yielding) mind accepts fear and allows its fantasies to spread unchecked. To rid yourself of passive, gullible thinking, renew your mind by keeping it strong with truth from God's Word. Fear is a liar. Learn to call its bluff.

"The plans of the righteous are just, but the advice of the wicked is deceitful" (Prov. 12:5).

"Buy the truth and do not sell it; get wisdom, discipline and understanding" (Prov. 23:23).

"We demolish arguments and every pretension that sets itself up against the knowledge of God, and we take captive every thought to make it obedient to Christ" (2 Cor. 10:5).

1. From whom should you accept advice?
2. Why is thinking the truth so important?
3. How can you bring every thought captive to obey the truth?
4. What lies has fear been telling you lately? Talk back with truth.

For the Frantic, Frazzled, and Frustrated

"Then Esther sent this reply to Mordecai: 'Go, gather together all the Jews who are in Susa, and fast for me. Do not eat or drink for three days, night or day. I and my maids will fast as you do. When this is done, I will go to the king, even though it is against the law. And if I perish, I perish'" (Esther 4:15, 16).

The championship football game is next Friday and you're the quarterback. Already the jitters are attacking your stomach.

Your clarinet solo at last week's regional contest received an *A* rating, so you'll be playing at the state contest. Instead of being happy you're worrying about playing in front of those judges.

The Christian clique at school has chosen you to ask the principal if your group can have a room for prayer each morning before school begins.

But your mind keeps playing a recording of Mr. Crabb at the last school assembly: "If you think I will allow students to run this school, you are mistaken."

You've just learned that your grandmother has only a few months to live—and you're not sure she's a Christian. You feel a tremendous responsibility to witness to her.

WHERE CAN YOU FIND SOME EXTRA COURAGE?

When Queen Esther chose to risk her life to plead for her people, she was afraid. But she knew courage came from God, so she spent some time with Him by fasting. In Jewish tradition fasting was a way of separating oneself from the routine of daily life in order to seek God. Esther didn't think about the supper menu because she wasn't going to eat supper. She didn't think about what to do in the evening because she wouldn't be going anywhere. The time was completely given over to God. Fasting gave unhurried time for prayer. The events in the story of Esther prove she prayed much during her three days of fasting.

Through fasting, Esther became a different person. When the king saw her come before him, he was pleased with her. Had she been frantic, frazzled and frustrated—and fearful (as she had been three days earlier), the king would have turned away from her in disgust. But that day Esther entered his court with dignity and poise. Discretely she withheld her request, rather than blurting it out. She had received God's wisdom for the problem, and was willing to wait for His perfect timing.

Esther's God is your God. He can replace your fear with courage. But, as Esther, you must spend enough time with Him to learn what He wants, and catch His attitude toward the situation. Often you've heard people say, "I'm scared to death," or "I always get nervous when I have to speak in front of a group," or "I never sleep well the night before I start a new job," etc. Maybe you say those same things. In order to reject such thinking and stop fanning the fire of fear with such remarks, you must catch some courage from God. You pick up the attitudes of the person you're closest to. Let that person be Jesus.

Instead of worrying about losing the football game or flubbing your solo, set aside a chunk of time to be alone with God. Here are a few suggestions on how to use that time. Think about the great ways in which God delivered frightened people in the past: the Israelites at the Red Sea, David facing Goliath, Daniel in the lions' den, Paul on a sinking ship, and Peter in prison waiting to be executed. Then think of the ways God has helped you and your friends. Then thank Him for being a God who helps His children. You also might do a Bible study on fear. Search in a concordance for all the verses which say, "Fear not." Then write them down, think about them, and let the Holy Spirit apply them to your situation. Soon your mind will overflow with courageous thoughts.

Once you've filled your mind with fear-killing thoughts, don't trust your emotions. The devil will whisper, "Your knees are shaking," or "You have a lump in your throat," or "You're scared to start the conversation."

If you listen to his voice you'll soon be as afraid as you were before. You can control your will, but not your emotions. So keep your mind on Jesus and His words, and charge ahead. Sooner or later the symptoms of fear will disappear.

You don't have to be frantic, frazzled, and frustrated. After all, God is not like that, and He lives inside you. He wants you to pick up His attitudes. Spend enough time with Him and you will.

"... the Moabites and Ammonites with some of the Meunites came to make war on Jehoshaphat. Alarmed, Jehoshaphat resolved to inquire of the Lord, and he proclaimed a fast for all Judah. Jehoshaphat bowed with his face to the ground, and all the people of Judah and Jerusalem fell down in worship before the Lord. Early in the morning they left ... As they set out, Jehoshaphat stood and said, '... Have faith in the Lord your God and you will be upheld; have faith in his prophets and you will be successful.' As they began to sing and praise, the Lord set ambushes against the men ... who were invading Judah, and they were defeated" (2 Chron. 20:1, 3, 20, 22).

1. After King Jehoshaphat and the people of Judah had spent enough time with God to catch His attitude, how did they fight the battle?
2. How did King Jehoshaphat, frightened by the huge invading army, become so courageous?
3. How did the people of Judah fight the battle?
4. What fear are you facing? Are you willing to spend enough time with God to catch His attitudes?

The World Revolves Around the Son

"I will go to the king, even though it is against the law. And if I perish, I perish" (Esther 4:16).

When Esther decided to attempt saving her people, regardless of what might happen to her, she discovered one of the secrets of courage: looking first to the needs of others. Fear is atheistic—it leaves God out. But fear is also selfish—it leaves other people out. So one way to destroy fear is to concentrate on the needs of others instead of thinking about yourself.

You've found yourself in situations like these:

The captain of the football team invited you to his party, so you went determined to make a good impression—but you were scared to death. In your nervousness you forgot the name of the hostess, stammered all over the place, and let your embarrassment spoil the whole evening. You feel like a fool.

You wanted so badly to play your best in the tennis tournament, but hundreds of people were watching the match, so you got stage fright. After a bad serve, you became so nervous you hardly held the racket.

Now you're sure the coach will never let you play again.

You were playing in the spring band concert, feeling certain the spotlight was on YOU! If you went flat or played a wrong note, you might ruin the whole concert. Surely everyone was noticing your shoes weren't polished and your collar had a spaghetti stain. Such anxiety! It must have been the worst night of your life.

Did you notice the common characteristic in each of the above self-made disasters? Self-centeredness. Fear and self-centeredness always go together.

But once you take your eyes off yourself and start caring about and praying for others, your fear will disappear. You'll experience the same principle of unselfishness that sends a father back into a burning building to save his son, that makes a soldier voluntarily risk his life for his country, and that keeps a nurse in the room with a patient suffering a contagious disease. God has built into the universe a principle that gives extra strength and ability to the person who will forget about himself and attempt to help others.

This principle applies in even the smallest situations. If you go to the party at the football captain's house after the game and try to make other people feel comfortable rather than try to be the center of attention, you will feel calm and poised. If you try to make your tennis partner feel at ease, you won't have time to get nervous yourself. If you try to make things easy for the band director and spend your energy encouraging other band members, you'll make the concert much more enjoyable for yourself.

As a Christian you can experience this principle on an even higher level. You can release your concern for others through prayer. Pray for all the people who will be at the party, asking God to make you able to help somebody in some way rather than spending ten minutes in front of the mirror wondering if you look okay. Pray for all the members of the tennis team, or the person who plays doubles with you instead of worrying about how you'll do. Pray that God will bless the concert and help everyone to play well.

Fear will trap you if you begin thinking only about yourself, because the world does not revolve around you. It revolves, instead, around the Son of God. He wants to take away your fear. But He won't do it unless you are intent on helping others.

"Be strong and courageous, because you will lead these people to inherit the land I swore to their forefathers to give them" (Josh. 1:6).

"The Lord turned to him and said, 'Go in the strength you have and save Israel out of Midian's hand. Am I not sending you?' 'But Lord,' Gideon asked, 'how can I save Israel? My clan is the weakest in Manasseh, and I am the least in my family.' The Lord answered, 'I will be with you, and you will strike down the Midianites as if they were but one man' " (Judg. 6:14–16).

"But you will receive power when the Holy Spirit comes on you; and you will be my witnesses in Jerusalem, and in all Judea and Samaria, and to the ends of the earth" (Acts 1:8).

1. In the above verses God offers you freedom from fear. He also offers power to do what kinds of things?
2. If you obeyed God's command in each of the above verses, who would receive the most benefit—you or the person you are helping?
3. If you constantly worry about personal performance and public opinion, will you gain power from God and freedom from fear?
4. In what areas of life has self-centeredness made you a prisoner of fear? Talk with God about those fears.

Eradicating Evil

" 'If it pleases the king,' replied Esther, 'let the king, together with Haman, come today to a banquet I have prepared for him.' So the king and Haman went to dine with Queen Esther, and as they were drinking wine on that second day, the king again asked, 'Queen Esther, what is your petition? It will be given you. What is your request? Even up to half the kingdom, it will be granted.' Then Queen Esther answered, 'If I have found favor with you, O king, and if it pleases your majesty, grant me my life— this is my petition. And spare my people—this is my request. For I and my people have been sold for destruction and slaughter and annihilation. If we had merely been sold as male and female slaves, I would have kept quiet, because no such distress would justify disturbing the king.' King Xerxes asked Queen Esther, 'Who is he? Where is the man who has dared to do such a thing?' Esther said, 'The adversary and enemy is this vile Haman.' Then Haman was terrified before the king and queen. Just as the king returned from the palace garden to the banquet hall, Haman was falling on the couch where Esther was reclining. The king exclaimed, 'Will he even molest the queen while she is with me in the house?' As soon as the word left the King's mouth, they covered Haman's face. . . . The king said, 'Hang him on it!' So they hanged Haman on the gallows he had prepared for Mordecai. Then the king's fury subsided" (Esther 5:4; 7:1–6, 8–10).

Sometimes evil seems so overwhelming that it frightens you, crippling your ability to live for Jesus. How can you witness to classmates whose talk centers on complaining, telling dirty jokes, and making fun of others? How can you maintain clean thoughts at the beach without a blindfold? How can you avoid getting caught up in the spirit of ruthless competition— comparing yourself with others, and exposing people's faults in order to advance yourself on the "good guy totem pole"?

Esther had to contend with Haman—evil on two legs—and his plan to kill all the Jews. But she didn't let fear overwhelm her. Instead of being crippled with fright, she faced Haman squarely and let God deal with him. She didn't close her eyes to Haman's scheme. She didn't run from him in terror. She didn't spend days whining about her predicament. Yet, she didn't deal with Haman herself by concocting a little assassination plot. Instead, she invited Haman to the banquet and looked him straight in the face!

How could she be so confident? She prayed. And as she prayed, Esther realized God would have to deal with evil—without her help. In this case God would administer justice to Haman through His appointed authority: the king. Esther only had to tell the king and Haman was as good as dead.

Because God has all power, He will defeat evil, so you don't have to be afraid. That, however, does not mean you should walk straight into temptation; you must continue to hate evil. But if evil comes your way, you can take God's hand knowing He can conquer all the forces of Satan. You don't have to hide, avoid all contact with non-Christians, or bury your head in the nearest sandpile. Instead, stick close to Jesus and let Him conquer evil for you.

Now that you know how to avoid being paralyzed by fear of evil, don't fall into the other extreme: trying to eradicate evil in your own strength. The devil is stronger than you, so by yourself you'll always lose. You must stay so close to Jesus; He can defeat the evil before it hurts you.

Close to Jesus you'll have amazing victories, because you'll have your eyes on Him and not on the evil around you. With Jesus you won't be intimidated by the sinful, scandalous, sickening things your classmates talk about. Instead, God will give you faith to see what they would be like if they gave their lives to Jesus. With Jesus you'll no longer be paranoid about the beach. He can keep your eyes on the right things; He'll change your heart so instead of seeing the scantily clad bather, you'll see a person who needs Jesus. And with Jesus you can squarely face the evil of comparing yourself with others. You can be free, living to please Jesus and ignoring what everybody else thinks.

Don't let evil terrify you. Let Jesus exterminate it for you.

"You, dear children, are from God and have overcome them, because the one who is in you is greater than the one who is in the world" (1 John 4:4).

"For everyone born of God has overcome the world. This is the victory that has overcome the world, even our faith. Who is it that overcomes the world? Only he who believes that Jesus is the Son of God" (1 John 5:4, 5).

"I have told you these things, so that in me you may have peace. In this world you will have trouble. But take heart! I have overcome the world" (John 16:33).

"To him who is able to keep you from falling and to present you before his glorious presence without fault and with great joy—to the only God our Savior be glory, majesty, power and authority, through Jesus Christ our

Lord, before all ages, now and forevermore! Amen" (Jude 24, 25).

1. Why don't you have to hide from evil?
2. What will happen if you fight evil in your own strength?
3. What is the right way to face evil?
4. Have you been guilty of a fearful, "What's the world coming to?" mentality? What should you do to change your thinking?

A Banquet for a Big Shot

"So the king and Haman went to dine with Queen Esther, and as they were drinking wine on that second day, the king again asked, 'Queen Esther, what is your petition? It will be given you. What is your request? Even up to half the kingdom, it will be granted.' Then Queen Esther answered, 'If I have found favor with you, O king, and if it pleases your majesty, grant me my life—this is my petition. And spare my people—this is my request. For I and my people have been sold for destruction and slaughter and annihilation. If we had merely been sold as male and female slaves, I would have kept quiet, because no such distress would justify disturbing the king.' King Xerxes replied to Queen Esther and to Mordecai the Jew, 'Because Haman attacked the Jews, I have given his estate to Esther, and they have hanged him on the gallows. Now write another decree in the king's name in behalf of the Jews as seems best to you, and seal it with the king's signet ring—for no document written in the king's name and sealed with his ring can be revoked' " (Esther 7:1–4; 8:7, 8).

Authority figures can cause a lot of fear—if you don't know how to relate to them. You know how it feels to be in situations such as these:

When the principal calls you to his office, you shake in your tennis shoes, even though you're certain you haven't broken a rule.

When the boss wants to see you, your stomach becomes an Olympic diving champion!

When your gym teacher yells your name, you're certain he'll criticize you for something you're not doing perfectly.

Fear is a common response to such situations. Some people decide that the best offense is a good defense, and start hurling word-darts at whoever is in authority. They figure this is the best way not to get hurt. Others turn into cowering "yes machines" or apple polishers. Neither method works very well.

There is a biblical way to handle authority: submission. God appointed each authority to keep peace. Whether it's the U.S. Government or Mr. White in typing class, that authority maintains sense and order. You must, therefore, be willing to obey the authority even if he or she is wrong. This attitude is submission. You can see this in Queen Esther. Rather than being rebellious, she was willing to obey the king's law.

"Authority figures can cause a lot of fear—if you don't know how to relate to them."

However, when Esther felt the king was about to do something wrong, she appealed to him and gave him all the facts so he could make a better decision. She did it with a humble, submissive attitude. She first spent time with God to discover the best way to present her petition. She then invited the king to a banquet where he relaxed. She wisely made the king coax her request out of her instead of laying it on the line. Because she hadn't forced her request on him, the king never doubted her respect for authority. And he granted her request. Esther's method can work for you.

If your teacher gives an unfair test, don't rush up and complain. Find a way to tactfully and respectfully suggest a solution to the problem. If your boss makes you work every Saturday night so his nephew can have time off, let God show you a way to appeal to him and reasonably work out the problem. If your gym teacher rides your case because you're a klutz, find a way to explain (without blaming him for anything) that you're not good at sports, but would appreciate any suggestions for improvement. (This will give him a chance to tell you what he wants without yelling.)

If authority figures frighten you so that you complain behind their backs, you have not learned how to appeal to authority. Asking a person in authority to change his mind requires four things: (1) showing utmost respect; (2) being willing to obey your authority if your petition fails; (3) praying for the person and asking God how to approach him; (4) giving the person in authority an alternate plan which will fulfill the same goal. To do this you must try to discover why the unfair decision was made. (Maybe the unfair test was given to make students realize they must study more. If so, suggest that students who improve their grades and hand in all homework be allowed to take another test. Such a plan would allow the teacher to accomplish his goal and still be fair to the students.)

But if your appeal to authority fails, you must obey, trusting God to deliver you—even as Esther was willing to die if her banquet for Haman the big shot didn't succeed. (This, however, does not apply if you're asked to break God's law. If, for example, your boss asks you to lie to a customer, you'll have to refuse. If he fires you, God will help you find a new job.) After all, God is all-powerful and well able to show you how to handle the consequences. He can help you live through a D- on the test or working every Saturday night. He has a wonderful way of protecting people who really want to obey Him.

Having God's view of authority cancels out fear because it prevents reacting wrongly to the person in charge. When you respect and obey authority, you're obeying the God you love, the God who always has your best interest at heart.

"Everyone must submit himself to the governing authorities, for there is no authority except that which God has established. The authorities that exist have been established by God. Consequently, he who rebels against the authority is rebelling against what God has instituted, and those who do so will bring judgment on themselves. For rulers hold no terror for those who do right, but for those who do wrong. Do you want to be free from fear of the one in authority? Then do what is right and he will commend you" (Rom. 13:1–3).

1. Why must you submit to governing authorities?
2. Whom are you actually rebelling against if you are rebelling against authority?
3. Are you rebelling against God by not obeying someone in authority over you? If so, confess it as a sin.
4. How can you stop fearing those in authority?

Faith Remembers What Fear Forgets

"This happened on the thirteenth day of the month of Adar, and on the fourteenth they rested and made it a day of feasting and joy. That is why

rural Jews—those living in villages—observe the fourteenth of the month of Adar as a day of joy and feasting, a day for giving presents to each other. These days should be remembered and observed in every generation by every family, and in every province and in every city. And these days of Purim should never cease to be celebrated by the Jews, nor should the memory of them die out among their descendants" (Esther 9:17, 19, 28). (The Jews still honor Esther every year during the feast of Purim, remembering how God used her to save His people.)

It's probably happened to you:

You trusted God completely for last year's biology final and He worked a miracle, giving you supernatural calm and peace as you studied for and took the test. This year, however, you're a nervous wreck before the first chemistry exam.

You trusted God to run your social life last year, and you thoroughly enjoyed yourself. But now you're desperate because all your friends seem to be happily dating. You feel left out.

You even trusted God as you witnessed to your friend who was moving to another state—and he accepted Christ. But now your hands become clammy when you think of telling the new neighbor kid about Jesus.

God hasn't changed! So what is the problem?

Yesterday's faith doesn't automatically cover today's fears. You have to continually stick close to Jesus, constantly renew your mind by letting the Bible speak to you, and daily receive the power of the Holy Spirit. Whenever your focus slips from God to yourself, you are in for instant trouble.

One way to keep your focus on God is to remember with joy and thanks what God has done in the past. God, in Old Testament times, decreed certain holidays so His people would regularly remind themselves of the great things He had done for them. Passover commemorates the last plague which forced the Egyptians to release God's people from slavery. Purim commemorates God's deliverance for the Jews in the Persian Empire. In the same way Christians celebrate Easter to recall Jesus' glorious resurrection. Recalling God's great deeds of the past focuses your mind on God's power. Obviously, there is the danger of treating these events as ancient history, and not receiving the assurance that God's power can also work for you. But recalling God's wonderful miracles as you expect future miracles destroys anxiety with nuclear force.

When fear threatens to smother your faith, recall how God has helped you in the past; then remind yourself how He will help you now. One of the Psalm writers did that. In the midst of discouragement he wrote: "These things I remember as I pour out my soul: how I used to go with the multitude, leading the procession to the house of God, with shouts of joy and thanksgiving among the festive throng. Why are you downcast, O my soul? Why so disturbed within me? Put your hope in God, for I will yet praise him, my Savior and my God" (Ps. 42:4, 11).

Learn to effectively use the memories of victories God has won for you. Certainly you shouldn't degenerate into a what-happened-to-the-good-old-days dreamer. But when troubles come, recall with joy and thanks how God helped you in the past, then receive His power for your present situation.

Fear is irrational and tends to overpower clear thinking, so a specific task may help put your thoughts in the right place. When fear invades, therefore, try this prescription: On a sheet of paper write in big letters across the top "Jesus Christ is the same yesterday and today and for ever" (Heb. 13:8). Beneath that verse, list all the times Jesus has given you victory. After each point add, ". . . and God can do it again." You'll find it impossible to think about the greatness of God and be afraid at the same time. Faith remembers what fear forgets.

"I will remember the deeds of the Lord; yes, I will remember your miracles of long ago. I will meditate on all your works and consider all your mighty deeds" (Ps. 77:11, 12).

"I remember the days of long ago; I meditate on all your works and consider what your hands have done" (Ps. 143:5).

"Look to the Lord and his strength; seek his face always. Remember the wonders he has done, his miracles, and the judgments he pronounced" (Ps. 105:4, 5).

"For this reason I remind you to fan into flame the gift of God, which is in you through the laying on of my hands. For God did not give us a spirit of timidity, but a spirit of power, of love and of self-discipline" (2 Tim. 1:6, 7).

1. Why should you remember the miraculous things God has done?
2. Why are God's miracles of the past so important to your present problems?
3. How does remembering what God has done for you overcome fear?
4. Consider a frightening situation you are facing. Reread the last paragraph before the scripture quotations and make the kind of list described there.

Week Thirteen

NEHEMIAH: WORKING WITH WALLS AND OTHER IMPOSSIBILITIES

Introduction

Do you ever feel that the task before you is impossible? Would you like to give up right now? Learning how to "stick with it" when the going gets tough, and to see a job through to the end, isn't easy. If a tendency to give up is one of your problems, take lessons from Nehemiah.

Giving Up a Lucrative Job

Someone hard up for jokes has called Knee-high-miah the shortest man in the Bible. Actually, he was a man of gigantic spiritual stature. He lived during the fifth century B.C., and was a member of the Jewish minority whose ancestors had chosen to stay in Persia rather than return to Israel after the Babylonian Captivity. In Susa, the capital of Persia (modern-day Iran), he worked for the king, waiting on him and tasting his food and beverages to make certain there was no poison in the royal soup. This was a top job given only to one whom the king trusted completely.

God had another job for Nehemiah, however. His brother, Hanai, had made a trip back to Jerusalem. Horrified by the condition of the city, he described the sight to Nehemiah when he returned to Susa: The city walls were heaps of rubble and the gates had been burned down. Nehemiah was deeply concerned, but not wanting to make a rash decision, he prayed. After four months of prayerful consideration, he concluded that God wanted him to travel the thousand-plus miles to Jerusalem and supervise the rebuilding of the wall. Nehemiah then asked the king for a leave of absence, official letters guaranteeing safe passage, and permission to use logs from the king's forest to rebuild the gates—promising to return when he had completed the task. The king gave him all he asked for, and even threw in an armed escort.

Facing Opposition

After arriving in Jerusalem, Nehemiah sneaked out one night and inspected the broken walls, then announced to the leaders why he had come. They agreed to help him rebuild the wall. Each family and each individual were given a specific job.

As the rebuilding progressed, the non-Jewish neighbors became angry, for they didn't want Jerusalem to become a strong city. Sanballat, governor of the nearby city of Samaria, and Tobiah, leader of the people called the Ammonites, rallied their people to stop the project, and tried every trick they could imagine: ridicule, rumors, threats of force, and attempts to kill Nehemiah. But opposition only made Nehemiah and his people work harder. They worked with weapons in their hands while others stood guard, all the while trusting God and refusing to give in to the enemy's threats. After fifty-two days of diligent work, they had completed the wall.

To celebrate, Nehemiah gathered his people and had the Word of God read to them. Then they had a big feast. To dedicate the walls, the people formed two parades which marched around the walls in opposite directions, and met at the temple for a Thanksgiving service.

Nehemiah spent twelve years in Jerusalem doing everything possible to make sure the Jews followed God's law. Then, true to his promise, he returned to serve the king of Persia. But after a couple of years, he returned to Jerusalem, trying to turn his disobedient countrymen back to the Lord. His primary concern was always the glory of God and the obedience of God's people.

Nehemiah was a man of action, organization, and responsibility, a natural leader who could have done many things well, and enjoyed material success and prestige. Instead, he spent his life helping others, and history is different because Nehemiah chose God's priorities and not his own.

The Time of Your Life

"They said to me, 'Those who survived the exile and are back in the province are in great trouble and disgrace. The wall of Jerusalem is broken down, and its gates have been burned with fire.' When I heard these things, I sat down and wept. For some days I mourned and fasted and prayed before the God of heaven" (Neh. 1:3, 4).

Someone has said, "Time is the stuff of which life is made. Waste your time and you waste your life." How you spend your time determines, to a large extent, what your life will be. But how should you decide, among all the demands for your time, what things are worthwhile doing? Should you sign up for Spanish II because Bill did? Should you apply for the first job you see in the want ads? Should you attend the college that's closest to home? Aren't you tired of making spur-of-the-moment decisions that get you into trouble?

Nehemiah made choices—good choices. When he heard the wall of Jerusalem was in shambles, he had to decide whether or not to go there to supervise its rebuilding—a job that would take much time and effort. How did he make such a big decision?

First he was willing to do God's will, no matter what the cost. He was willing to leave his prestigious palace job, with all its fringe benefits. He was willing to risk an "off-with-your-head" edict from a king who might be furious with him for requesting a leave of absence. God's will was worth any sacrifice.

Do you consider God's will that important? Would you give up daily tennis games, the evenings with your girlfriend, or your favorite TV programs in order to spend your time going God's way?

Second, Nehemiah prayed—extensively. Although he was willing to make any necessary sacrifices, he didn't proceed until he was sure it was God's will. He recognized he could give up everything to serve God and still be completely out of God's will, so Nehemiah spent four months praying about it before he took action.

You, too, have to ask God to show His plans for you. What you do for Jesus is not your choice, it's His. In fact, He might have a better idea about what you can do to build His kingdom than you do!

One man who, as a young person, was confused about choosing the right occupation, was told by a friend, "Spend five minutes each day praying about this decision." He took the advice and got his answer.

Why don't you try it? Instead of complaining to everyone, "I just can't decide what courses to take next year," pray about it every day. Instead of groaning that you can't find a part-time job, pray about it every day. Instead of broadcasting like a radio station, "I just don't know if I should break up with Jeff" (got the refrain?), pray about it every day.

Nehemiah was willing to make the necessary sacrifices, and then he spent enough time praying to discover God's plan for his life. God, in turn, took care of the king's attitude and marvelously opened the way for Nehemiah to go and rebuild the wall. If you will dedicate your time to God and ask Him what walls He wants rebuilt, you, like Nehemiah, will receive His guidance and see His miracles. But don't try to build the wrong wall. If you'll spend the time of your life for God, you'll have the time of your life.

"Why, you do not even know what will happen tomorrow. What is your life? You are a mist that appears for a little while and then vanishes" (James 4:14).

"Show me, O Lord, my life's end and the number of my days; let me know how fleeting is my life" (Ps. 39:4).

"Be very careful, then, how you live—not as unwise but as wise, making the most of every opportunity, because the days are evil" (Eph. 5:15, 16).

1. What is the danger of thinking, I'm young and have my whole life ahead of me. I shouldn't have to think about responsibility just yet?
2. Life is amazingly short, but instead of letting the shortness of life scare you, how should you react?
3. Why is it important to set your priorities now, while you are young?
4. Pray and ask God to show you how to use your time.

"But I Always Travel Without Roadmaps"

"The king said to me, 'What is it you want?' Then I prayed to the God of heaven, and I answered the king, 'If it pleases the king and if your servant has found favor in his sight, let him send me to the city in Judah where my fathers are buried so that I can rebuild it.' Then the king, with the queen sitting beside him, asked me, 'How long will your journey take, and when will you get back?' It pleased the king to send me; so I set a time. I also said to him, 'If it pleases the king, may I have letters to the governors of Trans-Euphrates, so that they will provide me safe-conduct until I arrive in Judah? And may I have a letter to Asaph, keeper of the king's forest, so he will give me timber to make beams for the gates of the citadel by the temple and for the city wall and for the residence I will occupy?' And because the gracious hand of my God was upon me, the king granted my requests" (Neh. 2:4–8).

How would you respond if someone told you, "I know I should go to New York, so I'm just heading in that general direction. I really don't need a roadmap"? It may *sound* super-spiritual to "live by faith," never giving a thought for the next moment, but it isn't. God doesn't usually work that way. Consider some of His great acts—instructions for building the ark, for conquering Jericho, and for crossing the Red Sea; all were step-by-step directions. If Noah had designed the ark, it may have sunk. Joshua's parade plans may have invited an enemy attack. Moses' foray into the Red Sea may have turned into a session of free swimming lessons!

When God gives a goal, He also outlines each step necessary to reach it—a roadmap! Planning ahead with God is right. Making a certain plan into an idol, however, and being unwilling to change it, is wrong. And expecting a risk-free roadmap shows lack of faith in God.

Nehemiah had spent time planning with God. He knew he needed two things from the king—a letter guaranteeing safe passage through countries on the way, and big trees from the king's forests for building the city's gates. He may have desired horses and chariots to give the trip some style (after all, God's servants need some luxuries). He may have wished for cattle and sheep to provide roast beef sandwiches for picnics and lamb chops for snacks (after all, he needed strength to do a good job). But Nehemiah did not make his own plans for wall-building. He got his plans from God.

If God has shown you a wall to build—taking college prep courses, developing your talent as a musician, or being president of the youth group, be a Nehemiah who plans with God. Find out what doing a good job will entail. Decide what sacrifices you must make to reach the goal. For instance, you can't work nights, attend football practices, and still keep your grades up—you'll have to sacrifice something. Ask God to set

your priorities, then you can forget about doing other seemingly important things. Ask Him what you should omit from your schedule so you
can practice your guitar each day—if He has told you to become a top-
notch guitarist. Don't start on a God-assigned project, then do a poor job
because you failed to follow instructions.

God can use you if, by faith, you receive step-by-step instructions
from Him. Don't be the guy or gal who says, "Oh, I know what God
wants me to do. Now I'll just figure out how to do it." That's like trying
to draw your own roadmap. A few miles down the road you'll be hopelessly lost. So don't draw your own roadmap and don't travel without one.
Get your directions from God. Spend as much time praying about how to
accomplish the goal God gave you to pursue as you did finding out what
your goal is.

*"Suppose one of you wants to build a tower. Will he not first sit down
and estimate the cost to see if he has enough money to complete it? In the
same way, any of you who does not give up everything he has cannot be my
disciple" (Luke 14:28, 33).*

*". . . and if you call out for insight and cry aloud for understanding,
and if you look for it as for silver and search for it as for hidden treasure,
then you will understand the fear of the Lord and find the knowledge of
God. For the Lord gives wisdom, and from his mouth come knowledge and
understanding" (Prov. 2:3–6).*

*"The Lord delights in the way of the man whose steps he has made firm;
though he stumble, he will not fall, for the Lord upholds him with his hand"
(Ps. 37:23, 24).*

1. Are you willing to make the sacrifice necessary to reach your goal?
2. How do you get step-by-step instructions from God?
3. What promises can you claim if you consistently seek God's guidance
   for each step?
4. Are you willing to put enough prayer into planning your life step by
   step with God? What things in your life need special prayer right now?

Act Like a Branch

*"Adjoining this, Jedaiah son of Harumaph made repairs opposite his
house, and Hattush son of Hashabneiah made repairs next to him. Malkijah
son of Harim and Hasshub son of Pahath-Moab repaired another section
and the Tower of the Ovens. Shallum son of Hallohesh, ruler of a half-
district of Jerusalem, repaired the next section with the help of his daughters.
The Valley Gate was repaired by Hanun and the residents of Zanoah. They
rebuilt it and put its doors and bolts and bars in place. They also repaired
five hundred yards of the wall as far as the Dung Gate" (Neh. 3:10–13).*

Boredom is probably the most common teen-agers' disease in the world. When the English teacher picks up her grammar book, the kids at school groan in unison, "Oh, not that again!" "There's nothing to do around here" is repeated in every town in this country. Most teen-agers say classes are boring and work is a drag.

The usual prescription for boredom is: "Do something exciting," or, "Change your life style," or "Move somewhere else." But those who try such solutions find that the new school also has boring classes; that the city isn't much more exciting than the small town; that the new job remains interesting for only the first month. So what *is* the cure for boredom? Ask Nehemiah.

When Nehemiah organized the rebuilding of Jerusalem's wall, he assigned each individual or family a section to build, or a responsibility to fulfill. No doubt, some workers wished they could be traveling to the king's forest to bring back logs, rather then laboring hour after hour, day after day on the same section of wall. But because each person stuck with his assignment, the wall was completed. Everyone worked wholeheartedly, in spite of boredom.

God has some high priority work for you—if you intend to help build His kingdom. He may be asking you to study extra hard in order to develop your Bible-teaching ability. He may want you to become the best worker at Burger King so your testimony to your boss will change his life. God may desire you to work hard on voice lessons so you can sing for His glory—not your own—and thus be used in His kingdom. He'd no doubt like to revamp your personality so people can see a reflection of Jesus in you. He wants to teach you right attitudes toward money and possessions so they won't sidetrack you from doing His will.

Do such projects seem boring and uninteresting? Compared to what the devil is baiting you with, they maybe do. Satan will always try to lure you away from God's priorities with promises of excitement. But if you ditch God's priorities and pursue some new thrill, you will eventually learn a painful lesson: Satisfaction and fulfillment come, not from what you do, but from how you do it. Doing something for your own satisfaction leads to a miserable dead end. Zilch. Performing a task for God's glory, however, brings supernatural blessing. If you cooperate wholeheartedly with God, He will miraculously turn you into a worker who glorifies Him. Nothing could be greater than teaching a Bible study in the power of the Holy Spirit—or more boring than lying on the beach thinking only of yourself.

How do you get in on this power of the Holy Spirit? Jesus said, "I am the vine; you are the branches . . . apart from me you can do nothing [worthwhile, deeply satisfying, or pleasing to God]" (John 15:5). A branch receives everything from the vine. So ask Jesus, the True *Vine*, how to listen in church, how to clean up the kitchen, how to do math problems, or how to really enjoy a picnic. Just act like a branch and receive from Jesus a life that's not boring.

"I am the vine, you are the branches. If a man remains in me and I in

him, he will bear much fruit; apart from me you can do nothing. If anyone does not remain in me, he is like a branch that is thrown away and withers; such branches are picked up, thrown into the fire and burned. If you remain in me and my words remain in you, ask whatever you wish, and it will be given you. This is to my Father's glory, that you bear much fruit, showing yourselves to be my disciples. As the Father has loved me, so have I loved you. Now remain in my love. If you obey my commands, you will remain in my love, just as I have obeyed my Father's commands and remain in his love" (John 15:5–10).

1. In what areas of your life are you frequently tempted to search for more excitement, rather than doing the best you can where you are?
2. Are you trying to find satisfaction in the wrong way? What is the right way?
3. What can you do this week to depend on God completely, as a branch would depend on the vine.

Sign Up for "Improving Your Work Habits, 101"

"The next section was repaired by the men of Tekoa, but their nobles would not put their shoulders to the work under their supervisors" (Neh. 3:5).

"Meanwhile, the people in Judah said, 'The strength of the laborers is giving out, and there is so much rubble that we cannot rebuild the wall'" (Neh. 4:10).

It's easy to begin a task with gusto, but the follow-through is often difficult. You determine to write the best term paper possible in order to glorify God, but then you find out how much time and work a good term paper requires. Discouragement sets in. You promise to help your father with the spring yard work, but then you realize what the job really involves. You consider trying to get out of it. You agree to phone twenty people to remind them about the youth group retreat, but as you discover, teen-agers are never home and you're wondering if you really want to keep your word. You get completely bummed out.

Discouragement seems to strike everywhere—so easily. Just looking at the long chapter you're supposed to read makes you decide the assignment is impossible. And as you view the mound of debris in your room, you know how the tribe of Judah felt when they said the quantity of trash made wall-building impossible! Often, the amount of physical work involved keeps you from sticking with the priorities God has given you.

The feeling of being overwhelmed, however, is not really what keeps you from reaching the goals God has set for you. The underlying reason

216

is laziness and pride. Laziness keeps you from doing the daily assignments and taking notes during each class period. Therefore, studying for the test *is* nearly impossible. Laziness makes you decide you're too tired to complete a hard or uninteresting job.

Pride made the nobles of Jerusalem consider wall-building beneath their dignity, and you may be guilty of the same attitude. After all, why should a straight "A" student who was just voted "Best All-Around" by the senior class have to carry out his family's garbage every night? And why should the runner-up for homecoming queen have to suffer dishpan hands?

The solution to laziness and pride is not covering up by saying, "I'm easily discouraged," or, "Laziness runs in my family," or, "There are some jobs I just don't like." You must face the problem which keeps you from accomplishing what God wants you to do.

You first must deal with laziness and pride as sin. If you are not willing to work hard, God can do nothing with you. If you refuse to tackle tough, thankless jobs, He'll find someone else to build His kingdom. Forget your excuses and confront the issue. Repent of your wrong attitudes.

You then must receive God's grace and power to overcome laziness and pride—and instill diligence in your life. Pray for God's step-by-step guidance in writing your term paper. Then obey at every point. Ask God where to begin on the long assignment, the messy room, or the over-grown yard. Ask Him for courage to tackle the next task He has for you.

In case you're discouraged, take courage. God wants to work a miracle in you—giving you organization, diligence, and a will to work. He knows if you find it harder than most people to be neat. He understands if you have a tendency to lose things. He will give you whatever you need to overcome the discouragement you feel in facing a big job, because He's got a course especially designed to improve your work habits. Why not sign up for it today?

" 'Be strong, all you people of the land,' declares the Lord, 'and work. For I am with you,' declares the Lord Almighty" (Hag. 2:4).

"If you are willing and obedient, you will eat the best from the land" (Isa. 1:19).

"Now that I, your Lord and Teacher, have washed your feet, you also should wash one another's feet" (John 13:14).

"Therefore, my dear brothers, stand firm. Let nothing move you. Always give yourselves fully to the work of the Lord, because you know that your labor in the Lord is not in vain" (1 Cor. 15:58).

1. What attitudes toward work does God want you to adopt?
2. What promises does God have for the diligent worker?
3. Which attitude do you need God to place in you? Ask Him to do it.
4. Ask God to show you how to apply something from these verses to a job you need to get done. Ask Him for His grace and instructions.

Orders from the General Himself

"When Sanballat heard that we were rebuilding the wall, he became angry and was greatly incensed. He ridiculed the Jews, and in the presence of his associates and the army of Samaria, he said, 'What are those feeble Jews doing? Will they restore their wall? Will they offer sacrifices? Will they finish in a day? Can they bring the stones back to life from those heaps of rubble—burned as they are?' Tobiah the Ammonite, who was at his side, said, 'What they are building—if even a fox climbed up on it, he would break down their wall of stones!' Hear us, O our God, for we are despised. Turn their insults back on their own heads. Give them over as plunder in a land of captivity. So we rebuilt the wall till all of it reached half its height, for the people worked with all their heart" (Neh. 4:1–4, 6).

Do you take opinion polls among your friends to decide if you should drop basketball, or to decide which outfit to buy? Or do you ask God? Do you fall apart if someone says you are "straight-laced, sober, and sad," and therefore a poor advertisement for Christianity? Or do you ask God what He thinks of you and what changes He would like you to make? Do you accept it as fact if one of your Christian friends says you're wasting your time by teaching the third grade Sunday school class? Or do you request an evaluation from the Lord? The devil loves using the opinions of others to mix up your priorities and keep you from accomplishing the jobs God assigns you. When the devil tried this tactic on Nehemiah, however, it failed. Nehemiah simply ignored the insults and continued building.

The devil uses two kinds of "public opinion" to make you ineffective. The first kind is ridicule from unbelievers. If you drop basketball so you can lead a Bible study, many people will suggest you're crazy. If you decide to get by on last year's wardrobe so you can give more money to missions, you're more apt to get a Bronx cheer than a standing ovation. Such mockery and disrespect can easily paralyze you.

Besides the teasing you may receive for a specific decision, Satan uses general ridicule to wear you down and deter you from following God's priorities. Such ridicule shows up in every school via the Don't-Need-No-Education Club. Its "members" threaten kids who won't join the sit-down strike in gym class, and constantly taunt Brian Bookworm and Heidi Homework.

God wants you to ignore them, to relax, and to keep God's priorities: obedience to authority and working to the best of your ability. When a member of the Ego Demolition Squad quips, "Did you get your haircut at the poodle boutique?" don't let Satan convince you to hide for a month because you look too terrible to witness to anybody. When some self-crowned princess remarks that your skirt must have come from your grandmother's attic, don't decide that all the kids hate you because your

"Do you take opinion polls among your friends to decide . . . which outfit to buy? Or do you ask God?"

wardrobe isn't up to date, and therefore you don't dare ask Sherri to attend church with you. Learn, as Nehemiah, to ignore the abuse and keep building the wall that God has given you to build.

The other kind of destructive public opinion is wrong advice and discouraging comments from Christian friends. How should you handle such opinions? Again, ignore them. Although God often will use the council of other Christians to confirm what He has already told you, you must be careful to always get your orders from God—first. When God has clearly given you His plan, ignore the doubts of other Christians and walk ahead in faith. If He wants you to be brave and to suffer for Jesus, you must not listen to the words of those who would rescue you from doing God's will.

In the army, the commander-in-chief's orders cancel all other suggestions and orders. A fellow private's advice can never outweigh the words of the general Himself.

"Then Pilate took Jesus and had him flogged. The soldiers twisted together a crown of thorns and put it on his head. They clothed him in a

*purple robe and went up to him again and again, saying, 'Hail, O king of
the Jews!' And they struck him in the face" (John 19:1–3).*

*"Who is going to harm you if you are eager to do good? But even if you
should suffer for what is right, you are blessed. 'Do not fear what they fear;
do not be frightened.' But in your hearts set apart Christ as Lord. Always
be prepared to give an answer to everyone who asks you to give the reason
for the hope that you have. But do this with gentleness and respect, keeping
a clear conscience, so that those who speak maliciously against your good
behavior in Christ may be ashamed of their slander" (1 Pet. 3:13–16).*

1. What comfort can you have when you are persecuted?
2. What are specific things to remember when you are ridiculed?
3. Why is it wrong to let ridicule stop you from completing the work God
   has given you?

Easy Street Is Boring

*"When our enemies heard that we were aware of their plot and that God
had frustrated it, we all returned to the wall, each to his own work. From
that day on, half of my men did the work, while the other half were equipped
with spears, shields, bows and armor. The officers posted themselves behind
all the people of Judah who were building the wall. Those who carried
materials did their work with one hand and held a weapon in the other, and
each of the builders wore his sword at his side as he worked. But the man
who sounded the trumpet stayed with me" (Neh. 4:15–18).*

Have you ever wished for push-button consecration, or a Complete-
Surrender-to-Jesus-in-Ten-Easy-Lessons course—with a lifetime guar-
antee, or a vaccination against temptation? Could you use a vacation from
Satan's attacks? Would you like to live on Easy Street, at least for a while?
Don't count on it.

Once you have completely given yourself to Jesus and received His
Holy Spirit, the devil will test your surrender mercilessly. Someone has
compared your initial commitment to entering the right gate—and finding
there a long road to your destination. Life is designed this way so you
can walk hand in hand with Jesus, trusting Him for every step. If there
were no obstacles or temptations, you'd try to walk that road by yourself.

Such a life, however, isn't unending misery. Overcoming constant
opposition gives life a certain excitement, a cutting edge. Nehemiah and
his people, for instance, weren't basket cases because an enemy was
harassing them. They decided that they could guard against danger and
continue to build the wall. The opposition inspired cooperation, a renewed
dedication to the job, and a greater trust in God. God allowed their priorities to be tested so they could strengthen their faith.

Life without a challenge is boring. Playing football against third graders would be easy—but not fun. Canoeing the kiddie canal at the amusement park or skiing the bunny hill would be effortless—but dull. That's why God allows constant challenges in your Christian life—so you'll grow, and no longer be a whining baby Christian.

The sooner you quit seeking a safe, boring, easy Christian life, the better. You must always be on guard against Satan's attacks; today's victory will not help you tomorrow. You will have to stay close to Jesus and let Him protect you, because wandering out on your own will get you into deep trouble.

In a way, the Christian life is like a science fiction cartoon, with you as the main character. God has given you secret power against the devil. But whenever you venture off on your own, any attack of Satan crashlands you on a hostile, lonely planet. But if you stay close to Jesus, He'll always win the battle for you—and everybody likes to be on the winning side.

"Watch and pray so that you will not fall into temptation. The spirit is willing, but the body is weak" (Matt. 26:41).

"So, if you think you are standing firm, be careful that you don't fall!" (1 Cor. 10:12).

"Be on your guard; stand firm in the faith; be men of courage; be strong" (1 Cor. 16:13).

"Be self-controlled and alert. Your enemy the devil prowls around like a roaring lion looking for someone to devour" (1 Pet. 5:8).

1. At what times do you find it easy to let down your guard?
2. Which areas in your life are you not guarding with prayer and faith?
3. Do you watch with courage or with fear?
4. How can you start being more alert for Satan's attacks?

First on Your Agenda

"So on the first day of the seventh month Ezra the priest brought the Law before the assembly, which was made up of men and women and all who were able to understand. On the second day of the month, the heads of all the families, along with the priests and the Levites, gathered around Ezra the scribe to give attention to the words of the Law" (Neh. 8:2, 13).

What would you have done after spending fifty-two days on backbreaking work and tense guard duty to rebuild the walls of Jerusalem? If a Mediterranean cruise or some other vacation weren't possible, you could do a lot of important work: building much-needed houses, and attending to overgrown farms.

All sorts of lesser jobs had been postponed so the wall could be built. But instead of caring for any of these pressing needs, Nehemiah and his people took two days off to hear the Word of God. Impractical! In addition, they set aside other days that month to observe the celebration God had prescribed in the Law of Moses. Returning to God and obeying His Word was more important to them than work that "just has to get done."

Maybe you're already aware that life can grind on like a relentless machine—classes, homework, part-time job, choir rehearsal, Sunday afternoon, and then you start another carbon-copy week. Maybe you've noticed that making time payments, keeping up with the Joneses—or the kid at school, and trying to accomplish too many things at once can imprison you. It can seem like a merry-go-round that never stops—and you're on the wrong horse! Life makes so many demands on a person.

A man once remarked to another, "Your greatest danger is letting the urgent things crowd out the important." You may be groaning in response, "If only I could discover what things are important." Straightening out priorities isn't impossible.

Jesus knew what His priority should be: glorifying God. When Jesus' ministry was nearing its end, He could honestly say to His Father, "I have brought you glory on earth by completing the work you gave me to do" (John 17:4). Jesus did not heal every leper or preach to every person in Palestine. He did not get to do everything He might have enjoyed. But He had confidence and peace despite big crowds and a busy schedule, because He did exactly what God wanted Him to do. His life made sense and was full of accomplishment. Yours can be too.

Start discovering God's priorities by reading and studying God's Word. If you are obeying God's general biblical teachings about money, or work habits, or heart attitudes, you can expect specific guidance about what is your next important step. So take time to study the Bible every day.

You will also discover God's priorities by praying. Rather than bolting out of bed at the last moment and dashing off to school or to a day of skiing, get up earlier and spend time talking to God about your activities. In his wonderful booklet, *Tyranny of the Urgent,* Charles Hummel suggests you take some time each week to pray and plan with God, choosing your priorities for that week. (You could start by spending ten minutes each Sunday morning.)

Be willing to obey God and stick so close to Him that you won't wander down a wrong path. Let Him decide what will be first on your agenda. Your life will be much better if you spend it doing only the things God has planned for you.

"Paul and his companions traveled throughout the region of Phrygia and Galatia, having been kept by the Holy Spirit from preaching the word in the province of Asia. When they came to the border of Mysia, they tried to enter Bithynia, but the Spirit of Jesus would not allow them to. So they passed by Mysia and went down to Troas. During the night Paul had a vision of a man of Macedonia standing and begging him, 'Come over to Macedonia and help us.' After Paul had seen the vision, we got ready at

once to leave for Macedonia, concluding that God had called us to preach the gospel to them" (Acts 16:6–10).

1. What priority did Paul and his friends establish?
2. (Read Mark 16:15, Acts 1:8.) What general plan of God were they already following?
3. Are you disobeying any of God's general biblical principles? Which ones?
4. Ask God to help you set top priorities for this week. Write them down.